D0222646

"RE-MEMBERING" HISTORY IN STUDENT AND TEACHER LEARNING

"*'Re-Membering' History* provides compelling examples of educators moving theory, ideas, and ideals into action. This book not only 'talks the talk,' it shows practitioners how to walk the talk."

H. Richard Milner IV, Helen Faison Endowed Chair in Urban Education, University of Pittsburgh, USA

"… a bold invitation for rethinking the purpose and representation of the grand narrative in teaching the history of the United States in elementary schools. "

Etta R. Hollins, Kauffman Endowed Chair for Urban Teacher Education, University of Missouri–Kansas City, USA

"*'Re-Membering' History in Student and Teacher Learning* comes as a gift to all educators who believe that it is still possible to modify, even radically change, our attitudes about culture-based teaching."

Molefi Kete Asante, Temple University, USA and Visiting Professor, Zhejiang University, Hangzhou, China. From the Foreword

What kind of social studies knowledge can stimulate a critical and ethical dialog with the past and present? *"Re-Membering" History in Student and Teacher Learning* answers this question by explaining and illustrating a process of historical recovery that merges Afrocentric theory and principles of culturally informed curricular practice to reconnect multiple knowledge bases and experiences. In the case studies presented, K-12 practitioners, teacher educators, preservice teachers, and parents use this praxis to produce and then study the use of democratized student texts; they step outside of reproducing standard school experiences to engage in conscious inquiry about their shared present as a continuance of a shared past.

Joyce E. King holds the Benjamin E. Mays Endowed Chair for Urban Teaching, Learning and Leadership at Georgia State University, USA.

Ellen E. Swartz is an Education Consultant in curriculum development and the construction of culturally informed instructional materials for K-12 teachers and students.

"RE-MEMBERING" HISTORY IN STUDENT AND TEACHER LEARNING

An Afrocentric Culturally Informed Praxis

Joyce E. King and Ellen E. Swartz

WITH
LINDA CAMPBELL, SHONDA LEMONS-SMITH, ERICKA LÓPEZ

Routledge
Taylor & Francis Group

NEW YORK AND LONDON

First published 2014
by Routledge
711 Third Avenue, New York, NY 10017

and by Routledge
2 Park Square, Milton Park, Abingdon, Oxon OX14 4RN

Routledge is an imprint of the Taylor & Francis Group, an informa business

© 2014 Taylor & Francis

The right of the Authors to be identified as authors of this work has been asserted by them in accordance with sections 77 and 78 of the Copyright, Designs and Patents Act 1988.

All rights reserved. No part of this book may be reprinted or reproduced or utilized in any form or by any electronic, mechanical, or other means, now known or hereafter invented, including photocopying and recording, or in any information storage or retrieval system, without permission in writing from the publishers.

Trademark notice: Product or corporate names may be trademarks or registered trademarks, and are used only for identification and explanation without intent to infringe.

Library of Congress Cataloging in Publication Data
King, Joyce Elaine, 1947–
    "Re-membering" history in student and teacher learning : an Afrocentric culturally informed praxis / Joyce E. King, Ellen E. Swartz.
    pages cm
    Includes bibliographical references and index.
    1. African Americans—Education. 2. African American schools—Curricula.
    3. Afrocentrism—Study and teaching—United States. 4. African American
    teachers—Training of. I. Swartz, Ellen. II. Title.
    LC2771.K56 2014
    371.829'96073—dc23
    2013035942

ISBN: 978-0-415-71512-6 (hbk)
ISBN: 978-0-415-71513-3 (pbk)
ISBN: 978-1-315-88206-2 (ebk)

Typeset in Bembo and Stone Sans
by EvS Communication Networx, Inc.

Printed and bound in the United States of America by Publishers Graphics, LLC on sustainably sourced paper.

Library
University of Texas
at San Antonio

This book is dedicated to the memory of Harriet Tubman and her African ancestors who taught her that freedom is inherent and shared, and that no one is free unless everyone is free. We acknowledge her self-determination and agency on the long road to freedom—and that of the millions of African men and women who came before and after her whose names we will never know—in the hope that we can begin to "re-member" the history they have made.

WITHDRAWN
UTSA LIBRARIES

WITHDRAWN
UTSA LIBRARIES

CONTENTS

FOREWORD

Molefi Kete Asante

A few years ago a frustrated school superintendent insisted that—given the low level of institutional competence and knowledge about culture—the task of radically changing the curriculum to reflect the increasingly diverse student populations' aspirations was nearly impossible. She confronted me with the proposal that mass retraining of administrators and teachers was essential, recognizing that even with the tremendous strides made in the last three decades to liberalize American education, we remained, for the most part, captured in the clutches of a stagnant conception of what education ought to be. The grand narratives of American education have always marginalized Africans, Latino people, Indigenous Nations, and women. This is why the work by Joyce E. King and Ellen E. Swartz, *"Re-Membering" History in Student and Teacher Learning: An Afrocentric Culturally Informed Praxis,* comes as a gift to all educators who believe that it is still possible to modify, even radically change, our attitudes about culture-based teaching.

Education should prepare us to live in a diverse world because that is the only world. Nothing in the work that is presented here is what Michael Tillotson, author and assistant professor of Africana Studies, calls an agency reduction formation; everything that these writers present to us is a capacity-building formation for living and working in an inspirational and culturally rich environment. A curriculum that takes away the agency of students and teachers is a vapid curriculum and the only way to confront it is to change it. What is so beautiful in this book is the attitude that Ellen Swartz and Joyce King have toward the extraordinary challenge we face as educators. Their attitude says, "We can do this!" Certainly, the teachers we need in the public schools of this nation are those with victorious consciousness who believe that an authentic education is possible.

Why must we feel defeated when it comes to the public schools? What is the reason for the disproportionality of tested achievement among schools and districts? How do we deliver meaningful education to a diverse population? In order to answer those questions we must seek refuge in what we have learned through research and practice. Indeed, in the best of times practice proves research and research guides practice. No other educators could have written with such deftness about the nature of teacher preparation and training as these veterans of the educational wars in urban schools. They have been joined by a cadre of outstanding educators who know that the master script in social studies must be challenged by extending the boundaries of what is included in the content of classes.

When we are confronted with limited achievement, lack of motivation, and inadequate creativity, we must examine the structure of our curriculum, question the imposition of the mythic vision of a monocultural society, and revise the social studies narrative of the United States. It is inevitable that we will become less successful if we do not have a culturally relevant curriculum. For many years we have insisted, as have especially the authors of this book, on challenging schools to establish a consistent attitude of success in the educational arena.

Re-Membering History in Student and Teacher Learning: An Afrocentric Culturally Informed Praxis combines the best skills of two educators with strong training and experience in writing history in order to demonstrate what is possible in the act of teaching. I am convinced that King and Swartz have given us the best possible work on Afrocentric practice in education not simply because they are knowledgeable about the structure of the educational system but because they also have the emotional commitment for creating a sane and rational society.

In July 2013, I became, for the second time, the chair of the Department of African American Studies at Temple University, and, on the day that I was moving books into my office, I met a young man and a young woman, both in their 20s, in the corridor outside my office. No other people were in the building and this was a Sunday so I asked, "What are you doing in the building on a Sunday? I am moving books into my office." The young man rushed to shake my hand and then to say, "I wanted my fiancée to see where I went to school and to walk the halls where I studied and to be in the presence of the familiar paintings, ancestors' photos, and faculty offices that helped to shape me." I was very pleased to see how happy the young woman was to be in the halls of the African American Studies department where the first doctoral degree in the field was offered. But there was another message that did not go unappreciated by me and that was that the young man held onto something that was worth remembering, how he felt being in the place that helped to bring him to consciousness.

Thus, any true experience of knowledge content is an encounter with all information one has experienced culturally. If this is not the case, then we have missed the point of being able to make our knowledge meaningful and rich. We all know that the authentic engagement with content comes from the ability to address our experiences in such a way that the knowledge becomes something that is a primary part of our being-ness. It exists in our reality because we have captured the knowledge and tied it to our experiences; it becomes our knowledge culturally and not something that we or students must "go get" because it is already present.

I will dare to say that this book will strike a lot of teachers as something that is true on face value; others I am afraid will claim that this is only a "feel good story" meant to make Africans, Native Americans, and Latinos feel good, and I will say to them that there is nothing wrong with feeling good if events, personalities, and communities that were locked out of the American narrative are now in place. What I have seen in education is that students are struck in a positive way by the magnetic force of culture and they are repelled when something is negative about culture. I embrace the intellectual and emotional dimensions of what King and Swartz and their colleagues have decided to share with us. This will become a standard book for teachers who want to expand their students' and their own views about social studies.

PREFACE

At the center of this volume is the concept of "re-membering"—a process for recovering history by putting back together the multiple and shared knowledge bases and experiences that shaped the past. We use an Afrocentric theoretical framework to reconnect these knowledge bases so that all students can experience more comprehensive and accurate accounts of the past compared to the limited and fragmented accounts and concepts still found in school curricula and state standards.

All cultures and groups—from the underrepresented to the overrepresented—have lived, acted, and produced knowledge that marks their presence. Accounts of the past that bring their presence into view are history at its best. Accounts of the past that dismember this presence are history at its worst, as dismembered accounts interfere with historical concurrence and derail the possibility of having comprehensive knowledge about the past. The previous century of struggle over the monocultural content of school curricula has resulted in only superficial alterations of standard accounts that fail to keep pace with available scholarship. For example, Indigenous names of once-conquered Peoples (e.g., Taíno, Wampanoag, Lakota, Haudenosaunee) have more recently been included in instructional materials, and there may be an occasional excerpt quoted from a speech of an Indigenous leader. However, the script of unquestioned colonial rule and manifest destiny remains intact, which invisibilizes the worldview, cultural knowledge, and socio-political practices of Indigenous Peoples. Likewise, the absence of Indigenous voice and accurate scholarship in school knowledge continues to position African people on the Continent and in the Diaspora in neo-Hegelian terms as a people without history—as if thousands of years of African cultural production did not create the earliest civilizations and set humanity on the pursuit of knowledge in every discipline (Asante, 2007; Carruthers, 1995; Diop, 1974; Hegel, 1900; Hilliard, 1997).

The process of "re-membering" not only provides an achievable alternative to what Michael Apple (1999) calls "official" knowledge—the knowledge that states and their corporate partners reproduce—but it also eschews the token multicultural inclusion that serves to reify grand narratives and the master scripts that teach them. While history contains silences by its very nature, there is a difference between these silences and silenced history. By using an Afrocentric culturally informed praxis of historical recovery, we have created a process that unearths the silenced narratives of omitted or underrepresented cultures and groups and brought them together with the narratives of dominant groups to produce what we refer to as democratized knowledge in the social studies. This knowledge is framed by Afrocentric concepts and written for students by applying the same set of culturally informed principles to all groups so that knowledge of the past is no longer distorted by hegemonic accounts that privilege some groups and silence others.

In *Hope and History*, Vincent Harding (1990) writes that American democracy cannot be realized and this country can never be whole unless there is equity in the experience of democracy, and "that the freedom struggle of its African American citizens has always been a gift of life and truth to the whole society. Always" (p. 108). Harding explains the many ways in which these African gifts—of ongoing resistance to systemic inequities, of raising contradictions between national rhetoric and unjust realities, of continuously challenging intellectual hegemony in education and other fields—have been and continue to be offered as a path toward human freedom—one that moves away from denial of the nation's anti-democratic and White supremacist past and present. Sylvia Wynter (1992, 1997) offers us a conceptual tool in response to this denial. Her concept of alterity—of learning from the vantage points or locations of liminal identity groups whose critical analysis of and engagement with the worldview and practices of dominant groups—increases the possibility of bringing truthfulness to the teaching of historical topics. As we demonstrate in this volume, liminal groups' perspective advantage of alterity gives us access to knowledge that has been hidden and denied, which allows us to produce a more discerning view of the connections among groups—one that more closely represents the past and present.

Many education authors view expanding curricular knowledge in the social studies as an imperative driven by the inevitability of demographic change. We frame the task differently, as an imperative of historical wholeness and integrity. Heritage knowledge and cultural knowledge loom large in this imperative. Heritage knowledge or group memory is the repository of knowledge, traditions, experiences, and cultural retentions of people of African ancestry and other liminal groups—long ignored and devalued as a strategy of oppression (Clarke, 1994; King, 2006). Cultural knowledge, which social studies educators need to learn about the cultures of students they are teaching, includes multiple knowledge bases, traditions, values, languages, and ways of knowing and being. This information exists in the historical record, but for liminal groups, in particular, has either been omitted or distorted in social studies knowledge.

Wade A. Boykin (1994, p. 244) explains that all cultures are normative and have cultural capital, and he describes how the "saturating cultural character of traditional schooling" typically positions only European culture as normative and worthy of bearing influence on teaching and learning. Through critical analysis of standard instructional materials and the state standards that underlie them, we demonstrate the problems with what we refer to as eurocratic limitations on social studies knowledge. (In this volume we use the term "euro" in the construction of words to provide more specificity about hegemony than the general term "Eurocentric.") These eurocratic or official constraints imposed by a hierarchal system of European domination, authority, and ensuing hegemony determine whose culture has influence and whose knowledge is worth knowing in the educational system we have inherited.

With this critical analysis in place, we go a step further to create a process that recovers the cultural knowledge that these limitations have obscured from educators, and the heritage knowledge that has been denied to various identity groups (King, 2006, 2008). In so doing, we move beyond the endless contestation of dominance to a space in which culturally singular knowledge can be replaced with democratized knowledge. The process of democratizing knowledge recognizes the importance of also drawing on the heritage knowledge of students and parents who have the right to be conscious of their place on the "map of human geography" (Clarke, 1998, p. 104).

Overview

This volume offers concepts and practices for teachers, students, and families at all levels. While many of our examples are at the elementary level, case studies involve elementary, middle, and higher education contexts. Hence, our intended audience would include elementary and middle school in-service teachers; teacher educators and their pre-service students in undergraduate and graduate programs (e.g., social studies, mathematics, and literacy methods, social foundations); English for Speakers of Other Languages (ESOL) and multicultural/culturally responsive education faculty and students at all levels; and professional development providers such as teacher centers, teacher unions, and social studies departments in districts across the country.

Our approach is to combine the clarity of theory with the efficacy of practice. Therefore the book has two sections: In Section I, "An Afrocentric Culturally Informed Praxis of Historical Recovery," four chapters describe the Afrocentric culturally informed praxis of historical recovery and the process of "re-membering"; Section II, "Studying the Use of 'Re-Membered' Texts," includes four chapters that report on practitioner inquiry case studies that explore what happens when "re-membered" student texts are used in classrooms and with parents. Readers are invited to enter this volume through either section. The final chapter is a coda that identifies additional insights that emerged from the findings and conclusions of the four case studies, connecting them to the Afrocentric culturally informed praxis described in Section I.

In Section I, chapter 1 defines and describes the grand narratives in social studies curricula, analyzes examples from master scripts that perpetuate these grand narratives, and introduces the three components of the Afrocentric culturally informed praxis of historical recovery. Chapter 2 describes the three components of the praxis of historical recovery—Afrocentric theory, principles of culturally informed curricular practice, and practitioner inquiry—with the first two framing and writing "re-membered" student texts, and the third studying their use in classrooms and community. Chapter 3 discusses the four phases in the "re-membering" process; identifies, refines, charts, and compares the salient themes in identity group narratives; and shows how the knowledge bases and experiences of identity groups that shaped freedom and democracy in colonial North America can be reconnected in the form of a student text entitled *Freedom and Democracy: A Story Remembered* (Swartz, 2013). Chapter 4 presents a "re-membered" standards model that supplements state standards with culturally informed standards, making it possible for teachers to select the standards they need to guide instruction rather than complying with standards that reproduce hegemony in the social studies.

In the Section II case studies, the teacher researcher in chapter 5 describes a study conducted in her third-grade classroom that examined how students responded when parents had an expanded role in curriculum and assessment using "re-membered" content. In chapter 6, a math methods professor examines how a "re-membered" social studies text informed pre-service teachers' choices of math concepts, the ways in which they structured lessons, and their ideas about historical content. In chapter 7, a pre-service ESOL teacher examines what a lesson plan looks like that uses culturally informed instructional materials and emancipatory pedagogy to encourage critical thinking. In chapter 8, a teacher educator and two of her doctoral students explore what happened when a teacher educator modeled Afrocentric curriculum and pedagogy to support doctoral students teaching middle school students and what happened when the parents of these students were invited to collaboratively reflect on what was taught to their children. The coda or final chapter 9 identifies a new theme: using "re-membered" texts to reveal how disconnected relationships and practices can be "re-membered," which has implications for changing the educational system.

In this neo-reform era of management-driven accountability, democratizing the content of the curriculum seems to be off the radar of considered reforms. Perhaps policy makers and practitioners within the dominant episteme see no need for reforming the curriculum, as monocultural content—as well as appropriated multicultural content—is well-suited to the assimilationist mission of schooling to produce a so-called Americanized citizenry and national unity based on Euro-American values and experiences. Or perhaps the curriculum has been sidelined by policies designed to distract educators from resisting the hegemony it perpetuates. In either case, the content of the curriculum represents harmful practice for students who either don't see themselves or see token or distorted representations of themselves, their communities, and their ancestors in the curriculum. These too-common experiences devalue their identity, compromise their interest and engagement in school, and teach a hierarchy of human worth that positions liminal identity groups at the bottom. In addition, when parents and families are disconnected from participation in the instructional process, valuable knowledge and experiences are silenced; and when "agreed-upon versions of knowledge" dictate the use of transmission pedagogy, students become receivers of scripted lessons, not critical thinkers and co-creators of knowledge (Swartz & Goodwin, 1992, p. 58). Monocultural content also disserves students whose heritage is privileged in the curriculum, as the social and curricular construction of dominance as inevitable diminishes their access to the human collective. Thus, it is the content of the curriculum, the mind-numbing pedagogy used to present it, and the absence of meaningful parent/family participation in the instructional process that are at the core of programming the probable destinies of children of African ancestry and all children according to how they are positioned on the hierarchy of human worth. Locking down schools as fortresses of grand narratives and the exclusionary ideologies and practices they produce ensures that this programming proceeds uninterrupted generation after generation.

It is not difficult to make a case for the inclusion and representation of students and parents and the use of inquiry-based pedagogy, and we do this. Yet our intention is to go beyond this need to "prove" what is systemically harmful to show how change can be made. Using an emancipatory paradigm that draws upon African and Indigenous knowledge bases and the Black Studies intellectual tradition, we identify what Molefi Kete Asante (1980/1988) calls cultural platforms as locations of the knowledge and experiences that describe an identity group's participation in any topic, era, or movement. With cultural platforms in place, it is possible to write group narratives; and with our process of "re-membering" it is also possible to combine these narratives in student texts. When these disconnected narratives are reconnected, this "re-membered" content about both dominant and dominated groups obviates the omissions and distortions that occur when history is viewed through only one lens or location. Thus, in an Afrocentric culturally informed praxis of historical recovery, the dominant episteme no longer controls accounts of the past. Our stories—that is, all of our stories, and how they connect to the stories of others—can now be told.

References

Apple, M. (1999). *Official knowledge: Democratic education in a conservative age* (2nd ed.). New York, NY: Routledge.

Asante, M. K. (1980/1988). *Afrocentricity*. Trenton, NJ: Africa World Press.

Asante, M. K. (2007). *The history of Africa: The quest for eternal harmony*. New York, NY: Routledge.

Boykin, W. A. (1994). Afrocultural expression and its implications for schooling. In E. R. Hollins, J. E. King, & W. C. Hayman (Eds.), *Teaching diverse populations: Formulating a knowledge base* (pp. 243–273). Albany, NY: State University of New York Press.

Carruthers, J. (1995). *Mdw Ntr: Divine speech: A historiographical reflection of African deep thought from the time of the Pharaohs to the present*. London, England: Karnak House/Lawrenceville, NJ: Red Sea Press.

Clarke, J. H. (1998). *Christopher Columbus and the Afrikan holocaust: Slavery and the rise of European capitalism*. Brooklyn, NY: A & B Publishers Group.

Diop, C. A. (1974). *The African origins of civilization: Myth or reality?* (M. Cook, Trans.). Westport, CT: Lawrence Hill Company.

Harding, V. (1990). *Hope and history*. New York, NY: Orbis Books.

Hegel, G. W. F. (1900). *The philosophy of history*. New York, NY: The Colonial Press. (rev. ed. from G. W. F. Hegel's original lecture manuscripts, 1830–1831)

Hilliard, A. G., III (1997). *SBA: The reawakening of the African mind*. Gainesville, FL: Makare Publishing.

King, J. E. (2006). "If justice is our objective": Diaspora literacy, heritage knowledge and the praxis of critical studyin' for human freedom. *Yearbook of the National Society for the Study of Education, 105*(2), 337–360.

King, J. E. (2008). Epilogue: Black education post-Katrina: "And all us we are not saved." In L. C. Tillman (Ed.), *Sage handbook of African American education* (pp. 499–510). Thousand Oaks, CA: Sage.

Swartz, E. E. (2013). *Freedom and democracy: A story remembered*. Rochester, NY: Omincentric Press.

Swartz, E. E., & Goodwin, S. (1992). Multiculturality: Liberating classroom pedagogy and practice. *Social Science Record, 30*(1), 43–69.

Wynter, S. (1992). Do not call us "Negroes": How multicultural textbooks perpetuate racism. San Francisco, CA: Aspire Books.

Wynter, S. (1997). Alterity. In C. Grant & G. Ladson-Billings (Eds.), *Dictionary of multicultural education* (pp. 13–14). New York, NY: Oryx.

ACKNOWLEDGMENTS

We are responsible for the words we have written, yet these words are a gathering of voices from the past and present who have taught us and called us to consciousness. We acknowledge family, both kindred and community who stand with us, always. We thank the late Dr. Martha E. Hennington—a Harriet of our times—for taking us steps closer to freedom; Dr. Susan Goodwin whose insight and actions create contexts for thoughtful and emancipatory work; and Dr. Molefi Kete Asante for producing and advancing the Afrocentric meta-theory that guides this work. We pay tribute to teachers and students who make our work meaningful, and we thank the Routledge editorial and production staff whose consistent support throughout the process of preparing, finalizing, and publishing this manuscript has carried us to our destination.

SECTION I

An Afrocentric Culturally Informed Praxis of Historical Recovery

This volume has two sections and readers can begin with either one. For some, the case studies in Section II will provide a practice-based context for then engaging with the chapters in Section I that explain and exemplify the emancipatory intent of historical recovery. Others will prefer the reverse—moving from explanations of praxis to its school-based implementation. Moving in either direction is a viable approach to using this volume.

The four chapters in Section I describe a praxis of historical recovery that produces democratized knowledge using Afrocentric theory and principles of culturally informed curricular practice. The need for democratized knowledge is demonstrated through examination of standard social studies materials that have historically perpetuated a culturally singular version of the past through grand narratives and master scripts. A four-phase process for re-connecting or "re-membering" the past is presented, as well as how to produce democratized knowledge in the form of student texts. Even though knowledge of the past cannot be known with empirical certainty, it can become more comprehensive when scholarship is informed by a range of diverse vantage points, voices, knowledge bases, and experiences. This section also provides a democratized standards model to guide teaching and measure student learning.

1

INTRODUCTION

What kind of social studies knowledge can stimulate a critical dialog with the past and present, and how can it be constructed?

A Democratized Vision of History: Who Will Benefit?

"Re-membering" history is a process enacted within an Afrocentric culturally informed praxis of historical recovery that reconnects the multiple and shared knowledge bases and experiences that shaped the past. This praxis has three components—Afrocentric theory, the principles of culturally informed curricular practice, and practitioner inquiry (Asante, 1980/1988; Cochran-Smith & Lytle, 2009; Swartz, 2012a). Together, these components are designed to actualize a democratized vision of history that steps outside of reproducing "history business" as usual by engaging teachers, teacher educators, students, and families in conscious inquiry about their shared present as a continuance of a shared past. This vision of the past—and the examples that bring it to life in this text—can enhance what social studies educators and those in other fields know and are able to do with historical knowledge. Importantly, a goal of this praxis for teacher learning and development is to cultivate teachers who (a) "are community minded—putting their knowledge, skills, and compassion at the service of themselves, peers, families, and communities;" (b) "are scholars who conceptualize and demonstrate learning as a communal practice"; and (c) "are imaginative, creative, critical, and reflective thinkers and builders" (RTC, 2007, p. 4).

These three standards are quoted from the Rochester Teacher Center *Cultural Learning Standards* (RTC, 2007), which describe what students are expected to know, be able to do, and be like. If educators are guided by these standards, they can model them for students. With a three-pronged focus on what teachers are expected to know (content), be able to do (pedagogy), and be like (ways of being), we invite teacher educators, pre-service teachers, and in-service teachers to use this volume in structured dialogues about the practical applications of using social studies knowledge in both classrooms and communities. PK-12 practitioners, teacher educators, and researchers affiliated with the Rochester Teacher Center have demonstrated the power of this way of learning as seen in their classrooms and professional development activities such as teacher research, an example of which is included in chapter 5 in this volume.

This chapter by Joyce E. King and Ellen E. Swartz is the first of four chapters in Section I. It defines and describes the grand narratives still found in social studies curricula and analyzes examples from the master scripts that continue to teach and perpetuate these grand narratives. Even though there is now an increased presence of historically omitted cultures and groups in social studies materials, we explain how their insertions serve to reify grand narratives and the master scripts that now include them. These narratives and scripts can be countered by producing and studying democratized knowledge, which refers to knowledge that is reconnected or "re-membered" through the Afrocentric culturally informed praxis of historical recovery introduced in this chapter.

Chapter 2, "Silenced History" by Ellen E. Swartz, examines the limitations and gatekeeping function of grand narratives and master scripts that silence history and the ways in which they teach and replicate a hierarchy of human worth. She describes and exemplifies the three components of the praxis of historical recovery: Afrocentric theory and its human-centric concepts that frame historical accounts able to center *all* cultures and groups, the six principles of culturally informed curricular practice that translate these Afrocentric concepts into the writing of student texts, and practitioner inquiry that examines the use of "re-membered" student texts in classrooms and community.

Chapter 3, "'Re-Membering' the Way to Content" by Joyce E. King and Ellen E. Swartz, discusses the four phases in the "re-membering" process; identifies, refines, charts, and compares the salient themes in each identity-group narrative; and shows how the alterity themes of Haudenosaunee and African people, and a marginalized theme of a sub-group of White colonists, provide knowledge that upends the silences in grand narratives and master scripts (King, 2004; Wynter, 2006). This chapter further explains how the knowledge bases and experiences of *all* identity groups that shaped freedom and democracy in colonial North America can be reconnected in the form of a student text entitled *Freedom and Democracy: A Story Remembered* (Swartz, 2013).

In chapter 4, "Standards "Re-Membered" by Ellen E. Swartz, we take up the question of standards in the current management driven era of neo-reform. State standards and culturally informed standards are presented in order to demonstrate their combined use in guiding teaching and measuring learning in the social studies. Just as Afrocentric theory and the principles of culturally informed curricular practice can democratize knowledge by "re-membering" it, standards for the social studies can be democratized if they too are informed by a range of diverse vantage points, knowledge bases, and experiences that shaped the past. Our standards model invites teachers to take hold of standards and use them in the best interests of teaching and learning, rather than be held hostage by standards that reproduce hegemonic narratives of the past.

Chapters 5 through 8 in Section II of this volume are examples of practitioner inquiry that demonstrate how elementary, higher education, and pre-service teachers have examined the use of "re-membered" texts. Together, these four practitioner studies provide feedback about pedagogy, student outcomes, family participation, and relationships among teachers, students, and families when using "re-membered" student texts. These studies also represent a new line of research on Afrocentric culturally informed praxis with the potential for systemic change.

In chapter 5, "Austin Steward: 'Home-Style' Teaching, Planning, and Assessment," Linda Campbell describes a study she conducted in her third-grade classroom that examined how students respond when parents have an expanded role in culturally responsive curriculum and assessment. (Note that in this volume the term "culturally responsive" is interchangeable with the term "culturally informed.") Family members were invited to participate in creating an assessment rubric, help students with homework, and co-produce a book about Austin Steward with their children based on a "re-membered" document-based learning chapter entitled "Austin Steward: Self-Determination and Human Freedom" (Goodwin & Swartz, 2009). The study's findings show the impact on a teacher, students, and parents—and on their relationships—when parents have an expanded role in a culturally informed curriculum.

In chapter 6, Shonda Lemons-Smith reports on an interdisciplinary study she conducted entitled "Using 'Re-Membered' Student Text as a Pedagogical Frame for Urban Pre-Service Mathematics Teachers." As a math educator she explores the ways in which the "re-membered" student text, *Freedom and Democracy: A Story Remembered* (Swartz, 2013) informs pre-service teachers' choices of math concepts, the structure of their lessons, and their ideas about historical content when writing lesson plans and discussing content. The study's findings echo those in the teacher preparation literature about how pre-service teachers engage with issues of cultural diversity and suggest the kind of learning situations pre-service teachers need when using culturally informed content. This study also underscores the value of teacher preparation that includes cultural knowledge in methods and other courses, not only in a designated diversity course.

In chapter 7, "Culturally Informed Lesson Planning," Ericka López describes a study she conducted when she was an English for Speakers of Other Languages (ESOL) pre-service teacher. This case study examines what a lesson plan looks like when a culturally informed text, *Freedom and Democracy: A Story*

Remembered (Swartz, 2013) and emancipatory pedagogy are used to encourage critical thinking. The study's findings indicate what teachers and students need to know, do, and be like in culturally informed lesson planning. López also identified how traditional lesson planning is linked to tracking and the systemic marginalization of ESOL students who are often placed in low ability or special education classes and experience high dropout rates.

In chapter 8, "Recovering History and the 'Parent Piece' for Cultural Well-Being and Belonging," teacher educator Joyce E. King and two of her doctoral students, Adrienne C. Goss and Sherell A. McArthur, co-investigate what happens when doctoral students and parents engage with Afrocentric curriculum and pedagogy in an afterschool program. King models Afrocentric curriculum and pedagogy for her doctoral students who are teaching middle school students, and, in a series of workshops, the research team discusses this same curriculum with the parents of these students. This curriculum represents an African worldview drawn from both classical Africa and the Diaspora. The study's findings indicate the impact of these interventions on doctoral students and parents related to historical recovery and cultural well-being and belonging.

Chapter 9 entitled "Coda: What 'Re-Membered' Texts 'Re-Member'" is assembled through the writings of all authors. We refer to this final chapter as a coda, because it not only connects the Afrocentric culturally informed praxis described in Section I with the summaries and findings of the four case studies in Section II, but it also identifies a new theme about the relationship between using "re-membered" texts and "re-membering" disconnected relationships and practices that when put back together have implications for changing the educational system.

Democratizing Knowledge

Democratized knowledge in the social studies is coalescent knowledge that reconnects or "re-members" the multiple and shared knowledge bases and experiences that shaped the past (Swartz, 2007a). Such knowledge eschews singular, agreed-upon, hegemonic constructions of knowledge that fragment and distort the past. A number of educators write about the democratization of knowledge (Asante, 2007; Fishman & McLaren, 2000; Freire, 1998; Giroux, 2001; Grande, 2004; Karenga, 2006). These scholars make clear cases for curricular and pedagogical reinventions aimed at changing everyday oppressive conditions, achieving social justice and equality, and/or producing examples of self-determination and collective responsibility instead of the more prevalent emphases on appropriation and assimilation. Unfortunately, this scholarship has had little impact on the "official knowledge" that corporate-owned textbook publishers and their state partners continue to produce for PK-12 teaching and learning (Apple, 1999; Buras, 2008). Nevertheless, these analyses of the democratization of knowledge constitute counter responses to the power hierarchy that controls school knowledge and determines whose knowledge is to be known and whose is to be suppressed (Buras, 2008; Popkewitz, 1992; Stanley, 1998). While we draw upon a range of these discourses, we focus more on the actual process of producing and studying social studies content and pedagogy for PK-12 students. Given the dearth of such developmentally appropriate curricular materials for younger children, we take the next step to write and study democratized instructional materials for school children. The alternatives to standard social studies knowledge that we provide in this volume permit readers to examine and experience the way content and pedagogy can either expand or shrink possibilities for engaging school children in a dialog with the past that has heretofore been unavailable to them.

Standard Social Studies Knowledge

We refer to the knowledge typically taught in the social studies as "standard," since its character and content—as seen in textbooks and related curricula and assessments—have been, for the most part, unchanged for generations (CIBC, 1977; Peterson, 2008; Spring, 2011; Swartz, 1996). Most of the scholarship related to standard social studies content has been produced by traditional historians whose writing supports a conservative socio-political agenda that fits well with the grand narratives that explain U.S. national development from a particular perspective (Appleby, Hunt, & Jacob, 1994; Buras, 2008). As seen in textbooks since the 1990s, a few revisionist historians and well-known multicultural/culturally responsive educators have also been employed as authors by corporate publishers (Armento, Nash, Salter, & Wixson, 1991; Banks et al., 2005; Boyd et al., 2011a-e). While these scholars have built careers and published work that challenge standard curricular practices (Banks, 2001; Gay, 2000) and brought additional perspectives to historical accounts (Nash, 1976/1990), the conservative context of PK-12 publishing has reduced their impact to an illusion of inclusion, that is, a form of inclusion that does not challenge standard narratives as we will see in examples throughout this volume (Buras, 2008; Cornbleth & Waugh, 1995; King, 2004). So, it comes as no surprise that educators in the discipline of social studies continue to impart a dismembered and fragmented record of errors, omissions, distortions, and misrepresentations of *all* cultures and groups.

Even after decades of critique from parents, community groups, and educators, the state and corporate publishers of social studies materials (including standards) have not changed grand narratives, which are the explanatory themes of national development that frame their products (Epstein, 2009; Swartz, 2009). In fact, as we will show, publishers' moves to multiculturalize social studies textbooks actually reify the grand narratives of U.S. history that have served as the framework for standard curricula, instructional materials, and assessments for generations. As soon as children enter school, their understandings of the past (and therefore the present) are shaped by such narratives, albeit in different ways (Epstein, 2009). These grand narratives—and the cumulative master scripts through which they are conveyed—define what students learn about national development, including such topics as European exploration and colonial settlement, slavery, freedom and democracy, manifest destiny, industrialization, economic development, immigration, and U.S. expansion. While the state/corporate partnership has appropriated and used some concepts from multicultural education to "colorize," "genderize," and in other ways tokenize the once excluded in grand narratives and master scripts, we acknowledge that multicultural education and other cultural knowledge practices have provided locations from which it is possible to critique this appropriation. In fact, advancing a praxis of historical recovery in this volume depends upon a range of cultural knowledge theories and practices that preceded this work.

A close look at one grand narrative will show the content and assumptions it contains. The topic of European exploration and colonial settlement of the Americas is typically introduced in kindergarten, often in October with the celebration of Columbus Day. Each year, students learn more about this topic. By the fifth grade, they are imprinted with the explanatory themes of this grand narrative, meaning that most students have internalized the messages it conveys. Table 1.1 provides the basic elements of the hegemonic grand narrative of European exploration and colonial settlement. It is a euro-driven account of what happened that also includes an unstated set of faulty assumptions about sovereignty, legitimacy, choice, right of conquest, difference, and development.

Children learn this grand narrative by reading master scripts that transmit and keep alive the hegemonic explanations of European exploration and colonial settlement. With only slight variations, this grand narrative and the master scripts that teach it can be found in *any* state social studies standards

TABLE 1.1 Grand Narrative of European Exploration and Colonial Settlement

Beginning in the 15th century, European rulers sent explorers on ocean voyages in search of shorter sea routes to other parts of the world and to find resources such as gold, salt, and spices. When they arrived in the Americas, they met native people who were unknown to Europeans at that time. Explorers claimed the lands they found, set up towns, and opened the way for European settlement. When they returned home, they reported what they learned on their often long and difficult journeys, which led to increased interest in settling the land and developing its abundant resources. Within a short period of time, colonies were established and thousands of Europeans came to settle in them. Many people came in search of opportunities and religious freedom. Native Americans often helped European settlers survive in the new land, yet there were conflicts between them due to their different ways of life. Some of these conflicts led to war, which brought about many changes for Native Americans. As time went on, Europeans and their descendants worked hard to develop the vast lands and natural resources they found. They established economic, political, and social systems that suited their new way of life in the Americas.

and corporate textbooks. These standards and scripts are ubiquitous and consistent in teaching arrangements of knowledge that assume the paramountcy of Europe in general and its wealthy, male, and abled descendants in particular. This assumption is maintained by presenting knowledge of the past through only one cultural lens or location.

What Master Scripts Teach about European Exploration and Colonial Settlement

In Table 1.1 the claiming of land upon which European explorers set foot and their ensuing conquest and empire building are described only in their voices and are in no way questioned in master scripts that convey this grand narrative. As foundational elements upon which European colonies and later the United States were established, exploration, conquest, and colonization have an assumed legitimacy. The capture and enslavement of Indigenous people—and soon after African people, the brutal imposition of Christianity, and the huge profits plantation owners made all occurred within a short time after the arrival of explorers and were often initiated by them. Master scripts present these historical developments as inevitable aspects of the colonial project and the so-called advance of "civilization" rather than as choices by sovereign European states that disregarded the sovereignty of Indigenous and African Peoples and Nations. (See the first section of chapter 3 for a detailed in-text explanation of the use and capping of "Nations" and "Peoples.") The language and concepts these master scripts use to refer to the Indigenous lands, lives, and cultures that Europeans claimed, disrupted, or destroyed misrepresent these events. For example, these scripts use seemingly innocuous statements such as "the native peoples' way of life changed" (Boyd et al., 2011a, p. 136). A primary reason given for this "change" that made European conquest more possible is said to be smallpox germs carried by Europeans, which killed large numbers of Indigenous people (Garcia, Ogle, Risinger, & Stevos, 2005). European germs did cause much death, yet focusing blame on microbes effectively masks the ideology and actions of cultural supremacy that, from the outset, drove European conquest and disregard for the lives of Indigenous people.

Master scripts virtually omit Indigenous people immediately following their initial encounters with European explorers and settlers. Students learn not only what explorers and early settlers did, but also what they thought and believed, while the thoughts and beliefs of Indigenous people about the colonial experience are absent, as if they didn't have any. European settlers traded with Native Americans, but there were often "conflicts" or "clashes" (the descriptive words of choice in textbooks), which are said to be the result of different ways of life. Thus, students are taught that it is difference that creates "conflict" and "clash," not unjust policies and dominating practices that create resistance. European actions are merely stated as facts—as just what happened—which obfuscates the European assumed right of conquest and domination.

Indigenous people were clearly the majority of people in the early colonial period, with mid-range estimates being around 75 million people in North and South America when Europeans arrived in the late 15th century (CIBC, 1977; Olson, 2002). Their majority is, however, impossible to perceive in state standards, curricula, and textbooks. Soon after the arrival of Europeans, there is a near absence of Indigenous people and communities and a predominance of explorers, settlers, and colonial settlements in standards, curricular guidelines, text, and images. From this point on, the central story of the Americas is a European story. Indigenous Americans appear as individuals, with a few such as Doña Marina, Pocahontas, Squanto, and Sacagawea being regularly included in master scripts. Their legitimacy appears to come only from the assistance they gave explorers or early settlers, since this is the only information provided about them. While this assistance is noted as helpful, it is through the hard work of European colonists that development of what is still called a "wilderness" in some textbooks is accomplished. Here we see an embedded Lockean assumption that developing "wild" and "unused" Indigenous land justifies its appropriation by any and all means, which reflects another unstated assumption about the European right of conquest leading to appropriation (Arneil, 1996; Locke, 1988; Tully, 1993). Texts communicate that with land and the development of farms and businesses, colonists built a way of life based on freedom and rights that were denied to them in Europe. Yet, their denial of freedom and rights to Indigenous Americans, Africans, poor Europeans, and all women is typically underplayed, but most often omitted. The hierarchy of whose knowledge is valued and whose assumptions and explanations are legitimate is quite clear in the grand narrative of European exploration and colonial settlement.

Master Scripts and Social Studies Textbooks

As illustrated above, grand narratives and the "agreed-upon versions of knowledge" found in their accompanying master scripts constrict thinking through the hierarchal assumptions, inaccuracies, and distorted explanations they contain—a function they have had since the beginning of mandatory state education in the mid-19th century (Gatto, 2003; Swartz & Goodwin, 1992, p. 58). Even though social studies organizations such as the National Council for the Social Studies (NCSS, 2010) encourage teachers to engage in critical approaches that can *uncover* history, most teachers continue to *cover* the version of history found in market-driven textbooks (Apple, 1988; Buras, 2008; Cherryholmes, 1988; Farrell & Tanner, 2012; Nieto, 2002). Less experienced teachers—whose numbers are increasing in urban schools due to high teacher turnover—more often exhibit this tendency (Levstik, 2008). As the central purveyor of master scripts, textbooks have become more visually and graphically stimulating, more interactive through online support and digital versions, and more dotted with pictures of people of color, women, and workers. This can be seen by reviewing publishers websites (Kessler, 2011; Pearson Education, 2011) and by comparing a representative sample of elementary, middle, and high school textbooks across the last three decades (see Boyd et al., 2011a, compared to Klein, 1983; Garcia et al., 2005, compared to Schwartz & O'Connor, 1981; and Cayton, Israels Perry, Reed, & Winkler, 2007, compared to Graff, 1985). Little has changed in terms of the misrepresentations of all cultures and groups that stem from whose voice *always* narrates, whose experiences are *always* central and normative, and whose story is *always* presented as the "real" story of U.S. development. Moreover, these textbook master scripts communicate more than history's storylines. They convey messages about a selected set of ontologies, epistemologies, ideologies, beliefs, and values, so that even when historically omitted groups are present, their incorporation takes the form of isolated "mentioning" (Apple, 1999) that fits within the values and beliefs of what Claude Denis (1997) and Sandy Grande (2004) call "whitestream" culture.

Just as corporations have pushed the advertising of their products into schools by providing "free" computer equipment and other resources, increasingly consolidated global textbook publishers push their versions of knowledge—which are tightly linked to state and local standards and curricular frameworks—into classrooms through a network of national distribution laden with technical support and offers to localize portions of text (Buras, 2008; Fishman & McLaren, 2000; Swartz, 2009). It is somewhat perplexing that voices ranging from classroom teachers to critical pedagogues in academia argue that even though these market-serving tomes are limited and limiting, they represent contexts for critical thinking and the negotiation of knowledge. There is no doubt much to gain from the analysis of corporatized knowledge, but advocating its critique—particularly by young students—ignores the vast omissions and distortions in textbooks that leave students and teachers virtually devoid of the knowledge needed for critical analysis to be possible. Why not replace the seemingly endless analysis of dominance—which, in effect, keeps us wedded to dominance—with critical analysis of democratized knowledge? Imagine that instead of thinking critically about the shortcomings of state-sanctioned standards and textbooks, students and teachers thought critically about texts that acknowledge the self-determination, sovereignty, and indigenous voices of *all* cultures and groups (Franklin, 1992; Grande, 2004; Karenga, 2006; King & Goodwin, 2006; Lomawaima & McCarty, 2006; Wynter, 2006). Needless to say, as we debate *how* to use these canonical texts—not *what* to use instead—the corporate textbook industry is busy churning them out. Year after year, rearranged versions appear, and year after year they fall profoundly short of a critical dialog with the past—the approach to writing history recommended by the American Historical Association (AHA, 2011). The large question percolating here is what kind of social studies content can facilitate the AHA's recommendation, and how can that content be constructed?

The Black Studies Intellectual Tradition

We turn to authorities within the Black Studies intellectual tradition—historians, educators, philosophers, authors, and civil and human rights advocates—whose systems of thought and broad conceptual frameworks of cultural representation, social justice, self-determination, and analysis of domination and resistance have challenged and rethought universalized grand narratives for over a century (Asante, 1980/1988, 1987/1998; Césaire, 1955/2000; Cooper, 1892/1969; Crawford, 2003; Du Bois, 1903, 1945; Fanon, 1963, 1965, 1967; Hilliard, 1978; King, 2005; Woodson, 1919, 1933/1990; Wynter, 1992, 2006). African and Diasporan scholars in this tradition—and others whose work has been informed by it—provide theoretical and empirical support for the democratization of knowledge, a process that relies on ethical integrity and concern for the human collective (Aptheker, 1951/1969, 1976/1990; Asante, 2007; Carruthers, 1972/1994; Clarke, 1990; Diop, 1967, 1974; Davidson, 1978; Du Bois, 1899, 1902, 1924, 1935/1972; Hilliard, 1986; Karenga, 2006; Thompson, 1990). For example, W. E. B. Du Bois and Herbert Aptheker have conducted historical and sociological studies that demonstrate the agency of African and European people in the Diaspora as they resisted injustice, contributed to the development of the United States, and created social, political, and economic institutions—all filling the void evident in the omission or marginalization of this knowledge in standard instructional materials. Importantly, these and earlier scholars and actionists such as Martin Delany (1972), Robert B. Elliott (1997), Henry Highland Garnet (1972), David Walker (1965), Ida B. Wells (1892), and Marcus Garvey (Clarke & Garvey, 1974) give us access to their distinct actions, knowledge, and experiences, including their analyses of the milieu in which they lived. Together, their work makes possible fuller representations of the past and lays a foundation for theoretically and practically expanding and transforming social studies knowledge in the present (C. M. Banks, 1995; J. A. Banks, 1992).

Afrocentric Theoretical Framework

One theoretical framework that has emerged from the Black Studies intellectual tradition and the scholarship noted above is Afrocentricity (Asante, 1980/1988). As a set of ideas, concepts, processes, and mode of analysis, this theoretical framework calls upon the knowledge bases of ancient to modern African/Diasporan history and culture to radically rethink and transform the centuries of misinformation and denigration of all things African (Asante, 2007; Diop, 1974; Karenga, 1990; Mazama, 2003). Afrocentricity is a theory of liberation for African people *as a group,* able to not only challenge racial oppression and the belief structures and hierarchies of power that sustain it, but able to construct emancipatory knowledge in the interests of African people and therefore in the interests of the human collective (Asante, 1987/1998; Dove, 2003; Karenga,

2006; Kershaw, 1992). There are applications of Afrocentric theory in diverse academic disciplines that are constructed with concepts that Afrocentric theorists hold in common. For this reason, we follow Molefi Kete Asante (2007) by calling Afrocentric theory a metatheory that "exists as a place in which Afrocentric theories can be generated to deal with practically any issue in the African world" (pp. 101–102). This metatheory posits that by locating African people at the center of phenomena, not on the periphery to be described and defined by others, the universalized knowledge of the hierarchal European episteme can be replaced with democratized knowledge (Asante, 1980/1988, 2003a & b). Concepts such as Centrality/Location, Subjects with Agency, and the Reclamation of Cultural Heritage—which are applicable to all cultures and groups—define the character of this metatheory, whose use has the capacity to broaden social studies knowledge by cutting through grand narratives and their master scripts in order to reimagine social studies knowledge devoid of the supremacies these narratives and scripts uphold. (These and other Afrocentric concepts are listed and defined in chapter 2, Table 2.3.) We will show how the Afrocentric culturally informed praxis of historical recovery democratizes knowledge production in the social studies by using Afrocentric metatheory and concepts in the production of knowledge about *all* cultures and groups.

Thus, Afrocentricity, which is more fully described in chapter 2, is a framework within which to construct curricular knowledge so that all cultures and groups speak for and about themselves through scholarship that unearths and centers their voices. For example, the historical record of the African press in the United States between 1827 and 1865 (called "African" here to reflect the indigenous naming of churches, schools, and mutual aid societies as African during that period) demonstrates the self-determination of African people who, as subjects with agency responded to the oppressive sociopolitical conditions of that period. Learning about the African press with Afrocentricity as a framework locates African people in the Diaspora as normative subjects at the center of engagement with the democratic spirit of the post-Revolutionary era. The editors of newspapers such as *Freedom's Journal* (1827–1830), *Mirror of Liberty* (1838-1840), and *The North Star* (1847–1851) demonstrated a twin commitment to liberation and education by informing readers of ongoing struggles for freedom and the achievements of African men and women in business, education, and other fields during a period of severe racial restrictions (Detweiler, 1922; Hutton, 1993). In cities and towns, the African press existed alongside the establishment of African mutual aid societies (e.g., New York African Society for Mutual Relief), African schools (e.g., New York African Free Schools, African Mutual Instruction Society), African churches (e.g., African Methodist Episcopal Church, African Methodist Episcopal Zion Church) as well as state and national conventions, anti–slavery societies, vigilance committees, literary societies, libraries, and reading rooms whose meetings and activities were often noted in these newspapers. The African press was itself a 19th century strategy for centering African people as subjects within and across communities at a time when they were excluded from and/or vilified in White newspapers and other institutions of the dominant society. As such, the early African press signifies a standing place or location from which African people represent Subjects with Agency, Collective Consciousness, and Collective Responsibility—three Afrocentric concepts. In this way, Afrocentric metatheory and concepts bring forward the ways in which newspaper editors, agents, and community members took actions that reflected their collective interests in and care for African people. Yes, these concepts were there, and yes, Afrocentric theory guides a writer to look for them in the historical record.

By comparison, standard social studies scholarship would produce an account of the early African press (if this topic were even included) that would miss these concepts. At best, it would mention one or two newspapers, their dates of operation, and perhaps provide a sound bite quote from an article by Frederick Douglass or a picture of *The North Star* masthead. It would fail to connect the African press to the establishment of other organizations in African communities. This fragmented view of a section of Diasporan history distorts the meaning of that period by missing how the conscious and collective efforts of African people produced interdependent community practices aimed at expanding people's opportunities and life chances. Afrocentricity guides the recovery of this heritage knowledge by using concepts such as Collective Consciousness, Collective Responsibility, Centrality/Location, Self-Determination, Subjects with Agency, and the Reclamation of Cultural Heritage that prompt us to look for that which is conceptually African in the African past and present—for what Asante (1980/1988) calls the cultural platform that carries sets of knowledge, beliefs, values, and ways of being that endure, in any culture, across time. When the past and present are constructed from the cultural platforms of its participants, we take a step closer to democratizing the social studies curriculum.

Culturally Informed Curricular Practice

Afrocentric theory provides the concepts that frame student texts that are "remembered," and six principles of culturally informed curricular practice bring those concepts to the page through words, images, and graphics. These principles—inclusion, representation, accurate scholarship, indigenous voice, critical thinking, and a collective humanity—are defined and exemplified in chapter 2. They are drawn from numerous criteria, guidelines in Black Studies scholarship, and analyses of multicultural education, culturally relevant/responsive teaching, and culturally centered education (ANKN, 1999; Banks, 1988, 2004; Cajete, 1994; CIBC, 1977; Gay, 2000, 2004; Karenga, 2003, 2006; King, 1994, 2004; Ladson-Billings, 1994, 2004). We have used and refined these principles over the past 25 years in critical evaluations of instructional materials (Swartz, 1989, 1992, 1996, 2009), the production of professional development materials

(Goodwin & Swartz, 2004, 2006, 2008, 2009), the writing and publication of instructional materials for students (Swartz, 2007b, 2008a & b, 2010, 2013), and in empirical research (Swartz, 2004, 2012a; Swartz & Bakari, 2005). Importantly, these principles have also been informed by teachers and teacher educators in professional development settings where cultural knowledge is the framework within which teaching and learning are studied (RTC, 2008). For example, when teachers design collegial learning circles, teacher research projects, and peer review sessions around gaining cultural knowledge related to the students they teach, their use and perceptions of the principles of culturally informed curricular practice add to what we understand from the conceptual and empirical literature. In the Afrocentric culturally informed praxis of historical recovery, we use these principles to identify relevant research and to write democratized accounts about *both* dominant and oppressed cultures and groups. For example, using the principles of indigenous voice and accurate scholarship in writing text about the above example of the African press, an Afrocentric concept such as the Reclamation of Cultural Heritage can be actualized by including the voices of newspaper editors and writers of the African press and the White press as they speak for, name, and define themselves so that their actions become a known part of our shared cultural heritage.

Linking the principles of culturally informed curricular practice to Afrocentric concepts can bring back the silenced voices and put back together the once-lived, contiguous, and interdependent strands of history. After all, various groups of people experienced past events, movements, or eras—often at the same time and in the same places. Historical records that hold this knowledge can speak about and exemplify how all cultures and groups have lived, acted, and produced in ways that mark their presence. And it is this knowledge that needs to be "re-membered," meaning that its members or pieces need to be put back together. Such re-connected knowledge—shaped by Afrocentric concepts and written using the principles of culturally informed curricular practice—is democratized knowledge; it brings together the voices and experiences of those who once *were* together. While the past is partial and incomplete, and its retrieval is constructed (Trouillot, 1995; Weinstein, 2005), democratized knowledge represents the possibility of coalescing knowledge that has been separated by grand narratives and master scripts. The etymology of the word "remember" can help to explain why this is so.

The Latin word *recordari* means to remember. In her analysis of the ways in which African bodies were itemized and "made into pieces" (p. 27) during enslavement, Barbara Christian (1995) reformulated remember as "re-member," meaning that the members or parts of bodies can be put back together. This reformulation is supported by knowing that the Greek word for *cord* in *recordari* is *chorde,* which means gut—a string or fiber made of braided strands. Christian's shift from "remember" to "re-member" suggests that the separation and profit-driven itemization of enslaved African's body parts on the auction block was one tool of subjugation that involved dismembering wholeness; and that putting those strands or parts back together is part of liberation from the residual effects of such inhumane practices. In the same sense, the "body" of the past (and therefore the present) has been dismembered and subjugated to the control of "whitestream" interests. While this "body" cannot be fully recovered, it can be made fuller through a process of reconnecting its cords or putting back together its once-connected strands that have been pulled apart (Swartz, 1998). By reconnecting these severed strands, the lived experiences, actions, and agency of all cultures and groups are brought to the surface and recovered as normative contexts in which to learn about the dialectical relationship between the past and present.

But, Haven't Things Changed?

Some will counter that change, albeit slow, is happening. Can we still say that school knowledge is held hostage by master-scripted, eurocratic accounts when historically omitted groups are present more than ever before in textbooks and curricula? In the last decade, for example, people of color and women are increasingly visible in social studies textbooks and the curricula that mirror them (Banks et al., 2005; Boyd et al., 2011a–e; Cayton et al., 2007; Danzer, Klor de Alva, Krieger, Wilson, & Woloch, 2005). As shown in two detailed examples below, however, the increased presence of the once omitted has had little effect on the grand narratives of U.S. history and the master scripts into which these "others" are now placed. As stated above, their insertions have served to maintain grand narratives and reify the master scripts that now include them.

The Ihánktunwan People, Zitkala-Ša, and the Grand Narrative of Manifest Destiny

Historically, the Ihánktunwan (Yankton) People are one of the seven Nations of the Očhéthi Šakówiŋ (Sioux Confederation or Seven Council Fires). Zitkala-Ša is an Ihánktunwan woman who lived in the late 19th and 20th centuries—a published author and lecturer who worked to maintain the cultural traditions of her people and to change federal policies that allowed land theft and exploitation of Indigenous Peoples (Fisher, 1979; Hafen, 1997; Rappaport, 1997). Her photograph and a sound bite quote about a painful childhood boarding school experience appear on a high school textbook page titled "Cultures Clash on the Prairie" (Danzer et al., 2005, p. 408). Cultural differences are presented as the reason for the "clash," as if differences inevitably lead to conflict. Signifying otherness, the image of Zitkala-Ša in traditional dress serves to represent these differences. And on the same page, the chapter's Main Idea states, "The cattle industry boomed in the late 1800s, as the culture of the Plains Indians declined." The textbook makes no connection between White settlers' actions and the "decline" of the Očhéthi Šakówiŋ. Instead, it carefully selects images and words of now-included "others" to fit within the grand narrative of manifest destiny. The accounts of Zitkala-Ša and her People as they would tell them are silenced. In their place are decontextualized fragments that support this grand narrative of imperialist expansion and bolster the master script that teaches it by multiculturalizing or making it appear more inclusive. While scholarship exists that could bring a more accurate presence of the Očhéthi Šakówiŋ and other Indigenous Peoples into PK-12 historical accounts, it is submerged in the westward and Whiteward movement emblazoned in the master script that continues to protect the grand narrative of manifest destiny (Deloria, 1970, 2004; Grande, 2004; Lomawaima & McCarty, 2006).

African People and the Grand Narrative of Freedom in the Revolutionary Era

African people are now present in instructional materials about the pre- and post-Revolutionary War period. For example, noteworthy individuals such as Prince Hall, Elizabeth Freeman, and Richard Allen are recently included in some textbooks. However, their stories are typically kept separate from the story of White colonial patriots fighting for freedom. This contradiction of White colonists seeking freedom from England while denying freedom to African people is a consistent theme in African petitions, letters, and other documents of this era—a theme that Hall, Freeman, and Allen acted upon (Aptheker, 1951/1969; Bennett, 1968; Kaplan, 1973; Walker, 1965). Yet, textbooks typically credit Abigail Adams with observing this contradiction in a section of her 1776 "Don't forget the ladies" letter to John Adams (Cayton et al., 2007). It is a rare case when an African person is given text space to voice the illogic of Europeans and their descendants wanting freedom and democracy while engaging in a system of slavery. In a recent fifth-grade textbook, Prince Hall is this rare case (Boyd et al., 2011a, p. 310). Let's look at how Hall is represented to see if this is an example of how things have changed.

Prince Hall's ideas about the contradiction of seeking freedom while maintaining slavery are placed in a special two-page section titled "Issues and Viewpoints," as if having freedom is a matter of viewpoint (Boyd et al., 2011a, p. 310). A painted image of Hall is placed on the symbolic backdrop of an American flag (that did not yet exist). Through symbolism and words, his actions are situated as part of (White) Americans "Seeking Freedom" (the page title) from England, rather than as part of his African understanding that freedom is a natural and shared right never forfeited by African people enslaved in the Americas. By so doing, the text severs Prince Hall from his ancestry; it also severs him from his community by inaccurately stating that "he sent a petition, or official written request [to end slavery], to the Massachusetts House of Representatives" (p. 310). In fact, he was one of seven African men who signed and sent this petition in 1777. Hall's leadership was informed by African traditions. He did not act alone, but in concert with others in the interests of his community. His efforts to bring congruency between the freedom and democracy rhetoric and the realities of his day were collective, but the price for inclusion in a master-scripted textbook account of Americans seeking freedom is erasure of the African conceptualizations, definitions, and communal pursuits of freedom that actually produced his ideas and actions (Bennett, 1975; Price, 1979). So, Prince Hall is included in ways that maintain the assimilationist assumption in the grand narrative of freedom, that is, that U.S. freedom is an absorptive concept that incorporates everyone equally. The master script that teaches this assumption emblematically incorporates Hall into the White pursuit of political freedom by excluding the African legacy of freedom and the collective orientations of his African identity. In other words, to maintain the assumption of assimilation in the grand narrative of freedom, that which is African about Prince Hall must be omitted from the master scripts that include him.

The two examples above show how the grand narratives of manifest destiny and freedom appropriate Indigenous and African people. Their increased insertions over the past decade might appear to be an improvement, yet the cost for this kind of inclusion is the theft (again) of their freedom—this time the freedom to speak and write accounts of *their* histories that relate *their* experiences and actions. Scott Richard Lyons (2000) refers to what has been stolen as "[r]hetorical sovereignty ... the inherent right and ability of *peoples* to determine their own communicative needs and desires in this pursuit, to decide for themselves the goals, modes, styles, and languages of public discourse" (pp. 449–450). While there is an abundance of scholarship to draw upon, it appears that corporatized and state-sanctioned school knowledge views the indigenously voiced presence of "others" as inconsistent with "whitestream" narratives of national development (Bennett, 1975; Denis, 1997; Grande, 2004; Price, 1979). So, Indigenous and African people are an absent presence—there, but not really there (Swartz, 1996). Actually, no grand narrative is more culpable of this dismissal and misrepresentation than the grand narrative of freedom and democracy, and it is this grand narrative that schoolchildren are diligently exposed to from their earliest years.

Is Change Possible?

While grand narratives and the master scripts that transmit them are still firmly in place, something *has* changed in the struggle over the curriculum. There is now general agreement—albeit more words than actions—among education leaders that inclusive and equitable accounts of diverse cultures and groups are needed in the social studies (AHA, 2011; Banks et al., 2001; NCSS, 2010; NYS Board of Regents, 1991). Yet, even after agreeing on the value of such accounts, decades of cosmetic changes by publishers and the absence of a method for producing democratized instructional materials has made minimal changes seem, to many, like all that can be expected. After all, how would textbook writers and curriculum specialists handle such "problems" as conflicting data and the resistance of dominant groups to altering their long-standing grand narratives? How would educators determine what is to be included or left out? How would they position concurrent narratives in relationship to each other? Is coherence (or what has passed for it) possible without dominance? This volume responds to these questions by using an Afrocentric culturally informed praxis of historical recovery that shows how to produce inclusive and equitable accounts of all cultures and groups in the form of "re-membered" texts. In so doing we move beyond the current rhetoric of agreement to accomplish democratized knowledge in the social studies.

A Caveat

It is important to note that while the need for democratized social studies materials is pressing, *we are not suggesting that teachers are responsible for producing these materials.* Teachers already have a job, and a very demanding one at that. The structure of schooling, with its current test and sanction environment keeps too many teachers anchored to a social efficiency, behaviorist model of schooling that dates to the early 20th century (Kliebard, 1986; Ravitch, 2010; Spring, 2011). With rare exceptions, teachers have little time and resources to conduct the necessary research and produce their own materials. So, while the process we propose can be taught, and some classroom teachers will be interested, teachers commonly experience that instructional materials are made available to them. In the same fashion, "re-membered" texts can be made available to teachers, teacher candidates, and teacher educators to enhance their content knowledge, to demonstrate how to "teach against the grain" using expanded content, and to underscore the need for social studies content and pedagogy that encourage critical thinking (Cochran-Smith, 1991; NCSS, 2010; Sleeter & Grant, 1988). As teachers learn what is limited about standard social studies materials, what democratized materials look like, and what happens when such materials are used, they will be better prepared to search for and request such materials—to expect more from the schools and districts in which they labor.

Merging Theory, Practice, and Practitioner Inquiry

In the chapters that follow, we present and use an Afrocentric culturally informed praxis of historical recovery that merges Afrocentric theory, the principles of culturally informed curricular practice, and practitioner inquiry to produce and study "re-membered" texts. The examples of practitioner inquiry in this volume demonstrate the pedagogy teachers and teacher educators use when these texts are the basis for constructing lessons and engaging parents in meaningful collaboration with teachers around instruction and assessment. In addition to a focus on social studies, interdisciplinary opportunities are presented for using "re-membered" texts produced with the praxis of historical recovery. In fact, one of our practitioner studies examines the use of a "re-membered" social studies text in teaching mathematics methods.

Pre-service and in-service teachers and teacher educators engaged in practitioner inquiry using three "re-membered" texts: *Freedom and Democracy: A Story Remembered* (Swartz, 2013), *Document-Based Learning: Curriculum and Assessment* (Goodwin & Swartz, 2009) and *Remembering Our Ancestors* (Swartz, 2012b). Their studies provide a range of instructive models for future teacher research about what happens when "re-membered" texts are used by teachers, students, and families. As explained in chapter 2, we anticipate varying iterations of practitioner inquiry to evolve from the diverse contexts and experiences of emergent to experienced educators who read this volume.

Recovering history by "re-membering" the topics that dominant accounts have steadily torn and kept apart interrupts the hegemonic versions of knowledge and knowing that are still being used to socialize children in schools across this nation. The process of "re-membering" presented in this volume demonstrates that it is possible to access a wide range of knowledge, experiences, claims, and practices from the historical record of all those cultures and groups that bore influence on a particular topic or era. Such democratized accounts are long overdue.

References

AHA (American Historical Association). (2011). *Statement on standards of professional conduct*. Washington, DC: Author.

ANKN (Alaska Native Knowledge Network). (1999). Guidelines for preparing culturally responsive teachers for Alaska's schools. Retrieved from http://www.ankn.uaf.edu/publications/teachers.html

Apple, M. (1988). *Teachers and texts: A political economy of class and gender relations in education*. Boston, MA: Routledge.

Apple, M. (1999). *Official knowledge: Democratic education in a conservative age* (2nd ed.). New York, NY: Routledge.

Appleby, J., Hunt, L., & Jacob, M. (1994). *Telling the truth about history*. New York, NY: W.W. Norton & Company.

Aptheker, H. (1951/1968). *A documentary history of the Negro people in the United States: From the Reconstruction era to 1910, Volume II*. New York, NY: The Citadel Press.

Aptheker, H. (1951/1969). *A documentary history of the Negro people in the United States: From colonial times through the Civil War* (Vol. I). New York, NY: The Citadel Press.

Aptheker, H. (1976/1990). *Early years of the republic: From the end of the Revolution to the first administration of Washington (1783–1793)*. New York, NY: International Publishers.

Armento, B. J., Nash, G. B., Salter, C. L., & Wixson, K. K. (1991). *America will be*. Boston, MA: Houghton Mifflin.

Arneil, B. (1996). *John Locke and America: The defence of English colonialism*. New York, NY: Oxford University Press.

Asante, M. K. (1980/1988). *Afrocentricity*. Trenton, NJ: Africa World Press.

Asante, M. K. (1987/1998). *The Afrocentric idea*. Philadelphia, PA: Temple University Press.

Asante, M. K. (2003a). Locating a text: Implications of Afrocentric theory. In A. Mazama (Ed.), *The Afrocentric paradigm* (pp. 235–244). Trenton, NJ: Africa World Press.

Asante, M. K. (2003b). African American studies: The future of the discipline. In A. Mazama (Ed.), *The Afrocentric paradigm* (pp. 97–108). Trenton, NJ: Africa World Press.

Asante, M. K. (2007). *An Afrocentric manifesto*. Malden, MA: Polity Press.

Banks, C. A. McGee (1995). Intellectual leadership and the influence of early African American scholars on multicultural education. *Educational Policy, 9*(3), 260–280.

Banks, J. A. (1988). *Multiethnic education, theory and practice*. Newton, MA: Allyn and Bacon.

Banks, J. A. (1992). African American scholarship and the evolution of multicultural education. *Journal of Negro Education, 61,* 273–286.

Banks, J. A. (2001). Multicultural education: Goals, possibilities, and challenges. In C. F. Diaz (Ed.), *Multicultural education for the 21st century* (pp. 11–22). New York, NY: Longman.

Banks, J. A. (2004). Multicultural education: Historical development, dimension, and practice. In J. A. Banks & C. A. McGee Banks (Eds.), *Handbook of research on multicultural education* (2nd ed., pp. 3–29). San Francisco, CA: Jossey-Bass.

Banks, J. A., Beyer, B. K., Contreras, G., Craven, J., Ladson-Billings, G., McFarland, M. A., & Parker, W. C. (2001). *United States: Adventures in time and place*. New York, NY: McGraw-Hill School Division.

Banks, J. A., Boehm, R. G., Colleary, K. P., Contreras, G., Goodwin, A. L., McFarland, M. A., et al. (2005). *Our nation*. New York, NY: Macmillan/McGraw-Hill.

Bennett, L., Jr. (1968). *Pioneers in protest*. Chicago, IL: Johnson Publishing.

Bennett, L., Jr. (1975). *The shaping of Black America*. Chicago, IL: Johnson Publishing.

Boyd, C. D., Gay, G., Geiger, R., Kracht, J. B., Ooka Pang, V., Risinger, C. F., & Sanchez, S. M.. (2011a). *The United States*. Boston, MA: Pearson.

Boyd, C. D., Gay, G., Geiger, R., Kracht, J. B., Ooka Pang, V., Risinger, C. F., & Sanchez, S. M. (2011b). *All together*. Boston, MA: Pearson.

Boyd, C. D., Gay, G., Geiger, R., Kracht, J. B., Ooka Pang, V., Risinger, C. F., & Sanchez, S. M. (2011c). *People and places*. Boston, MA: Pearson.

Boyd, C. D., Gay, G., Geiger, R., Kracht, J. B., Ooka Pang, V., Risinger, C. F., & Sanchez, S. M. (2011d), *Communities*. Boston, MA: Pearson.

Boyd, C. D., Gay, G., Geiger, R., Kracht, J. B., Ooka Pang, V., Risinger, C. F., & Sanchez, S. M. (2011e). *Regions*. Boston, MA: Pearson.

Buras, K. L. (2008). *Rightist multiculturalism: Core lessons on neoconservative school reform*. New York, NY: Routledge.

Cajete, G. (1994). *Look to the mountain: An ecology of Indigenous education*. Durango, CO: Kivaki Press.

Carruthers, J. H. (1972/1994). *Science and oppression*. Chicago, IL: Kemetic Institute.

Cayton, A., Israels Perry, E., Reed, L., & Winkler, A. M. (2007). *America: Pathways to the present*. Boston, MA: Pearson Education/Prentice Hall.

Césaire, A. (1955/2000). *Discourse on colonialism*. New York, NY: Monthly Review Press. (Original work published 1955, Présence Africaine)

Cherryholmes, C. H. (1988). *Power and criticism: Poststructural investigations in education.* New York, NY: Teachers College Press.

Christian, B. T. (1995). All of we are one: A conversation with B. T. Christian with discussants S. Goodwin & G. Shakes. *Raising Standards, Journal of the Rochester Teachers Association, 3*(1), 21–31.

CIBC (The Council on Interracial Books for Children) (1977). *Stereotypes, distortions, and omissions in U.S. history textbooks.* New York, NY: CIBC.

Clarke, J. H. (1990). African-American historians and the reclaiming of African history. In M. K. Asante & K. Welsh Asante (Eds.), *African culture: The rhythms of unity* (pp. 157–171). Trenton, NJ: Africa World Press.

Clarke, J. H., & Garvey, A. J. (1974). *Marcus Garvey and the vision of Africa.* New York, NY: Vintage Books.

Cochran-Smith, M. (1991). Learning to teach against the grain. *Harvard Educational Review, 61*(3), 397–336.

Cochran-Smith, M., & Lytle, S. L. (2009). *Inquiry as stance: Practitioner research in the next generation.* New York, NY: Teachers College Press.

Cooper, A. J. (Haywood) (1892/1969). *A voice from the South, by a black woman of the South.* New York, NY: Negro Universities Press.

Cornbleth, C., & Waugh, D. (1995). *The great speckled bird, multicultural politics and education policymaking.* New York, NY: St. Martin's Press.

Crawford, M. (2003). African American intellectual history: Philosophy and ethos. In J. L. Conyers, Jr. (Ed.), *Afrocentricity and the academy: Essays on theory and practice* (pp. 129–140). Jefferson, NC: McFarland & Company.

Danzer, G. A., Klor de Alva, J. J., Krieger, L. S., Wilson, L. E., & Woloch, N. (2005). *The Americans.* Evanston, IL: McDougal Littell.

Davidson, B. (1978). *Discovering Africa's past.* London, England: Longman.

Delany, M. R. (1972). The political destiny of the colored race. In S. Stuckey (Ed.), *The ideological origins of Black nationalism* (pp. 195–236). Boston, MA: Beacon Press. (Originally delivered as a report to the delegates of the Emigration Conference in Cleveland, 1854)

Deloria, V., Jr. (1970). *We talk, you listen.* New York, NY: Dell.

Deloria, V., Jr. (2004). Promises made, promises broken. In G. McMaster & C. E. Trafzer (Eds.), *Native universe: Voices of Indian America* (pp. 143–159). Washington, DC: National Museum of the American Indian, Smithsonian Institution/National Geographic Society.

Denis, C. (1997). *We are not you.* Toronto, Canada: Broadview

Detweiler, F. G. (1922). *The Negro press in the United States.* Chicago, IL: The University of Chicago Press.

Diop, C. A. (1967). *Anteriority of Negro civilizations.* Paris, France: Presence Africaine.

Diop, C. A. (1974). *The African origins of civilization: Myth or reality?* (M. Cook, Trans.). Westport, CT: Lawrence Hill Company.

Dove, N. (2003). Defining African womanist theory. In A. Mazama (Ed.), *The Afrocentric paradigm* (pp. 165–183). Trenton, NJ: Africa World Press.

Du Bois, W. E. B. (1899). *The Philadelphia Negro, a social study.* New York, NY: Schocken Books.

Du Bois, W. E. B. (1902). *The Negro artisan.* Atlanta, GA: Atlanta University Press.

Du Bois, W. E. B. (1903). *The souls of Black folks.* Greenwich, CT: Fawcett Publications.

Du Bois, W. E. B. (1924). *The gift of Black folk, the Negroes in the making of America.* Boston. MA: The Stratford Company.

Du Bois, W. E. B. (1935/1972). *Black reconstruction in America*. New York, NY: Atheneum.

Du Bois, W. E. B. (1945). *Color and democracy*. New York, NY: Harcourt Brace.

Elliott, R. B. (1997). Speech in the House of Representatives addressing the Civil Rights Bill of 1875. New York, NY: G. K. Hall & Co./Simon & Schuster Macmillan. (Original work published 1874, *Congressional Record*, January 6)

Epstein, T. (2009). *Interpreting national history: Race, identity, and pedagogy in classrooms and communities*. New York, NY: Routledge.

Fanon, F. (1963). *The wretched of the earth*. New York, NY: Grove Press.

Fanon, F. (1965). *A dying colonialism*. New York, NY: Grove Press.

Fanon, F. (1967). *Black skin, white masks*. New York, NY: Grove Press.

Farrell, J. P., & Tanner, D. (2012). *Overview, school textbooks in the United States*. Retrieved from http://education.stateuniversity.com/pages/2507/Textbooks.html

Fisher, D. (1979). Zitkala-Ša: The evolution of a writer. *American Indian Quarterly, 5*(3), 229–238.

Fishman, G., & McLaren, P. (2000). Schooling for democracy: Toward a critical utopianism. *Contemporary Sociology, 29*(1), 168–179.

Franklin, V. P. (1992). *Black self-determination: A cultural history of African American resistance*. Chicago, IL: Lawrence Hill Books.

Freire, P. (1998). *Teachers as cultural workers: Letters to those who dare to teach*. Boulder, CO: Westview Press.

Garnet, H. H. (1972). Speech to the Colored citizens of Boston, 1859. In S. Stuckey (Ed.), *The ideological origins of Black nationalism* (pp. 174–194). Boston, MA: Beacon Press. (Originally printed in *The Weekly Anglo African*, Volume 1, No. 9, September 19, 1859)

Garcia, J., Ogle, D. M., Risinger, C. F., & Stevos, J. (2005). *Creating America: A history of the United States*. Evanston, IL: McDougal Littell.

Gatto, J. T. (2003). *The underground history of American education: A schoolteacher's intimate investigation into the prison of modern schooling*. Oxford, NY: The Oxford Village Press.

Gay, G. (2000). *Culturally responsive teaching: Theory, research, and practice*. New York, NY: Teachers College Press.

Gay, G. (2004). Curriculum theory and multicultural education. In J. A. Banks & C. A. McGee Banks (Eds.), *Handbook of research on multicultural education* (2nd ed., pp. 30–49). San Francisco, CA: Jossey-Bass.

Giroux, H. A. (2001). Pedagogy of the depressed: Beyond the new politics of cynicism. *College Literature, 28*(2), 1–32.

Goodwin, S., & Swartz, E. E. (Eds.) (2004). *Teaching children of color: Seven constructs of effective teaching in urban schools*. Rochester, NY: RTA Press.

Goodwin, S., & Swartz, E. E. (2006). *Guide to understanding the seven constructs of effective teaching*. Rochester, NY: RTA Press.

Goodwin, S., & Swartz, E. E. (2008). *Culturally responsive practice: Lesson planning and construction*. Rochester, NY: RTA Press.

Goodwin, S., & Swartz, E. E. (2009). *Document-based learning: Curriculum and assessment*. Rochester, NY: RTA Press.

Graff, H. (1985). *America, the glorious republic*. Boston, MA: Houghton Mifflin.

Grande, S. (2004). *Red pedagogy: Native American social and political thought*. Lanham, MD: Rowman & Littlefield.

Hafen, J. P. (1997). Zitkala-Ša: Sentimentality and sovereignty. *Wicazo Sa Review, 12*(2), 31–41.

Hilliard, A. G., III (1978). *Free your mind, return to the source: The African origin of civilization.* San Francisco, CA: Urban Institute for Human Services.

Hilliard, A. G., III (1986). Pedagogy in ancient Kemet. In M. Karenga & J. H. Carruthers (Eds.), *Kemet and the African worldview: Research, rescue, and restoration* (pp. 130–148). Los Angeles, CA: University of Sankore Press.

Hutton, F. (1993). *The early Black press in America, 1827 to 1860.* Westport, CT: Greenwood Press.

Kaplan, S. (1973). *The Black presence in the era of the American Revolution, 1770–1800.* Greenwich, CT: New York Graphic Society Ltd. in association with the Smithsonian Institution Press.

Karenga, M. (1990). *Kawaida theory.* Los Angeles, CA: Kawaida Publications.

Karenga, M. (2003). Afrocentricity and multicultural education: Concept, challenge and contribution. In A. Mazama (Ed.), *The Afrocentric paradigm* (pp. 73–94). Trenton, NJ: Africa World Press.

Karenga, M. (2006). Philosophy in the African tradition of resistance: Issues of human freedom and human flourishing. In L. R. Gordon & J. A. Gordon (Eds.), *Not only the master's tools: African American studies in theory and practice* (pp. 243–271). Boulder, CO: Paradigm Publishers.

Kershaw, T. (1992). Afrocentrism and the Afrocentric method. *The Western Journal of Black Studies, 16*(3), 160–168.

Kershaw, T. (2003). The Black Studies paradigm: The making of scholar activists. In J. L. Conyers, Jr. (Ed.), *Afrocentricity and the academy: Essays on theory and practice* (pp. 27–36). Jefferson, NC: McFarland & Company Publishers.

Kessler, S. (2011). Publishers launch first digital-only textbook for K-12. Retrieved from http://mashable.com/2011/06/27/iste-textbooks-k-12/

King, J. E. (1994). The purpose of schooling for African American children: Including cultural knowledge. In E. R. Hollins, J. E. King, & W. C. Hayman (Eds.), *Teaching diverse populations: Formulating a knowledge base* (pp. 25–56). Albany, NY: State University of New York Press.

King, J. E. (2004). Culture-centered knowledge: Black studies, curriculum transformation, and social action. In J. A. Banks & C. A. McGee Banks (Eds.), *Handbook of research on multicultural education* (2nd ed., pp. 349–378). San Francisco, CA: Jossey-Bass.

King, J. E. (Ed.). (2005). *Black education: A transformative research and action agenda for the new century.* Mahwah, NJ: Erlbaum for the American Educational Research Association.

King, J. E., & Goodwin, S. (2006). *Criterion standards for contextualized teaching and learning about people of African descent.* Rochester, NY: Authors.

Klein, S. (1983). *Our country's history.* Austin, TX: Steck-Vaughn.

Kliebard, H. M. (1986). *The struggle for the American curriculum 1893–1958.* New York, NY: Routledge.

Ladson-Billings, G. (1994). *The dreamkeepers: Successful teachers of African American children.* San Francisco, CA: Jossey-Bass.

Ladson-Billings, G. (2004). New directions in multicultural education: Complexities, boundaries, and critical race theory. In J. A. Banks & C. A. McGee Banks (Eds.), *Handbook of research on multicultural education* (2nd ed., pp. 50–65). San Francisco, CA: Jossey-Bass.

Levstik, L. S. (2008). What happens in social studies classrooms? Research on K-12 social studies practice. In L. S. Levstik & C. A. Tyson (Eds.), *Handbook of research in social studies education* (pp. 50–62). New York, NY: Routledge.

Locke, J. (1988). *Two treatises of government* (P. Laslett, Ed.). New York, NY: Cambridge University Press. (Original work published 1690)

Lomawaima K. T., & McCarty, T. L. (2006). *To remain an Indian: Lessons in democracy from a century of Native American education.* New York, NY: Teachers College Press.

Lyons, S. R. (2000). Rhetorical sovereignty: What do American Indians want from writing? *College, Composition and Communication, 51*(3), 447–468.

Mazama, A. (Ed.) (2003). *The Afrocentric paradigm.* Trenton, NJ: Africa World Press.

Nash, G. B. (1976/1990). Social change and the growth of pre-Revolutionary urban radicalism. In A. F. Young (Ed.), *The American Revolution: Explorations in the history of American radicalism* (pp. 3–36). DeKalb: Northern Illinois University Press.

NCSS (National Council for the Social Studies). (2010). *National curriculum standards for social studies: A framework for teaching, learning, and assessment.* Silver Spring, MD: Author.

Nieto, S. (2002). *Language, culture, and teaching: Critical perspectives for a new century.* Mahwah, NJ: Erlbaum.

NYS Board of Regents. (1991). *One nation, many peoples.* A report of the Social Studies Syllabus Review and Development Committee. Albany: New York State Department of Education.

Olson, S. (2002). *Mapping human history: Discovering the past through our genes.* Boston, MA: Houghton Mifflin.

Pearson Education (2011). *Textbook resources.* Retrieved from http://www.phschool.com/atschool/

Peterson, R. (2008). Whitewashing the past: A proposal for a national campaign to rethink textbooks. *Rethinking Schools, 23*(1), 34–37.

Popkewitz, T. S. (1992). Culture, pedagogy, and power: Issues in the production of values and colonialization. In K. Weiler & C. Mitchell (Eds.), *What schools can do: Critical pedagogy and practice* (pp. 133–148). Albany: State University of New York Press.

Price, R. (Ed.). (1979). *Maroon societies: Rebel slave communities in the Americas* (2nd ed.). Baltimore, MD: The Johns Hopkins University Press.

Rappaport, D. (1997). *The flight of Red Bird: The life of Zitkala-Ša.* New York, NY: Dial Books.

Ravitch, D. (2010). *The death and life of the great American school system: How testing and choice are undermining education.* New York, NY: Basic Books.

RTC (Rochester Teacher Center). (2007). *Cultural learning standards: What students are expected to know, be able to do, and be like.* Rochester, NY: Author.

RTC (Rochester Teacher Center). (2008). *Evaluation of the Institute on Teaching and Learning Informed by Cultural Knowledge: What do teachers need to know, be able to do, and be like.* Rochester, NY: Author.

Schwartz, M., & O'Connor, J. R. (1981). *The new exploring American history.* New York, NY: Globe Book Company.

Sleeter, C. E., & Grant, C. A. (1988). *Making choices for multicultural education.* Columbus, OH: Merril.

Spring, J. (2011). *The American school: A global context from the Puritans to the Obama era* (8th ed.). Boston, MA: McGraw-Hill.

Stanley, T. (1998). The struggle for history: Historical narratives and anti-racist pedagogy. *Discourse: Studies in the Cultural Politics of Education, 19*(1), 41–52.

Swartz, E. E. (1989). *Multicultural curriculum development: A practical approach to curriculum development at the school level.* Rochester, NY: Rochester City School District.

Swartz, E. E. (1992). Emancipatory narratives: Rewriting the master script in the school curriculum. *The Journal of Negro Education, 61,* 341–355.

Swartz, E. E. (1996). Emancipatory pedagogy: A postcritical response to "standard" school knowledge. *Journal of Curriculum Studies, 28*(4), 397–418.

Swartz, E. E. (1998). Using dramaturgy in educational research. In S. R. Steinberg & J. L. Kincheloe (Eds.), *Students as researchers, creating classrooms that matter* (pp. 113–135). Bristol, PA: Falmer Press, Taylor & Francis.

Swartz, E. E. (2004). Casing the self: A study of pedagogy and critical thinking. *Teacher Development, An International Journal of Teachers' Professional Development, 8*(1), 45–65.

Swartz, E. E. (2007a). Stepping outside the master script: Re-connecting the history of American education. *The Journal of Negro Education, 76*(2), 173–186.

Swartz, E. E. (2007b). *Reconstruction: Moving toward democracy.* Rochester, NY: RTA Press.

Swartz, E. E. (2008a). *Journeys to freedom: Self-determination, abolition, and the Underground Railroad.* Rochester, NY: RTA Press.

Swartz, E. E. (2008b). *People of African descent petition for justice: Putting democratic principles into practice.* Rochester, NY: RTA Press.

Swartz, E. E. (2009). Diversity: Gatekeeping knowledge and maintaining inequalities. *Review of Educational Research, 79*(2), 1044–1083.

Swartz, E. E. (2010). *Early African Presence in the Americas.* Rochester, NY: Omnicentric Press.

Swartz, E. E. (2012a). Distinguishing themes of cultural responsiveness: A study of document-based learning. *The Journal of Social Studies Research, 36*(2), 179–211.

Swartz, E. E. (2012b). *Remembering our ancestors.* Rochester, NY: Rochester City School District.

Swartz, E. E. (2013). *Freedom and democracy: A story remembered.* Rochester, NY: Omni-centric Press.

Swartz, E. E., & Bakari, R. (2005). Development of the teaching in urban schools scale. *Teaching and Teacher Education, 21*(7), 829–841.

Swartz, E. E., & Goodwin, S. (1992). Multiculturality: Liberating classroom pedagogy and practice. *Social Science Record, 30*(1), 43–69.

Thompson, R. F. (1990). Kongo influences on African American artistic culture. In J. E. Holloway (Ed.), *Africanisms in American culture* (pp. 148–184). Bloomington: Indiana University Press.

Trouillot, M.-R. (1995). *Silencing the past: Power and the production of history.* Boston, MA: Beacon Press.

Tully, J. (1993). Placing the 'Two Treatises.' In N. Phillipson & Q. Skinner (Eds.), *Political discourse in early modern Britain* (pp. 253–280). New York, NY: Cambridge University Press.

Walker, D. (1965). *David Walker's appeal* (C. M. Wiltse, Ed). New York, NY: Hill and Wang. (Original work published 1829)

Weinstein, B. (2005). History without a cause? Grand narratives, world history, and the postcolonial dilemma. *International Review of Social History, 50,* 71–93.

Wells, I. B. (1892). *Southern horrors: Lynch law in all its phases.* New York, NY: The New York Age Print.

Woodson, C. G. (1919). Negro life and history as presented in the schools. *The Journal of Negro History, IV,* 273–280.

Woodson, C. G. (1933/1990). *The mis-education of the Negro.* Trenton, NJ: Africa World Press.

Wynter, S. (1992). *Do not call us "Negroes": How multicultural textbooks perpetuate racism.* San Francisco, CA: Aspire Books.

Wynter, S. (2006). On how we mistook the map for the territory, and re-imprisoned ourselves in our unbearable wrongness of being, of Désêtre: Black studies toward the human project. In L. R. Gordon & J. A. Gordon (Eds.), *Not only the master's tools: African American studies in theory and practice* (pp. 107–169). Boulder, CO: Paradigm.

2

SILENCED HISTORY

How can we recover and mend the torn and unquestioned history that is still standard in the social studies?

Can We Know the Past?

As we examine historical narratives—grand or otherwise, the concern about what can really be known with any certainty looms large. In this regard, the past is like the present. The moments we are living and the moments historians and the public identify and call history are multiply informed complexities that are difficult to track and never fully accessible (Trouillot, 1995). Given that history is filled with varying power relations in the production of knowledge and varying interpretations and conflicts, historian Michel-Rolph Trouillot suggests that "… any historical narrative is a particular bundle of silences, the result of a unique process, and the operation required to deconstruct these silences will vary accordingly" (p. 27). He explains that some facts and events are noted and others are not; and some facts and events leave traces, while others do not—all which result in the ambiguities of history. Other historians suggest that the imposing of order and structure by historical narrators produces constructed points of view that are located more in language than in the reality of the past (research notwithstanding), and that these constructions run the risk of silencing some voices (Bonnell & Hunt, 1999; Lorenz, 1998; Weinstein, 2005). Given these factors, history as anyone comes to know it, is not "the past" in any empirically certain sense.

In the absence of empirical certitude, is it possible to democratize historical knowledge by unearthing the narratives of invisibilized and misrepresented groups and joining them together with the narratives of dominant groups when history contains, by its very nature, so many silences and impositions? The work of "re-membering" history for PK-12 students, teachers, and families turns on this question, the response to which is shaped by the answer to a related question: What is the difference between silences in history and silenced history? While it makes good postpositivist sense that the past cannot be known with certainty, corporate publishers uphold the positivist tradition with fervor. They lay down "facts," not only with certainty but with claims of objectivity (Apple, 1999; Buras, 2008). They present the dominant paradigm of modernity as a singular line of progression, beginning with European expansion in the 15th century, thereby denying the anteriority of similarly advanced or more advanced civilizations in the Americas, Africa, and Asia (Diop, 1967; Grande, 2004; Weinstein, 2005). Students may retain few particulars from these volumes, but they "get" two basic messages: (a) What's in these texts is "the way it was"; and (b) Europeans and their descendants have done most of what's worth knowing about. Of course teachers can interrupt such fiction, and many do. Our point here, however, is that there is only consensus across 12 or more years of these market-driven texts—which are used by most teachers—about whose narratives are to be heard and whose are not. Even a cursory examination of these texts reveals how the history they "make" distributes silences unevenly across race, class, gender, language, and other social markers (Buras, 2008; Sleeter & Grant, 1991). These are not silences due to the inherent partiality and interpretive complexities of knowing the past; these are *silenced narratives*. And the engines that drive these narratives into silence are the grand narratives that explain the overarching themes of U.S. national development.

We agree that the recovery of history is inherently a project of partiality, yet we assert that a process of "re-membering" history provides a fuller view of the past—an ever increasing democratized view—as it is told through a broader range of knowledge and experiences, and is admittedly unfixed and unfinished. While the unequal distribution of social, political, economic and other "goods" in the actual past needs to be told and explored, a specific approach—such as the one proposed in this volume—is needed to avoid reproducing these unequal distributions in the way the past is written and re-presented to students in the present.

So, what are we to do with the grand narratives of U.S. national development that impose selective silences on what occurred and who was involved? Postmodern historians have advocated throwing out the grand narrative baby with its bath water of explanations, but we suggest that the problem is not the existence of macro-narratives with explanatory power. The problem is in their grandness—in their rank of foremost status, which is used not only to explain "what happened," but to justify an unquestioned dominance. In other words, social studies knowledge continues to use *hierarchal* national narratives with a fixed and pre-determined order of leadership based on hegemonic patterns and unquestioned practices that position European/White people and their favored descendants above all "others." If we step outside this grand scheme and its hierarchy of human worth, narrative leadership becomes relational—to be determined among numerous possibilities, rather than predetermined based on a particular race, class, gender, nationality, language, or other group identity (Stanley, 1998). Such narratives are *heterarchal,* which means that there is a shifting order of narrative leadership determined by multiple factors such as knowledge, experience, vantage point, context, and expertise (Lincoln & Guba, 1985; Swartz, 2009; Schwartz & Ogilvy, 1980). Moving from hierarchal to heterarchal national narratives is not a call to reconstitute positivist history—to replace one set of grand narratives with another. Rather, it is a call to hold on to the possibility of explaining a *shared* past without the hegemony of grand narratives. If macro-narratives that explain historical events, topics, and eras are not fixed—if they can shift and change due to a shared and continuously expanding knowledge base—we can democratize social studies knowledge by eclipsing eurocratic constructions that have "stood" for history.

Changing Trends, but Not For Children

Grand narratives have been used since the 19th century to explain the origins, causes, and consequences of macro-historical events. In so doing, they have provided authoritative seemingly coherent explanations of the past (Megill, 1995; Weinstein, 2005). Yet, there is no longer general agreement among historians about what constitutes a "good" explanation. More recent approaches to the study of history and social trends suggest that the consensus-driven character of the traditional historical paradigm has capitulated to a multiplicity of narrative practices (Burke, 2001). Not surprisingly, however, PK-12 school knowledge is one of the last outposts of the traditional paradigm of history. "Good" explanations in the form of grand narratives are still found in social studies textbooks and other instructional materials written by selected European/White historians and others who identify with their conservative socio-political agenda. These enduring narratives are codifications of the dominant episteme—the one that organizes whose knowledge is to be known and whose is to be silenced. As a result, Europeans and their progeny play leading roles in each grand narrative. In their omnipresence, they have become, in the United States, the semiotic signifier of "the American people" who came, conquered, settled, and built social, political, and economic institutions in a seemingly "empty" and "unused" land that they claimed (and still do) to be theirs. While postmodern, postcolonial, and cultural historians have discredited the limitations of these eurocratic descriptions and explanations, children are still held in their tenacious grip. Could it be that the inculcation of these grand narratives is linked to the historic mission of schooling to produce a so-called Americanized citizenry and national unity based on Euro-American values and experiences (Buras, 2008; Grande, 2004; Hirsch, 1987; Schlesinger, 1992; Spring, 2011)? In the next sub-section, we describe the hierarchal grand narrative of freedom and democracy and provide some additional corporate-state tactics that use knowledge of the past to reproduce in the present the power relations between already privileged and subordinated groups (Apple, 1999; Stanley, 1998).

The Hierarchal Grand Narrative of Freedom and Democracy

After several years of exposure, students—particularly engaged students—have internalized the grand narrative of freedom and democracy that we have constructed and placed in Table 2.1.

Indigenous and African Peoples are omitted from the above hierarchal grand narrative of freedom and democracy that positions only Europeans and their descendants as originators and leaders on this topic. Indigenous Americans are typically presented in the master scripts of current textbooks as museum figures drawn from a compendium of anthropological data. Not only does this produce distortions, it suggests that Indigenous Americans belong to an earlier cultural epoch. Also, a deculturalizing (Spring, 1997) and objectifying categorization scheme still identifies Indigenous Peoples with geographic regions such as Eastern Woodlands and Great Plains. Students learn what people in these regions ate, the clothes they wore, their forms of shelter, and whether they rode horses or traveled by canoe; and there may be a few details about customs and traditions in the form of festivals, music, and dancing (see Boyd et al., 2011a, for recent examples of this practice). With this focus on material culture, students learn, for example, about the longhouses of the Haudenosaunee—their size, how many people lived in them, and how many longhouses were in one community, but not about the ontological orientations (e.g., collectivity, collective responsibility, cooperation, interdependence) that produced these communal

TABLE 2.1 Hierarchal Grand Narrative of Freedom and Democracy

When White colonists won freedom from England in the late 18th century, they developed democracy in North America with a conceptual foundation provided by French and English Enlightenment philosophers whose ideas were drawn from a Greek model. English documents such as the Magna Carta and the Mayflower Compact also influenced the development of democracy in the United States. The Declaration of Independence, the Constitution, and the Bill of Rights are three major documents that define U.S. democracy. An important feature of this form of government is its ability to change based on the will of the people. Another feature is that freedom and democracy are inextricably linked, with the latter being a government ruled by the majority of the people, and the former occurring in a system of representation with free and fair elections. While improvements are viewed as possible, the United States exemplifies the most advanced form of freedom and democracy in the world. The absence of freedom and democracy in other countries can result in U.S. interventions (e.g., political, economic, military) for the purpose of encouraging and establishing democratic practices in other parts of the world.

living spaces (Boykin, 1986; Cajete, 1994). The design of homes varies across cultures. Those with a communal ethos, such as the Haudenosaunee, create homes that reflect that ethos. Both the reason for longhouses *and* their physical characteristics are important for students to know about.

In terms of freedom and democracy, Haudenosaunee tenets are observable in demonstrations of freedom as an inherent right and shared responsibility; and in Haudenosaunee participatory democracy, with its protocols and practices based on peace, justice, consent, and gender equity (Grinde, 1992; Lyons, 1992; Tehanetorens, 1970/1999). While these orientations and practices existed *centuries before* the arrival of Europeans in North America—and their later influence on shaping freedom and democracy in the new United States is well documented—this scholarship has not affected accounts of freedom and democracy in the writing of K-12 textbooks (Barreiro, 1992; Grinde, 1989; Grinde & Johansen, 1991; Lyons & Mohawk, 1992; Van Doren & Boyd, 1938). It appears that corporate publishers are unable to find a way to make this Indigenous knowledge and practice of participatory democracy fit with the grand narrative of freedom and democracy and the master scripts that perpetuate it. Thus, they only give freedom and democracy a European origin.

The absence of African people from this hierarchal grand narrative of freedom and democracy is also accomplished by ignoring chronology. For example, while the positions and actions taken by free and enslaved African people to define and make human freedom a reality *preceded* and continued apace with White colonial interests in freedom from England (Aptheker, 1951/1969; Bennett, 1975; Hart, 1985/2002), this content is excluded in textbooks. In one first-grade textbook, a 6-year old African American child is used to mask this omission (Boyd et al., 2011b, p. 205). At the beginning of a lesson entitled "The Colonies Become Free" (p. 202), James, clad in a three-cornered colonial hat, polo shirt, and jeans, smiles at the readers. He is holding a scroll and quill pen as if about to participate in penning the Declaration of Independence, which is written about in the text and depicted in a painting on the opposite page of the White men who wrote that document (p. 203). Two pages later, James holds up a picture of George Washington and says, "George Washington was a hero" (p. 205). Need it be said that this was a man who not only supported the system of slavery as president of the United States but was a slave owner himself, which clearly does not make him a hero to people of African ancestry. What is being communicated to and hidden from the 6-year-old readers of this text? The false inference of participation in writing a founding document at a time when there were severe restrictions placed on free and enslaved African people in colonial America uses an African American child to hide racial oppression and suggest egalitarian possibilities that did not exist. Adorning pages of colonial history with smiling Black children—an approach that repeats in several texts in this Pearson/Scott Foresman series—but excluding the real and earlier participation of their ancestors in pursuing human freedom mocks the process of writing history.

Using language to elide the participation and cultural traditions of Indigenous and African Peoples is an example of what Scott R. Lyons (2000) calls "… rhetorical imperialism: the ability of dominant powers to assert control of others by setting the terms of debate. These terms are definitional—that is, they *identify* the parties discussed by describing them in certain ways" (p. 452). Just as the language of court decisions, treaties, and laws sought to replace Indigenous and African sovereignty and self-determination with dependence (Bennett, 1975; Franklin, 1992; Lyons, 2000; Prucha, 1994), the grand narratives and master-scripted language of textbooks replace the "rhetorical sovereignty" of Indigenous and African Peoples with "rhetorical imperialism" by excluding their self-determined definitions and descriptions of their Peoplehood, collective traditions, and interactions with others. In this way, grand narratives and master scripts use knowledge of the past to reproduce the power relations between already privileged groups and everyone else.

Countering Grand Narratives

Our response to the "rhetorical imperialism" of standard school knowledge is to produce knowledge about *all* cultures through an Afrocentric culturally informed praxis of historical recovery. This praxis is framed by Afrocentric theory, which locates African people—and all groups of people—at the center of phenomena, not on the periphery to be described and defined by others (Asante, 1980/1988, 1991; 2003a & b). We will show how this praxis counters grand narratives by producing democratized knowledge.

Now that we are familiar with the hierarchal grand narrative of freedom and democracy in Table 2.1, what does a heterarchal macro-narrative look like on this topic? This type of macro-narrative is also explanatory, but it shifts the leadership related to freedom and democracy to a shared one that includes historical content that the grand narrative of freedom and democracy submerges. It should be noted here that both types of narratives sit within different paradigms or philosophical frameworks. Grand narratives sit within a traditional historical paradigm grounded in scholarship that reflects the euro-epistemic order. Heterarchal macro-narratives sit within an historical paradigm grounded in scholarship that reflects multiple knowledge bases, voices, and experiences—an epistemic order that arranges knowledge and knowing by using emancipatory theories and practices such as Afrocentric theory and culturally informed practices (Asante, 2007; Goodwin, 2004; Swartz, 2009). Heterarchal macro-narratives are concise explanatory descriptions of national development themes—as are grand narratives—but they are based on expanded scholarship. Even so, they are not fixed; they too can be revised and expanded as new scholarship becomes available. In Table 2.2, we have constructed a heterarchal macro-narrative that generally explains the development of freedom and democracy by including and representing the four cultural groups that shaped this topic.

TABLE 2.2 Heterarchal Macro-Narrative of Freedom and Democracy

Freedom and democracy in North America originated with the knowledge and experiences of Indigenous Peoples. The Haudenosaunee developed a participatory democracy recorded in the Great Law of Peace that involved participation, equity, the right to speak, and consensus, and was set up to foster unity and protect freedom. African Peoples experienced centuries of freedom in their homelands, with elders as leaders who were publicly accountable for just treatment of people. They brought these ideas about freedom with them when they were kidnapped in Africa and enslaved in the Americas, claiming that they had never given up their right to be free. Both Indigenous and African Peoples understood freedom as an inherent right and shared responsibility. During the same period, Europeans experienced monarchy and tyranny by rulers and landed aristocracy. Shortly after their arrival in North America, their colonial practices resulted in the disruption and later destruction of many Indigenous Nations and maintenance of the system of slavery. White colonial leaders observed and documented Haudenosaunee freedom and governance practices and experienced African people's consistent actions for freedom and equality. However, upon ending English rule, they wrote a Constitution that included some aspects of the Great Law of Peace, but excluded African and Indigenous people, poor White men, and all women. Rights and freedom were only for wealthy, White, landowning men. The framework for these structured inequalities was provided by Enlightenment philosophers who viewed European cultures as more advanced and therefore more worthy of continuance than Indigenous and African cultures. In response to inequalities, African and Indigenous Peoples and a sub-group of White colonists resisted subjugation, modeled democratic practices, and advocated for freedom and justice.

The Pedagogy of Praxis

The heterarchal macro-narrative in Table 2.2 and the "re-membered" texts that convey it are outcomes of the proposed Afrocentric culturally informed praxis of historical recovery. While praxes differ, what they hold in common is the presence of some pedagogy—some set of assumptions, ideas, and approaches to selecting theory and engaging in actions and inquiry that are instructive to those who read about or are involved with the praxis. In other words, it is pedagogy that propels the three elements (theory, action, inquiry) of any praxis. We chose emancipatory pedagogy—a question-driven approach to instruction that liberates all participants from "agreed-upon versions of knowledge"—to act upon the praxis of historical recovery because it critically questions and challenges the hegemony of standard social studies content, seeking to transform it. As our instructional framework, emancipatory pedagogy guided (a) the selection of Afrocentric theory and a culturally informed curricular practice, (b) the writing of identity-group narratives (found in Appendix A) and student texts, and (c) the conducting of practitioner inquiry. This pedagogy is based on the assumption that all individuals and groups have knowledge worth knowing.

Acting on this assumption makes it possible to transform dominant and privileging relations of power that have for too long defined students as empty vessels, the researched as objects, theory as euro-bound, and content as fixed and given (Asante, 1987/1998; Bernard, 2000; Freire, 1970; Swartz, 2009). As the instructional energy behind our Afrocentric culturally informed praxis of historical recovery, emancipatory pedagogy guides us to be mindful that the three components of this praxis are shaped with a broad array of knowledge.

Afrocentric Culturally Informed Praxis of Historical Recovery

Prior to discussing each praxis component, a diagram of the praxis of historical recovery may be useful. While Figure 2.1 will have more meaning after reading the three sub-sections that follow it, the diagram is useful here as it graphically indicates the relationship among praxis components. In the sections that follow Figure 2.1, you will see how Afrocentric metatheory and the principles of culturally informed curricular practice join together to guide a process of "re-membering." This process has four phases: (a) identifying a topic and the identity groups that shaped its development; (b) researching and writing identity-group narratives; (c) identifying and comparing identity-group themes; and (d) writing a heterarchal macro narrative and a "re-membered" student text that reconnect the knowledge bases and experiences of identity groups. The student texts—the products created with this "re-membering" process—are then examined by practitioner inquiry, which illuminates what happens among teachers, students, and parents when they engage with democratized knowledge. In this way, practitioner inquiry accesses the knowledge of teachers, students, and families, thereby readjusting the power differentials in who controls ideas about effective teaching and learning. Another anticipated outcome is that practitioner inquiry will stimulate iterations by others. These outcomes are described in more detail later in this chapter.

We now turn to a more detailed look at the three components of an Afrocentric culturally informed praxis of historical recovery.

Afrocentricity

The importance of cultural knowledge is a common focus in the Black Studies intellectual tradition, multicultural education, culturally relevant/responsive teaching and learning, and Afrocentricity. However, it is Afrocentricity—the first component of the praxis of historical recovery—that has sharpened this focus on the role of cultural knowledge in consciously locating and centering African people as subject participants and agents in all phenomena of the past and present. Afrocentricity posits that by locating African people at the center of phenomena, not on the periphery to be described and defined by others, the universalized knowledge of the hierarchal European episteme can be replaced with democratized knowledge (Asante, 1980/1988, 2003a & b). This is a human-centric theory of representation and action that is open and applicable to other cultures and groups (Asante, 2007, 1991; Karenga, 2003). This

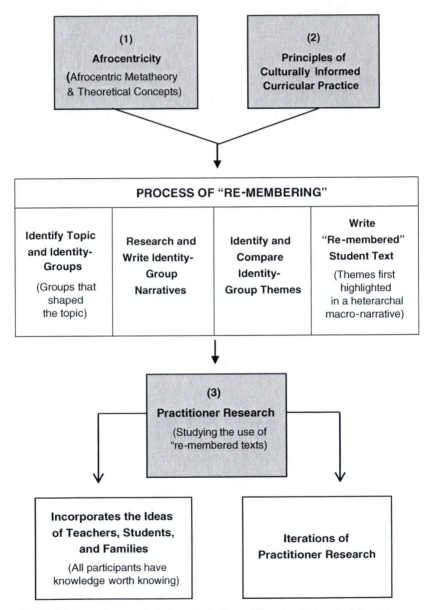

FIGURE 2.1 An Afrocentric Culturally Informed Praxis of Historical Recovery

metatheory positions African Peoples on the Continent and in the Diaspora as normative subjects of their own experiences—as are all human groups—with each necessarily defining, describing, and acting upon its own realities and knowledge bases as opposed to being defined, described, and acted upon by others (Diop, 1967, 1974; Karenga, 2006). In this sense, Afrocentric theory guides us toward a new approach to producing knowledge about any culture and group as well as toward a solution to the problem of European/White cultural supremacy.

Structurally, Afrocentricity is a paradigm or particular philosophical approach within the discipline of Africology (Asante, 2007; Kershaw, 1992; Mazama, 2003a). As a paradigm, it is a conceptual system or framework for organizing and ordering information—one that a community of scholars agree upon, including sets of assumptions that shape concepts, theories, methods, and analyses (Kershaw, 2003). As such, Afrocentricity represents a radical shift from European conceptual systems that continue to universalize all things European as the standard against which all other conceptual systems are measured in the social, political, personal, interpersonal, spiritual, economic, historical, and other realms. Asante (2007) characterizes the Afrocentric paradigm as revolutionary (not evolutionary) in that it locates African people as subjects with agency, not objects in relation to socio-political, economic, and cultural processes. He credits Ama Mazama with adding a functional aspect to earlier formulations of Afrocentricity so that it now has a "doing" aspect. As a result, Mazama (2003a) has expanded the Kuhnian (Kuhn, 1970) definition of paradigm beyond its cognitive and structural aspects to include the activation of consciousness, which is the functional aspect needed for mental liberation. Mazama explains that gaining knowledge is for the purpose of liberation, not for the sake of knowledge itself, so that without consciousness, new ideas in science or any other epistemology have no capacity to move people or to serve them. Prince Hall exemplifies this activation of consciousness to serve people in his actions for human freedom. As discussed in chapter 1 of this volume, the collective orientation of his African identity—in the context of the African legacy of freedom—guided him to act with others to end the system of slavery.

Having evolved since its first theoretical framework was presented by Molefi Kete Asante (1980/1988), the Afrocentric paradigm now includes numerous theories and methodologies in such fields as psychology, sociology, sociolinguistics, womanism, text analysis, aesthetics, and library classification and cataloging (Bethel, 2003; Cokely, 2003; Mazama, 2003b). The theories in this paradigm postulate ways in which scholars in diverse fields examine aspects of the world—all grounded in African history, cultural knowledge, and experiences (Alkebulan, 2007; Asante, 2003b; Karenga, 2003; Rabaka, 2005). As stated above, we follow Asante (2007) in referring to Afrocentric theory as a metatheory because it has fundamental concepts held in common by Afrocentric theorists in various fields. These concepts—which include but are not

limited to Collective Consciousness, Collective Responsibility, Centrality/
Location, Self-Determination, Subjects with Agency, Reclamation of Cultural
Heritage, and Anteriority of Classical African Civilizations—define the character of this metatheory and are all used in the interest of African liberation
and a humanistic vision of the world (Asante, 1987/1998, 1990, 2007; Mazama,
2003b). Importantly, several Afrocentric theoretical concepts can be used in the
construction of knowledge about all cultures and groups. As we will show, this
component of the praxis of historical recovery is an emancipatory framework
within which democratized knowledge can be produced. Table 2.3 provides
brief descriptions of Afrocentric concepts drawn from the cited scholarship in
this section.

There are specific connections between the Afrocentric theoretical concepts
in Table 2.3 and the curricular component we use in the praxis of historical
recovery. The next sub-section describes this culturally informed curricular
component and exemplifies how its principles are linked to Afrocentric theoretical concepts.

TABLE 2.3 Afrocentric Theoretical Concepts

Afrocentric Theoretical Concepts

- **Collective Consciousness** – This epistemology refers to the "retention of ancestral sensibilities" within and across generations (Nobles, 2005, p. 199). This way of knowing conveys the historic continuity of African essence, energy, and excellence; is sustained through relationships within the collective African family that make awareness, knowledge, and meaning possible; and elicits value for the human collective.
- **Collective Responsibility** – There are reciprocal and interconnected relationships among African people who together make and are made by the "best" practices within African culture. These "best" practices are emancipatory in that their collaborative enactment increases justice and right action for African people and the whole of humanity.
- **Centrality/Location** – Placing Africa and African people and experiences at the center of phenomena means that African knowledge, cultural ideals, values, and ways of knowing and being are a location or standing place from which the past and present can be viewed and understood.
- **Self-Determination** – African individuals make decisions, decide their fate, and control their lives within the context of considering the collective needs and interests of African people and maintaining the sovereignty of African and other cultures.
- **Subjects with Agency** – African people and ideas are subjects when and where they are present. They have the will and capacity to act in and on the world—not only as individuals, but as members of their cultural group.
- **Reclamation of Cultural Heritage** – The conscious recovery of African history, culture, and identity that is grounded in knowledge of African cosmology, ontology, epistemology, and axiology and presented with a culturally authentic lexicon is a model for reclaiming the heritage of diverse cultures and groups.
- **Anteriority of Classical African Civilizations** – Ancient Kemet and prior African civilizations developed and exhibited the earliest demonstrations of excellence in foundational disciplines such as philosophy, mathematics, science, medicine, the arts, and architecture.

Culturally Informed Curricular Practice

All cultures and groups are normative and have cultural capital (Boykin, 1994; Gay, 2000; King, 2004). However, the "saturating cultural character" of traditional school practices in the United States indicates that schools typically position children of European descent, particularly upper socioeconomic White males, as the normative students who possess cultural capital (Boykin, 1994, p. 244; Sleeter, 2005). Efforts to expand this limited cultural character of schooling are not new as seen in Black Studies scholarship dating from the 19th century. This scholarship was the fount of 20th century theories and practices such as intercultural and multicultural education, culturally congruent/relevant/responsive education, the modern Black Studies movement, and Afrocentricity (King, 2004; Swartz, 2009). Culturally informed curricular practice—the second component of the praxis of historical recovery—builds on these earlier efforts, with its emancipatory focus on expanding the knowledge of schooling. As explained in chapter 1, this curricular practice is the result of refining a set of six aphoristic principles drawn from numerous criteria, guidelines, and analyses found in the educational approaches just named. While each principle of culturally informed practice refers to distinct knowledge assertions, combining several principles strengthens their capacity to bring Afrocentric theoretical concepts to the pages of written texts. Thus, we typically link several principles of culturally informed curricular practice with Afrocentric concepts to select scholarship and construct the identity-group narratives from which "re-membered" student texts are written. Along with describing these principles below, we show how each one can be linked to specific Afrocentric concepts. It should be noted that the example(s) provided under each principle were constructed using more than one culturally informed principle, but for heuristic purposes, we only discuss the principle being described in each sub-section.

Inclusion

Inclusion, the first principle, refers to content in which cultures and groups are present in more than token ways and centered as the subjects of accounts (Asante, 1980/1988; Banks, 1988). This principle asserts that all cultures and groups are substantive participants in human development. For example, in standard social studies content, the rise of industry in the United States is characterized as occurring through the genius and excellence of the White male icons of industrialization, with a few token people of color and women more recently included. To democratize knowledge about this topic, we would frame a "re-membered" student text using the Afrocentric concepts of Centrality/Location, Self-Determination, and Subjects with Agency. These three concepts guide us to search out who was involved in the rise of industry, the actions they took, and what kinds of decisions they made that demonstrated their agency in shaping and/or responding to industrialization. In writing about this topic, the principle of inclusion is used to actualize these concepts in text and images—avoiding tokenism and showing not only the range of inventors, scientists, business owners, and workers without whom industrialization would not have been possible—but also the union activists and members who resisted their exploitation as workers, including the often inhumane conditions they experienced (Bennett, 1975; Hayden, 1970, 1972; Kass-Simon & Farnes, 1990; Van Sertima, 1986; Warren, 1999; Zinn, 1980/2003). In this way, using the principle of inclusion to write "re-membered" student texts contributes to the Reclamation of Cultural Heritage (another Afrocentric concept) for the diverse cultures and groups who have been omitted or put in the margins of standard social studies content about industrialization.

Representation

The second principle refers to comprehensive portrayals that provide enough content and context about individuals or groups to avoid distorted and stereotypic characterizations (CIBC, 1977). Representation locates individuals as normative subjects within, not separate from, their cultural communities; and it asserts that when portrayals of individuals or groups are contextualized, their ways of knowing, being, and doing are manifest (Mazama, 2003b; Swartz, 2009). For example, portrayals of Crispus Attucks are representational when they avoid assigning him only the role of the "first to die in the Boston Massacre." When he is presented as he was—a self-liberated man of African and Indigenous descent, well known by other sailors and dock workers in Boston—his leadership of White and Black working people against abusive British soldiers is contextualized (Swartz, 1996). Attucks becomes a normative subject, a man of his culture/race and class experiences (Bennett, 1968). A "re-membered" student account of Crispus Attucks and his pre-Revolutionary War actions would be framed by Afrocentric concepts such as Centrality/Location, Collective Responsibility, Self-Determination, and Subjects with Agency. These four concepts guide us to more fully examine how Attucks fits within this historical period, his relationships with his peers, the decisions he made, and the actions he took for human freedom. Using the curricular principle of representation helps us to actualize these Afrocentric concepts in writing "re-membered" student texts so that portrayals of Crispus Attucks allow students to examine his ways of being (communally oriented), knowing (relational and group based), and doing (making decisions and acting with agency on his personal, political, and culturally driven belief in freedom). In this way, using the principle of representation in writing "re-membered" texts keeps Attucks the individual connected to working people and to his African and Indigenous heritage—contexts that define him as more than a marginal character in Revolutionary War history and the nation's development.

Accurate Scholarship

The third principle asserts that when omissions or errors are avoided and relevant knowledge is present, curricula become a reflection of the past rather than an appropriation of it. While what is considered accurate can change based on new information, accuracy is identifiable when knowledge is examined with integrity (Karenga, 2003). For example, there is evidence of (a) White colonists, including some leaders, such as Charles Thomson and Anthony Benezet who spoke out against enslavement and advocated for just relations with Native Americans, and (b) poor White farmers and urban workers who resisted their exploitation in response to the growing socioeconomic chasm between rich and indebted poor following the Revolutionary War (Aptheker, 1993, 1956; Brookes, 1937; Foner, 1947; Hendricks, 1979; Szatmary, 1980). (See the European/White Colonists Narrative in Appendix A for more details about this sub-group.) For colonial history to be based on accurate scholarship, this knowledge needs to shape curriculum—especially because dominant accounts of White colonial interests in democracy position these actions far from the colonial patriot norm. The omission of individuals and groups who contested the dominant practices of their racial group reproduces one of the exclusionary outcomes in current presentations of that era.

To democratize knowledge about this period, we would frame a "re-membered" student text with the Afrocentric concepts of Centrality/Location, Subjects with Agency and the Reclamation of Cultural Heritage. These three concepts focus attention on the scholarship needed to present content about the decisions, actions, and values of both wealthy and poor White people who stood on the side of justice. The principle of accurate scholarship can "write" these Afrocentric concepts onto the pages of "re-membered" texts by ensuring that relevant knowledge is present about the White men and women who chose, in some measure, to stand outside of dominance.

In another example of accurate scholarship, errors result from using the omnipresent Mercator map, which does not show equal land areas equally. Drawn in 1569 by a cartographer in Germany, this map places that country at the center of the world, thereby falsely enlarging the Northern hemisphere and shrinking the Southern hemisphere (Gutstein, 2001). Simple calculations demonstrate that the Mercator map distorts size and deforms shapes, but this inaccurate map continues to be bought by U.S. school districts and used in classrooms across the country. Its use communicates ethnocentric messages by falsely centering and enlarging world areas primarily inhabited by Europeans and their descendants. In contrast, the Peters Projection map exhibits equality of area and fidelity of axis and position, which avoids enlarging the world areas of dominant groups while shrinking the world areas colonized by them (Kaiser, 1987). Depending on grade level, teachers can engage students in a critical comparison of these two maps (Gutstein, 2001) or, particularly for younger students, can put their Mercator maps in the closet along with the ethnocentric messages they send. To democratize map knowledge, we would use the Afrocentric concept, Collective Consciousness, to bring value for the human collective to maps. The principle of accurate scholarship—in particular the avoidance of errors—is used to actualize this concept by choosing to use the Peters Projection map as a graphic representation that challenges and disputes hegemony in how the world is represented. Knowing about this map can encourage teachers to engage in right action, not only by using a more accurate map, but also by advocating that districts and schools purchase it.

Indigenous Voice

Indigenous voice, the fourth principle, refers to the curricular portrayal of cultures and groups through the experiences of their members and historical events using the voices and actions of those who were present (ANKN, 1999; CIBC, 1977; Grande, 2004). Indigenous voice asserts that when cultures and groups speak for, name, and define themselves, their textual presence as historical agents mirrors their agency in life. For example, portrayals of the "mill girls" of Lowell, Massachusetts, are typically the backdrop for an account of the industrial revolution and manufacturing in New England towns in the early to mid-1800s. "Mill girls" are presented as unmarried, available, and unskilled farm girls who provided needed labor (Boyd et al., 2011c; Garcia, Ogle, Risinger, & Stevos, 2005), a hiring practice that one high school text unquestioningly states "made economic sense to mill owners" as they could be paid half the salary of men (Cayton, Israels Perry, Reed, & Winkler, 2007, p. 282). The agency of White girls and women in resisting oppressive working conditions—an important part of the slow but steady gains of workers in the 19th century (Zinn, 1980/2003)—is not mirrored in master-scripted textbooks where the absence of their indigenous voices keeps them from speaking for and defining themselves. Instead, the economic logic of White mill owners de-voices girls and women as an absent presence in their own story. To democratize knowledge about the development of the textile industry in the United States, we would frame a "re-membered" student text on this topic with the Afrocentric concepts of Centrality/Location, Subjects with Agency, and the Reclamation of Cultural Heritage that includes women and girls. The principle of indigenous voice actualizes these three concepts in "re-membered" texts by reproducing the agency of the women and girls who spoke for, named, and defined themselves in Lowell. Students learn about their significant role in textile manufacturing as well as their decisions to engage in right action by resisting the abuses of mill owners. In this way, the voices of girls and women as conscious actors in and authors of their own story reproduce—in current texts for students—the agency they demonstrated in their 19th century lives.

Critical Thinking

The fifth principle refers to instructional materials and curricula that avoid "agreed-upon versions of knowledge" by providing broad and typically omitted content (Swartz & Goodwin, 1992, p. 58). Critical thinking asserts that when students have enough information to develop questions, see connections and patterns, and evaluate and synthesize information, they can identify areas of significance and produce knowledge (Banks, 1991; Swartz, 2004). Critical thinking is often obstructed in standard social studies materials that mask the interests of the one side they show. For example, textbooks present only a U.S. version of Commodore Mathew Perry's forced opening of trade with Japan in 1854 (Cayton et al., 2007; Garcia et al., 2005). These accounts position Japan as merely *there* for the opening and *there* for the trade desired by the United States (Williams, 1980/2007). In this unquestioned and objectifying version of manifest destiny, Japan is the unknown frontier—one to be crossed, rather than a sovereign country to be respected. In this way, 21st century texts maintain the 1850s framework and "logic" of U.S. imperialism that obscures the motivations and interests of the United States. To democratize knowledge in an account of this interaction between the United States and Japan, we would frame a "re-membered" text using the Afrocentric concepts of Centrality/Location, Self-Determination, and Subjects with Agency. These three concepts guide us to more fully examine evidence that locates Japan and Japanese leaders as actors in the world, making decisions to control their lives and protect their nation's sovereignty. Writing a "re-membered" text that is informed by a Japanese account of this 1854 event invites students to think critically about who gained from this "opening" of Japan, what it means to have your "frontier" crossed by force, and how this was experienced by people in Japan. By objectifying Japan and Japanese people, standard social studies materials xenophobically position them outside of human consideration; Afrocentric concepts and the principle of critical thinking bring them back in as normative subjects.

A Collective Humanity

The sixth principle refers to the oneness of all humanity, meaning that all groups of people equally belong to the human collective (Christian, 1995; Karenga, 2006). A collective humanity asserts that all cultures and groups are normative based on knowing that the whole of humanity is one—even though equity is not presently a societal reality. The use of this principle is rarely evident in standard social studies materials. For example, the typical focus on individuals of African ancestry who resisted injustice (e.g., Frederick Douglass, Martin Luther King, Jr., Rosa Parks) excludes their understanding of freedom as a human entitlement. Omitting this understanding obscures one of the ways in which African people have modeled the oneness of humanity (Clark,

1962; Douglass, 1881/1983; Grant, 1998; Karenga, 2006; King, J. E., 2005; King, M. L. 1958). Teaching that incorporates historic practices of a collective humanity counteracts the illogic of a hierarchy of human worth that remains entrenched in standard school knowledge. Thus, "re-membered" accounts of well-known individuals of African ancestry are framed with the Afrocentric concepts of Collective Consciousness, Collective Responsibility, Centrality/Location, and Reclamation of Cultural Heritage. These four concepts "ask" writers of "re-membered" texts to keep these individuals—who were mindful about their relationships with all others—connected to their cultural platform (Asante, 1980/1988). From this location, their collective orientation of caring for and protecting self and others in the search for justice and right action are sources of their knowing that reciprocal and interconnected relations are a human norm (Hilliard, 1997; King, 1994; Kohl, 2005). The principle of a collective humanity is used to actualize these Afrocentric concepts by writing and picturing how African people have historically practiced this principle. When "re-membered" texts show how Frederick Douglass, Rosa Parks, and Martin Luther King, Jr. pursued human freedom as a shared entitlement of all people, they demonstrate how their *being* African informed who they were, what they did, and how their actions modeled that we are one humanity.

Practitioner Inquiry

The third component of the praxis of historical recovery is practitioner inquiry. As an integral part of teachers' everyday classroom lives, they reflect on: "What worked, what didn't, and what can I do differently?" Practitioner inquiry formalizes this daily questioning and is particularly well-suited to use with Afrocentric theory and the principles of culturally informed curricular praxis. This is the case, as all three praxis components aim to democratize knowledge by readjusting the power differentials in who controls historical content and who controls ideas about effective teaching and learning—differentials that have heretofore obstructed equity and excellence across schools and schooling (Cochran-Smith & Lytle, 2009; Lee, 2007; Urbanski, 2004). While practitioner inquiry is varied—ranging from approaches that retain traditional assumptions, policies, and practices to approaches that challenge and rethink them—there is a steady thread within the movement that supports the democratic focus of researchers as collaborative agents of change engaged in a more inclusive, knowledge-expanding process that Appadurai (2006) refers to as the "right to research." As a right, research is a boundary-crossing process of inquiry that includes a wide range of contexts and people and can be conducted inside or outside the walls of academia. As for practitioner inquiry, its seeds were sewn in action research, a social science dating to the 1940s that studies, and at the same time, empowers those being studied (Carr & Kemmis, 1986; Carson,

1990; Goodnough, 2008; Kemmis & McTaggart, 2000; Lewin, 1946). As practitioners at all levels conduct research, their findings are steadily adding to the
professional literature on topics such as gender and writing, pedagogy and critical thinking, language, parent engagement, developing authentic relationships,
performance-based assessment, and accountability (Bernard, 2000; Goldstone,
2003; Lee, 2007; MacLean & Mohr, 1999; McElroy, 1990; McPhail, 2009;
Price, 2003; Swartz, 2004).

The practitioner inquiry in this volume reflects what Cochran-Smith and
Lytle (2001, 2009) call "inquiry as stance"—a moniker that refers to the collective gathering of local knowledge as learned from critical, transformative, and
dialectical inquiry in classrooms and community. This gathering of knowledge
views the practitioner as having the capacity to challenge and change societal/
global hegemonies as they exhibit themselves in local educational contexts—all
in the interests of increasing the life chances of participants (Appadurai, 2006;
Cochran-Smith & Lytle, 2009). Our practitioner "stance" has an emancipatory intent also found in the other two components of the praxis of historical recovery: people are subjects not objects—in theory, practice, and in the
research process. We learn about various aspects of using "re-membered" student texts in the four practitioner studies in this volume. These studies focus on
(a) family engagement in curriculum and assessment; (b) interdisciplinarity as
experienced by pre-service teachers; (c) lesson planning, including content and
pedagogy; and (d) Afrocentric curriculum and pedagogy as modeled, taught,
and reflected upon by teachers and parents.

Practitioner inquiry also has another more general function. Whereas
theory and practice have long been understood as different and separate in
social science, with the former being a way to produce knowledge and the
latter being its quotidian third cousin, practitioner inquiry represents a different understanding with a different function. According to Cochran-Smith
and Lytle (2009), teachers are always theorizing, either informally or formally,
as an inherent aspect of their practice; and they are always reflecting on their
practices. This suggests that teaching *is* praxis. Whether teachers are conscious
of it or not, they already and always connect theory, practice, and reflection.
However, when they formalize this everyday process by conducting teacher
research, their studies demonstrate to other educators the value of such work.
Thus, it is our hope that the case studies in this volume will result in iterations
of teacher research. If, after reading this book, you view the praxis of historical
recovery as a viable approach to democratizing social studies knowledge, and if
you are looking to orient your social studies program in this direction, practitioner inquiry is an avenue to follow. Conducting such research positions teachers as leaders in their profession and contributes to strengthening our collective
capacity to democratize the social studies curriculum, that is, to reimagine it
as one that represents the whole of humanity rather than only a portion of it.

Toward a Critical Dialog

With emancipatory pedagogy as the "stance" that drives the three components of our praxis of historical recovery, it becomes possible to mend and recover the torn and unquestioned history that is still standard in the social studies. Grand narratives can be replaced with heterarchal macro narratives, and master scripts can be replaced with democratized knowledge in "re-membered" texts that provide a fuller view of the past. By constructing the past from multiple knowledge bases and experiences, once-silenced narratives now speak about the actions and actors that together "made" history. As we have explained in this chapter, the praxis of historical recovery uses Afrocentric metatheory and concepts to frame historical accounts. The principles of culturally informed curricular practice "write" these Afrocentric concepts onto the pages of "re-membered" texts. And the case studies of teacher researchers inform us about the use of these texts that may result in iterations of research by other educators. As you observe the process and outcome of writing "re-membered" texts in the next chapter, we invite you to think about the following question: When comparing the "re-membered" account of freedom and democracy described in chapter 3 to standard accounts of this topic, which one might lead to a critical dialog with the past and present and why?

References

Alkebulan, A. A. (2007). Defending the paradigm. *Journal of Black Studies, 37,* 410–427.

ANKN (Alaska Native Knowledge Network). (1999). Guidelines for preparing culturally responsive teachers for Alaska's schools. Retrieved from http://www.ankn.uaf.edu/publications/teachers.html

Appadurai, A. (2006). The right to research. *Globalisation, Societies and Education, 4*(2), 167-177.

Apple, M. (1999). *Official knowledge: Democratic education in a conservative age* (2nd ed.). New York, NY: Routledge.

Aptheker, H. (1951/1969). *A documentary history of the Negro people in the United States: From colonial times through the Civil War* (Vol. I). New York, NY: The Citadel Press.

Aptheker, H. (1956). *Toward Negro freedom.* New York, NY: New Century.

Aptheker, H. (1993). *Anti-racism in U.S. history: The first two hundred years.* Westport, CT: Praeger.

Asante, M. K. (1980/1988). *Afrocentricity.* Trenton, NJ: Africa World Press.

Asante, M. K. (1987/1998). *The Afrocentric idea.* Philadelphia, PA: Temple University Press.

Asante, M. K. (1990). *Kemet, Afrocentricity, and knowledge.* Trenton, NJ: Africa World Press.

Asante, M. K. (1991). The Afrocentric idea in education. *Journal of Negro Education, 60*(2), 170-180.

Asante, M. K. (2003a). Locating a text: Implications of Afrocentric theory. In A. Mazama (Ed.), *The Afrocentric paradigm* (pp. 235-244). Trenton, NJ: Africa World Press.

Asante, M. K. (2003b). African American studies: The future of the discipline. In A. Mazama (Ed.), *The Afrocentric paradigm* (pp. 97–108). Trenton, NJ: Africa World Press.

Asante, M. K. (2007). *An Afrocentric manifesto.* Malden, MA: Polity Press.

Banks, J. A. (1988). *Multiethnic education, theory and practice.* Newton, MA: Allyn and Bacon.

Banks, J. A. (1991). A curriculum for power, action, and change. In C. Sleeter (Ed.), *Empowerment through multicultural education* (pp. 125–141). Albany: State University of New York Press.

Barreiro, J. (1992) (Ed.). *Indian roots of American democracy.* Ithaca, NY: Akwe:Kon Press.

Bennett, L., Jr. (1968). *Pioneers in protest.* Chicago, IL: Johnson Publishing.

Bennett, L., Jr. (1975). *The shaping of Black America.* Chicago: Johnson Publishing.

Bernard, W. T. (2000). Participatory research as emancipatory method. Challenges and opportunities. In D. Burton (Ed.), *Research training for social scientists* (pp. 167–185). London, England: Sage.

Bethel, K. E. (2003). Afrocentricity and the arrangement of knowledge. In J. L. Conyers, Jr. (Ed.), *Afrocentricity and the academy: Essays on theory and practice* (pp. 50–65). Jefferson, NC: McFarland & Company.

Bonnell, V. E., & Hunt, L. (1999). Introduction. In V. E. Bonnell & L. Hunt (Eds.), *Beyond the cultural turn: New directions in the study of society and culture* (pp. 1–32). Berkeley: University of California Press.

Boyd, C. D., Gay, G., Geiger, R., Kracht, J. B., Ooka Pang, V., Risinger, C. F., et al. (2011a). *The United States.* Boston, MA: Pearson.

Boyd, C. D., Gay, G., Geiger, R., Kracht, J. B., Ooka Pang, V., Risinger, C. F., et al. (2011b). *All together.* Boston, MA: Pearson.

Boyd, C. D., Gay, G., Geiger, R., Kracht, J. B., Ooka Pang, V., Risinger, C. F., et al. (2011c). *Regions.* Boston, MA: Pearson.

Boykin, W. A. (1986). The triple quandary and the schooling of Afro-American children. In U. Neisser (Ed.), *The school achievement of minority children* (pp. 57–92). Hillsdale, NJ: Erlbaum.

Boykin, W. A. (1994). Afrocultural expression and its implications for schooling. In E. R. Hollins, J. E. King, & W. C. Hayman (Eds.), *Teaching diverse populations: Formulating a knowledge base* (pp. 243–273). Albany: State University of New York Press.

Brookes, G. S. (1937). *Friend Anthony Benezet.* Philadelphia, PA: University of Pennsylvania Press.

Buras, K. L. (2008). *Rightist multiculturalism: Core lessons on neoconservative school reform.* New York, NY: Routledge.

Burke, P. (2001). Overture, the new history: Its past and its future. In P. Burke (Ed.), *New perspectives on historical writing* (2nd ed., pp. 1–24). University Park: The Pennsylvania State University Press.

Cajete, G. (1994). *Look to the mountain: An ecology of Indigenous education.* Durango, CO: Kivaki Press.

Carr, W., & Kemmis, S. (1986). *Becoming critical: Education and action research.* London, England: Falmer Press.

Carson, T. (1990, Summer). What kind of knowing is critical action research, *Theory Into Practice, 29*(3), 167–173.

Cayton, A., Israels Perry, E., Reed, L., & Winkler, A. M. (2007). *America: Pathways to the present.* Boston, MA: Pearson Education/Prentice Hall.

Christian, B. T. (1995). All of we are one: A conversation with B. T. Christian with discussants S. Goodwin & G. Shakes. *Raising Standards, Journal of the Rochester Teachers Association, 3*(1), 21–31.

CIBC (The Council on Interracial Books for Children). (1977). *Stereotypes, distortions, and omissions in U.S. history textbooks.* New York, NY: Author.

Clark, S. (1962). *Echo in my soul.* New York, NY: E. P. Dutton & Co.

Cochran-Smith, M., & Lytle, S. L. (2001). Beyond certainty: Taking an inquiry stance. In A. Lieberman & L. Miller (Eds.), *Teachers caught in the action: Professional development that matters* (pp. 45–58). New York, NY: Teachers College Press.

Cochran-Smith, M., & Lytle, S. L. (2009). *Inquiry as stance: Practitioner research in the next generation.* New York, NY: Teachers College Press.

Cokely, K. (2003). Afrocentricity and African psychology. In J. L. Conyers, Jr. (Ed.), *Afrocentricity and the academy: Essays on theory and practice* (pp. 141–162). Jefferson, NC: McFarland & Company.

Diop, C. A. (1967). *Anteriority of Negro civilizations.* Paris, France: Presence Africaine.

Diop, C. A. (1974). *The African origins of civilization: Myth or reality?* (M. Cook, Trans.). Westport, CT: Lawrence Hill Company.

Douglass, F. (1881/1983). *The life and times of Frederick Douglass.* Secaucus, NJ: Citadel Press.

Foner, P. (1947). *History of the labor movement in the United States. Vol. 1: From colonial times to the founding of the American Federation of Labor.* New York, NY: International Publishers.

Franklin, V. P. (1992). *Black self-determination: A cultural history of African American resistance.* Chicago, IL: Lawrence Hill Books.

Freire, P. (1970). *Pedagogy of the oppressed.* New York, NY: The Seabury Press.

Garcia, J., Ogle, D. M., Risinger, C. F., & Stevos, J. (2005). *Creating America: A history of the United States.* Evanston, IL: McDougal Littell.

Gay, G. (2000). *Culturally responsive teaching: Theory, research, and practice.* New York, NY: Teachers College Press.

Goldstone, L. (2003). The mother tongue: The role of parent-teacher communication in helping students reach new standards. In E. Meyers & F. Rust (Eds.), *Taking action with teacher research* (pp. 63–78). Portsmouth, NH: Heinemann.

Goodnough, K. (2008). Dealing with messiness and uncertainty in practitioner research: The nature of participatory action research. *Canadian Journal of Education, 31*(2), 431–457.

Goodwin, S. (2004). Emancipatory pedagogy. In S. Goodwin & E. E. Swartz (Eds.), *Teaching children of color: Seven constructs of effective teaching in urban schools* (pp. 37–48). Rochester, NY: RTA Press.

Grande, S. (2004). *Red pedagogy: Native American social and political thought.* Lanham, MD: Rowman & Littlefield.

Grant, J. (1998). *Ella Baker: Freedom bound.* New York, NY: Wiley.

Grinde, D. A., Jr. (1989 Winter). Iroquoian political concept and the genesis of American government. *Northeast Indian Quarterly, 6*(4), 10–21.

Grinde, D. A., Jr. (1992). Iroquois political theory and the roots of American democracy. In O. Lyons & J. Mohawk (Eds.), *Exiled in the land of the free: Democracy, Indian nations, and the U.S. Constitution* (pp. 228–280). Santa Fe, NM: Clear Light.

Grinde Jr., D. A., & Johansen, B. E. (1991). *Exemplar of liberty: Native America and the evolution of democracy.* Los Angeles: American Indian Studies Center, University of California, Los Angeles.

Gutstein, E. (2001). Math, maps, and misrepresentation. *Rethinking Schools, 15*(3), 6–7.

Hart, R. (1985/2002). *Slaves who abolished slavery: Blacks in rebellion.* Kingston, Jamaica: University of the West Indies Press.

Hayden, R. C. (1970). *Seven Black American scientists.* Reading, MA: Addison-Wesley.

Hayden, R. C. (1972). *Eight Black American inventors.* Reading, MA: Addison-Wesley.

Hendricks, J. E. (1979). *Charles Thomson and the making of a new nation, 1929–1824.* Cranbury, NJ: Associated University Presses.

Hilliard, A. G., III (1997). *SBA: The reawakening of the African mind.* Gainesville, FL: Makare Publishing.

Hirsch, E. D., Jr. (1987). *Cultural literacy: What every American needs to know.* Boston: Houghton Mifflin.

Kaiser, W. L. (1987). *A new view of the world: A handbook to the world map, Peters Projection.* New York, NY: Friendship Press.

Karenga, M. (2003). Afrocentricity and multicultural education: Concept, challenge and contribution. In A. Mazama (Ed.), *The Afrocentric paradigm* (pp. 73–94). Trenton, NJ: Africa World Press.

Karenga, M. (2006). Philosophy in the African tradition of resistance: Issues of human freedom and human flourishing. In L. R. Gordon & J. A. Gordon (Eds.), *Not only the master's tools: African American studies in theory and practice* (pp. 243–271). Boulder, CO: Paradigm.

Kass-Simon G., & Farnes, P. (Eds.). (1990). *Women of science: Righting the record.* Bloomington: Indiana University Press.

Kemmis, S., & McTaggart, R. (2000). Participatory action research. In N. K. Denzin & Y. S. Lincoln (Eds.), *Handbook of qualitative research* (pp. 567–605). Thousand Oaks, CA: Sage.

Kershaw, T. (1992). Afrocentrism and the Afrocentric method. *The Western Journal of Black Studies, 16*(3), 160–168.

Kershaw, T. (2003). The Black Studies paradigm: The making of scholar activists. In J. L. Conyers, Jr. (Ed.), *Afrocentricity and the academy: Essays on theory and practice* (pp. 27–36). Jefferson, NC: McFarland & Company.

King, J. E. (1994). The purpose of schooling for African American children: Including cultural knowledge. In E. R. Hollins, J. E. King, & W. C. Hayman (Eds.), *Teaching diverse populations: Formulating a knowledge base* (pp. 25–56). Albany: State University of New York Press.

King, J. E. (2004). Culture-centered knowledge: Black studies, curriculum transformation, and social action. In J. A. Banks & C. A. McGee Banks (Eds.), *Handbook of research on multicultural education* (2nd ed., pp. 349–378). San Francisco, CA: Jossey-Bass.

King, J. E. (2005). A transformative vision of Black education for human freedom. In J. E. King (Ed.), *Black Education: A transformative research and action agenda for the new century* (pp. 3–17). Mahwah, NJ: Erlbaum for the American Educational Research Association.

King, M. L., Jr. (1958). *Stride toward freedom: The Montgomery story.* New York, NY: Harper.

Kohl, H. (2005). *She would not be moved: How we tell the story of Rosa Parks and the Montgomery bus boycott.* New York, NY: The New Press.

Lee, C. D. (2007). *Culture, literacy, and learning: Taking bloom in the midst of the whirlwind.* New York, NY: Teachers College Press.

Lewin, K. (1946). Action research and minority problems. *Journal of Social Issues, 2,* 34–46.

Lincoln, Y. S., & Guba, E. G. (1985). *Naturalistic inquiry.* Beverly Hills, CA: Sage.

Lorenz, C. (1998). Can histories be true? Narrativism, positivism, and the "metaphorical turn." *History and Theory, 37*(3), 309–329.

Lyons, O. (1992). The American Indian in the past. In O. Lyons & J. Mohawk (Eds.), *Exiled in the land of the free: Democracy, Indian nations, and the U.S. Constitution* (pp. 14–42). Santa Fe, NM: Clear Light.

Lyons, O., & Mohawk, J. (Eds.) (1992). *Exiled in the land of the free: Democracy, Indian nations, and the U.S. Constitution.* Santa Fe, NM: Clear Light.

Lyons, S. R. (2000). Rhetorical sovereignty: What do American Indians want from writing? *College, Composition and Communication, 51*(3), 447–468.

MacLean, M. S., & Mohr, M. M. (1999). *Teacher-researchers at work.* Berkeley, CA: National Writing Project.

Mazama, A. (2003a). The Afrocentric paradigm, an introduction. In A. Mazama (Ed.), *The Afrocentric paradigm* (pp. 3–34). Trenton, NJ: Africa World Press.

Mazama, A. (2003b). *The Afrocentric paradigm.* Trenton, NJ: Africa World Press.

McElroy, L. (1990, Summer). Becoming real: An ethic at the heart of action research. *Theory Into Practice, 29*(3), 209–213.

McPhail, G. (2009). The "bad boy" and the writing curriculum. In M. Cochran-Smith & S. L. Lytle (Eds.), *Inquiry as stance: Practitioner research for the next generation* (pp. 193–212). New York, NY: Teachers College Press.

Megill, A. (1995). 'Grand narrative' and the discipline of history. In F. Ankersmit & H. Kellner (Eds.), *A new philosophy of history* (pp. 151–173). Chicago, IL: The University of Chicago Press.

Nobles, Wade W. (2005). Consciousness. In M. K. Asante & A. Mazama (Eds.), *Encyclopedia of Black Studies* (pp. 197–200). Thousand Oaks, CA: Sage.

Price, J. R. (2003). The empire state strikes back: Portfolio culture in the Regents era. In E. Meyers & F. Rust (Eds.), *Taking action with teacher research* (pp. 115–155). Portsmouth, NH: Heinemann.

Prucha, F. P. (1994). *American Indian treaties: The history of a political anomaly.* Berkeley: University of California Press.

Rabaka, R. (2005). Afrocentricity. In M. K. Asante & A. Mazama (Eds.), *Encyclopedia of Black studies* (pp. 72–74). Thousand Oaks, CA: Sage.

Schlesinger, A. M., Jr. (1992). *The disuniting of America.* New York, NY: W.W. Norton.

Schwartz, P., & Ogilvy, J. (1980, June). *The emergent paradigm: Toward an aesthetics of life.* Paper based on a report written by J. Ogilvy & P. Schwartz and supported by the clients of SRI International's Values and Lifestyles Program; presented by P. Schwartz at the ESOMAR meeting (keynote speech, session IV), Barcelona, Spain.

Sleeter, C. E. (2005). *Un-standardizing curriculum: Multicultural teaching in the standards-based classroom.* New York, NY: Teachers College Press.

Sleeter, C. E., & Grant, Carl A. (1991). Race, class, gender, and disability in current textbooks. In M. Apple & L. Christian-Smith (Eds.), *The politics of the textbook* (pp. 78–110). New York, NY: Routledge.

Spring, J. (1997). *Deculturalization and the struggle for equality: A brief history of the education of dominated cultures in the United States.* New York, NY: McGraw-Hill.

Spring, J. (2011). *The American school: A global context from the Puritans to the Obama era* (8th ed.). Boston. MA: McGraw-Hill.

Stanley, T. (1998). The struggle for history: Historical narratives and anti-racist pedagogy. *Discourse: Studies in the Cultural Politics of Education, 19*(1), 41–52.

Swartz, E. E. (1996). Emancipatory pedagogy: A postcritical response to "standard" school knowledge. *Journal of Curriculum Studies, 28*(4), 397–418.

Swartz, E. E. (2004). Casing the self: A study of pedagogy and critical thinking. *Teacher Development, An International Journal of Teachers' Professional Development, 8*(1), 45–65.

Swartz, E. E. (2009). Diversity: Gatekeeping knowledge and maintaining inequalities. *Review of Educational Research, 79*(2), 1044–1083.

Swartz, E. E., & Goodwin, S. (1992). Multiculturality: Liberating classroom pedagogy and practice. *Social Science Record, 30*(1), 43–69.

Szatmary, D. P. (1980). *Shay's rebellion: The making of an agrarian insurrection.* Amherst: The University of Massachusetts Press.

Tehanetorens (Fadden, R.) (1970/1999). *Kaianerekowa Hotinonsionne: The Great Law of Peace of the Longhouse People.* Rooseveltown, NY: Akwesasne Notes/Mohawk Nation.

Trouillot, M.-R. (1995). *Silencing the past: Power and the production of history.* Boston, MA: Beacon Press.

Urbanski, A. (2004). Teachers as professionals. In S. Goodwin & E. E. Swartz (Eds.), *Teaching children of color: Seven constructs of effective teaching in urban schools* (pp. 3–12). Rochester, NY: RTA Press.

Van Doren, C., & Boyd, J. P. (Eds.). (1938). *Indian treaties printed by Benjamin Franklin 1736–1762.* Philadelphia: Historical Society of Pennsylvania.

Van Sertima, I. (Ed.). (1986). *Blacks in science: Ancient and modern.* New Brunswick, NJ: Transaction Books.

Warren, W. (1999). *Black women scientists in the United States.* Bloomington: Indiana University Press.

Weinstein, B. (2005). History without a cause? Grand narratives, world history, and the postcolonial dilemma. *International Review of Social History, 50,* 71–93.

Williams, W. A. (1980/2007). *Empire as a way of life: An essay on the causes and character of America's present predicament along with a few thoughts about an alternative.* New York, NY: Ig Publishing.

Zinn, H. (1980/2003). *A people's history of the United States: 1492–present.* New York, NY: Harper Collins.

3

"RE-MEMBERING" THE WAY TO CONTENT

In a praxis of historical recovery, how can dominance be told, but not continue its reign in the telling?

Presence and Influence

We have used Afrocentric theory and the principles of culturally informed curricular practice to create a process of "re-membering" with four phases: (a) identifying a topic and the identity-groups that shaped its development; (b) researching and writing identity-group narratives; (c) identifying and comparing identity-group themes; and (d) writing a heterarchal macro narrative and "re-membered" student texts that reconnect the knowledge bases and experiences of identity-groups (see Figure 2.1 in chapter 2). This chapter enacts these four phases to generate a product—a "re-membered" student text on the development of freedom and democracy in North America. This topic is ripe for historical recovery for several reasons: (a) the grand narrative used to teach it is enmeshed in dominant cultural assumptions, (b) there are agreed-upon contours for teaching about freedom and democracy that consistently omit and/ or relegate Indigenous and African Peoples to the margins, and (c) this topic is diligently taught throughout 12 or more years of schooling—driven by the same grand narrative and transmitted through master scripts at different developmental levels. Our task is to broaden the contours and content related to teaching about the development of freedom and democracy by accessing and incorporating the ideas and actions of those whose presence and influence are well documented.

In the first phase of the "re-membering" process, we use the Afrocentric concept of Centrality/Location to frame and guide our search for the identity-groups that shaped freedom and democracy in colonial North America. Centrality/Location asks us to place Africa and African people and experiences at the center of phenomena, which means that African knowledge, cultural ideals, values, and ways of knowing, being, and doing are a location or standing place from which the past and present can be viewed and understood. While Afrocentricity does not claim universality for the knowledge it produces, it does suggest that a concept such as Centrality/Location is logically applicable to all cultures. Viewing the knowledge, orientations, values, and productions of any culture as a location from which to know something about the past and present avoids sole reliance on the accounts of those with the most power and resources to produce and disseminate knowledge. Thus, the concept of Centrality/Location is an antidote for the false assumption that there is only one center—the one occupied by Europeans, and that European culture is "the measure by which the world marches" (Asante, 1987/1998, p. 3). Applying Centrality/Location to identity-groups who were present in colonial North America means that each group is placed at the center of phenomena so that our understanding of the development of freedom and democracy is informed by the knowledge, traditions, beliefs, values, and actions of each group.

To begin, we identified groups with a physical or ideological presence in the American colonies according to categories such as culture/Nation, race, class, gender, and geopolitical nationality. These categories were major social markers in that era, with each representing more than one group. For example, the Huron, Haudenosaunee, Lenni-Lenape, Mahican, Susquehanna, and Erie were several of the Indigenous cultures/Peoples or Nations in the American Northeast during the colonial period. Likewise, the Hausa, Wolof, Akan, Fulbe, Yoruba, and Igbo were several of the West African Peoples or Nations represented in the same region and time period (Blakey, 1998; Frohne, 2000). Calling Indigenous American and African cultures Peoples or Nations refers to their unifying organizational structure. These cultures (often referred to in the literature as ethnicities or pejoratively as tribes) each include large numbers of people indigenous to a specific region. Common lineage, traditions, language, and values define their Nationhood or Peoplehood as much as the governments they created. The Netherlands, England, France, Scotland, Ireland, and Germany were European nations represented in the same region and time period. While each of these nations included large numbers of people under a single government, and each had common traditions, language, and values, their geopolitical status as a nation state was their unifying factor and primary organizational structure. A small "n" is used for European nations as it is standard usage throughout the world for countries with geopolitical boundaries. To distinguish this usage from earlier and extant African and Indigenous Nationhood or Peoplehood as an organizational structure, a capital "N" and capital "P" are used for African and Indigenous Nations or Peoples.

Class was also increasingly relevant in colonial America, with a class structure mirroring the one in Europe. Among Europeans and their White descendants, the wealthy landowners were the upper class who controlled colonial policies and government practices to serve their interests. Merchants, craftsmen, lawyers, and small landowning farmers were a class with considerably less wealth and influence who would later emerge as a middle class; and indentured servants and poor rural farmers and urban workers formed a dispossessed class at the bottom of this hierarchy.

Group-identity is composed of numerous social markers that overlap. For example, if you lived in 17th-century colonial America, several social markers would shape your identity. You could be Songhoy (culture/Nation or People), Black (race), speak Songhoy-senni and African American Language (languages), be descended from an African family line of leaders, craftsmen, healers, scholars, or farmers (lineage), be female or male (gender), and practice traditional spirituality and/or Islam (religion). Convergence also occurs across social markers. For example, race (White), gender (male), nationality (British), language (English), religion (several forms of Protestantism), and class (upper) converged to signify the majority of colonial patriot leaders in the British colonies of North America. Standard school knowledge still credits these leaders as members of the group that originated freedom and democracy in colonial America. However, knowing who was present during the era and using the Afrocentric concept of Centrality/Location—that each culture is a location from which to know about the past—we identified four groups who shaped the development of freedom and democracy: Haudenosaunee, Africans in the Diaspora, European/white colonists, and European Enlightenment philosophers. The work of a diverse group of Indigenous-, African-, and European-descent scholars supports our selection of these four identity-groups as significant in shaping the development of freedom and democracy in this region. These scholars range the political spectrum, and their disciplines include economic history, social ethics, Black Studies, ethnohistory, anthropology, Africology, Native American studies, gender studies, cultural history, social history/people's history, and philosophy. Their scholarship is cited in this chapter, but more fully in the identity-group narratives in Appendix A.

Excuse Me, But Isn't This Political?

Yes. The process of historical recovery is decidedly political. Notwithstanding the expanded voice in "re-membered" texts, the writing of history is a political process that selects from among numerous pieces of data to produce an account contextualized by the worldview and political interests of its authors (Somekawa & Smith, 1988). The national grand narratives conveyed in the master scripts of standard social studies materials are also political works—even though corporate textbook publishers continue to claim objectivity and neutrality as their hallmark. Acknowledging that the writing of "re-membered" texts is political work avoids making the same error of falsely claiming or inferring neutrality and objectivity. Even though "re-membered" texts are written with an eye to including accounts of those who were present, there is no neutrality in recounting the past. As stated in the American Historical Association's *Statement of Standards of Professional Conduct:*

> Practicing history with integrity does not mean being neutral or having no point of view. … the very nature of our discipline means that historians also understand that all knowledge is situated in time and place, that all interpretations express a point of view, and that no moral mind can ever aspire to omniscience.
>
> *(2011, pp. 4–5)*

Disingenuously, neutrality has been claimed as the province of those corporate entities who seek to control the knowledge available to students. Instead, we propose creating more comprehensive accounts—a vision of the past constructed through a process that brings back together and into view the diverse cultures and groups that concurrently bore influence on any topic. All groups have knowledge and experiences worth knowing about the topics they were part of shaping, and our task is to demonstrate how to reconnect or "re-member" them through democratized knowledge production.

To exemplify how an interpretive political process results in the selection of identity-groups, we initially considered making a separate group narrative for women, since European/White colonial men imposed a lower social, political, and economic status on all women (Norton, 1980). However, in our interpretation of colonial data, women had more in common with their cultural groups than with each other, which resulted in the decision not to make women a separate identity-group. We found that White women, as a group, upheld internal class distinctions among themselves as well as distinctions across race—that is to say, they reproduced European hierarchies of social class, race, and power. As a result, this group expressed only limited denunciation of race and class exploitation and oppression (Hoff Wilson, 1976). With only a few exceptions, these demonstrated relations of power align White women's assumptions, ideas, and actions about racial and class status more with, than separate from, their male counterparts. During the same period, Haudenosaunee and African men and women were familiar with normative socio-cultural traditions and practices of right action across gender and were also engaged together in the pursuit and maintenance of human freedom (Bennett, 1968, 1975; Grinde, 1992; Tehanetorens, 1970/1999). Thus, knowledge about Haudenosaunee, African, and White women's involvement in the development of freedom and democracy is included in their respective cultural group narratives.

Narratives of Four Identity-Groups

The second phase of the "re-membering" process produces narratives of the four identity-groups that shaped the development of freedom and democracy in North America. These detailed narratives are found in Appendix A. We highly recommend reading these narratives along with this chapter, as this expanded content will clarify the process of "re-membering" described in this chapter and the discussion of standards in chapter 4. As you will see, these narratives provide content that is typically absent from or misrepresented in state social studies standards, local curricular frameworks, and standard instructional materials.

Following are brief overviews of the four identity-groups. Numerous Indigenous cultures could exemplify freedom and democratic practices. However, the Haudenosaunee was selected as the first identity-group because it produced, modeled, and documented a Confederacy that was/is a participatory democracy based on knowledge of and experience with freedom as an inherent right (Barreiro, 1992; Mohawk, 1992). Scholars have documented links between Haudenosaunee democracy and democracy designed for the new American republic (Grinde & Johansen, 1991; Lyons & Mohawk, 1992). Furthermore, since the 17th century, European and White American colonists developed policies and practices for specifically dealing with the Haudenosaunee in trade, war, treaty making around land acquisitions, economic development, and political relations, which put them in regular contact with each other (Colden, 1727/1922; Fenton, 1998; Grinde, 1992; Jennings, 1984; Johansen, 1982; Lyons, 1992; Mohawk, 1992; Van Doren & Boyd, 1938). Given that the Haudenosaunee are one of the four identity-groups, our demonstration of historical recovery focuses on events that took place in the northeastern region of what today is the United States, but not to the exclusion of related activities in other regions.

People of various African cultures/Nations were present in the American colonies and influenced the development of freedom and democracy. They came either directly from an African culture/Nation or were born on the colonial mainland or in one of the Caribbean colonies. African Peoples shared a common experience of cultural unity, and, once in the Americas, they also shared a common experience of racial oppression (King & Goodwin, 2006). This unity and coherence of experiences led to grouping Africans in the Diaspora together and selecting this group as the second identity-group (Asante, 2007a; Hilliard, 1997; Semmes, 1992). As detailed in Appendix A, whether free or enslaved, the African population's commitment to freedom and democracy is seen in writing, speech, and civil and social actions, including the institutions and organizations they established (Aptheker, 1951/1969, 1976/1990; Bennett, 1968, 1975). Scholars have studied individual and collective African resistance to enslavement, the denial of their human and civil rights, and the transference of the African legacy of freedom to the pursuit of freedom and democracy in the Americas (Blakey, 1998; Hart, 1985/2002; Karenga, 2006; Piersen, 1993; Quarles, 1961; Thompson, 1987).

The third identity-group is European/White colonists. While colonists came from several distinct geopolitical European nations and classes—ranging from gentry to indentured laborers—they merged in colonial North America as an increasingly distinct and separate identity-group. Wars existed among colonists from different European nations and disagreements occurred across class differences, but Europeans eventually formed common bonds based on survival, their agreed-upon drive to appropriate Indigenous lands, the emerging fixated binary of Europeans as "White" and superior, Africans as "Black" and inferior, and Europeans and their descendants as civilized and all "others" as not (Deloria, 2004; Mills, 1997; Morrison, 1992; Wynter, 1992). Scholars have examined the emergence of these bonds of whiteness and the ideas of (in)civility, including the social, legal, economic, and military policies and practices of European/White colonists, and the influence that the idea of whiteness bore on their freedom and the (un)freedom of Indigenous, African, and indentured White men and women; and they have studied this group's articulation of freedom and democracy in the nation's founding documents (Aptheker, 1976/1990; Beard, 1914; Deloria, 1992; Drinnon, 1980/1997; Franklin, 1992; Grinde & Johansen, 1991; Hoff Wilson, 1976; Millican, 1990; Nash, 1976/1990).

The fourth identity-group is European Enlightenment philosophers. These men did not have a lived experience in the colonies like the other three groups. Yet, European Enlightenment philosophers had extensive influence on shaping the ideology of dominance and empire building that led European/White colonists to view themselves as superior to all "others" in colonial America (Arneil, 1996; Biddiss, 1966; Gould, 1981; Kliewer & Fitzgerald, 2001; Keita, 2000; Mills, 1997; Williams, 1980/2007). While ontologically linked to European/White colonists, the influence of these upper-class intellectuals of mostly English and French nationality was and remains so profound and particular that they require a separate identity-group status. In terms of their impact on school knowledge, their ideas and ideologies were used to shape European thought about Europe's imperial reach beyond its borders, colonial settlement, and the practices of nation building and governance. Thus, these philosophers have had a major influence on the grand narrative of freedom and democracy and the master scripts that convey it. In fact, standard instructional materials still extol Enlightenment philosophers as the intellectual foundation for the colonists' interest in and pursuit of freedom and democracy. In the narrative of this group in Appendix A we explain why some scholars have questioned this claim (Di Nunzio, 1987; Lyons, 1992; Mohawk, 1992).

Identifying four predominant identity-groups is a heuristic for learning about the presence and influence of groups on the development of freedom and democracy in colonial America. It is important to note that settling on four identity-groups does not ignore varied intra-group identities. For example,

17th-century European/White colonists were far from homogeneous. While the concept of Whiteness served to unify them, their other identities, such as nationality, religion, gender, class, language, and regionality (e.g., urban, rural, colony affiliation) affected their experiences, practices, and interactions with others (Martin, 1973; Young, 1976). Likewise, Indigenous Americans and Africans in the Diaspora were not homogenous groups. Other group-identities such as Nation of origin, spirituality/religion, language, gender, lineage, and regionality variously affected their experiences, practices, and interactions with others (Bennett, 1975; Grande, 2004; Holloway, 1990; Mankiller, 2004; Piersen, 1993; Tayac, 2004; Walker, 2001). Thus, we are not suggesting that the four groups we selected are the only identity-groups to consider. In fact, content about gender, class, spirituality/religion, nationality/Nationhood, etc. adds particulars to an account of freedom and democracy that can help to illuminate and clarify broad trends. Also, these particulars—examples of which are found in the group narratives in Appendix A—are quite useful at higher grade levels. Care must be taken, however, not to reproduce the fragmentation that the praxis of recovering history seeks to overcome. Our challenge, therefore, is to make sure that outcomes of including particular identities is not, inadvertently, as fragmenting as outcomes of eurocratic scholarship. Our main focus as we begin the process of "re-membering" is on the idea that people have "made" history together as the result of their physical proximity, cultural interactions, and political engagements. By locating four main identity-groups—with attention to holding on to their within-group diversity—as sources of knowledge about the development of freedom and democracy, the stage is set for learning how they shared and shaped historical developments.

Selecting Scholarship

Afrocentric metatheory and concepts and the principles of culturally informed curricular practice guided our examination of historical records as well as the writing of identity-group narratives. Just as we used the Afrocentric concept of Centrality/Location (that each group is a location for knowing about the past) to select identity-groups, we also used it to select scholarship and frame narratives that locate each identity-group as the subject of its own experiences and the author of its own accounts (Asante, 2007b). Keeping in mind that Afrocentric theory is a human-centric theory, its use makes it possible to locate all groups as subjects with agency, not as objects described and defined by others. Thus, when the knowledge in the four identity-group narratives in Appendix A is put together, it becomes democratized, as it taps into the knowledge bases and experiences of those cultures and groups who shaped the development of freedom and democracy in North America. It is important to note here that the process of "re-membering" the past produces knowledge about each identity-group *under the same conditions*. That is, Afrocentric concepts are used to select scholarship that frames each narrative, and the principles of culturally informed curricular practice are then used to write the narratives. This means that all groups are located as the subjects of accounts about them, but *being the subject of an account no longer means being the only voice speaking.*

Collective Consciousness and Scholarship

Collective Consciousness is an Afrocentric concept and attribute of scholars of history who demonstrate a collective (not individual) orientation to knowledge and knowing as well as a value for the human collective in their work. They approach their work by mindfully considering self and others, including the spiritual realm of fostering ancestral continuity in dialogic relationship to the community being written about (Harris, 2003; Kershaw, 2003; Nobles, 2005). Scholars with Collective Consciousness seek knowledge from the perspective advantage of alterity that is afforded by the liminal location or vantage point of those who have been/are positioned at the bottom of the social hierarchy and misrepresented or disregarded in dominant scholarship (King, 2004; Wynter, 1997). According to Sylvia Wynter (2000, 2006). The perspective advantage of alterity refers to the knowledge, experiences, insights, claims, and actions of liminal cultures and groups, with their alterity being a location or vantage point from which to view any topic. Some knowledge is only available from such liminal locations, which produce critical responses to phenomena that are not available within the worldview of dominant groups (King, 2006). This critical agency is a perspective advantage, and the knowledge it produces increases the possibility of a comprehensive and truthful presentation of historical events. Below are examples of two scholars who exhibit Collective Consciousness in their work.

Maulana Karenga Presents Harriet Tubman

Maulana Karenga (2006) is a scholar of African ancestry who demonstrates Collective Consciousness as seen in his presentation of Harriet Tubman's Self-Determination (another Afrocentric concept) as a communal practice compared to typical presentations of her as a courageous individual. Positioning Tubman in the context of her collectively oriented history and culture indicates how Karenga locates her within the continuity of the African family. His Collective Consciousness guides him to produce an account of Harriet Tubman from a perspective advantage of alterity that conceptualizes how she was also guided by Collective Consciousness and Collective Responsibility (another Afrocentric concept) in her reciprocal and interdependent relationships with the people she lead to freedom. Once a text about Tubman is framed with these concepts, three principles of culturally informed curricular practice—representation, accurate scholarship, and indigenous voice—can be used to write about Tubman so that (a) she remains connected to the ontological and epistemological orientations of the African community that was the source of her strength, and (b) she names and defines her interactions with White people—both enslavers and abolitionists—so that her textual presence as an historical agent mirrors her agency in life. In this way, it is possible to not only write a more holistic portrayal of Harriet Tubman, but also to Reclaim the Cultural Heritage (another Afrocentric concept) through which she expressed her being and her humanity. Her "retention of ancestral sensibilities" (Nobles, 2005, p. 199), and her actions constitute a counter response to the power hierarchy of her day, and Karenga's analysis is a counter response to the power hierarchy of standard school knowledge that tells her story in our day, absent her voice and the voice of her people.

Donald A. Grinde Presents Canassateego

Donald A. Grinde (1992) is a Native American scholar who exhibits Collective Consciousness as he recounts the presence of Canassateego, a Haudenosaunee leader, at the 1744 Lancaster Treaty Council in Pennsylvania. On the last day of the treaty negotiations, Canassateego spoke to colonial governors about the principle of Haudenosaunee unity and advised them to pursue a similar course. Grinde provides Canassateego's words and explains how they were often referred to throughout the colonial period to inspire American colonists to stand against French and British control. The full text of Canassateego on the topic of unity was written as follows in the Lancaster Treaty printed by Benjamin Franklin in 1744:

> We have one Thing further to say, and that is, We heartily recommend Union and a good Agreement between you our Brethren. Never disagree, but preserve a strict Friendship for one another, and thereby you, as well as we, will become the stronger.
>
> Our wise forefathers established Union and Amity between the Five Nations; this has made us formidable; this has given us great Weight and Authority with our neighboring Nations.
>
> We are a powerful Confederacy; and by your observing the same Methods, our wise Forefathers have taken, you will acquire such Strength and Power; therefore whatever befalls you, never fall out with one another.
>
> *(Van Doren & Boyd, 1938, p. 78)*

As Grinde (1992) describes Canassateego's teaching about unity as a model worthy of emulation, he brings indigeneity into his scholarship by presenting Canassateego as he was commonly understood by his People. In this way, Grinde maintains historic continuity by locating Canassateego in the present as he was in the past—a respected Haudenosaunee leader who understood the power of interdependent relationships and reciprocity.

Standard Scholarship

The research that informs grand narratives and the master scripts that transmit them is not conducted by scholars with Collective Consciousness. And this standard scholarship fails to center all cultures and groups as locations for knowing about the past. So, can any of this scholarship be used in an Afrocentric culturally informed praxis of historical recovery? The answer is yes, with caution. Many scholars study groups and events as outsiders. They may or may not be members of the groups about which they are writing, but their direction of thought seems to ever elude producing knowledge that considers the worldview and cultural orientations of historically liminal identity-groups. This type of scholarship is not framed by Afrocentric theoretical concepts, yet it can provide needed details, offer observations, or provide primary sources that shed further light on a topic as seen in the example below.

Cadwallader Colden (1727/1922), an 18th-century European colonial administrator, scientist, author, and landowner in the colony of New York, wrote *The History of the Five Indian Nations* to "teach the King and Council, Lords of Trade and other ruling powers, the real position, influence and power of the Iroquois Confederacy" (from the 1922 introduction to *The History* written by Robert Waite, p. vi). Colden and other 18th-century colonial authors provide primary source accounts from their own observations and experiences that refer to the Haudenosaunee Nations as republics based on ideas of liberty and the absence of coercion (Grinde & Johansen, 1991). Listen to Colden's words:

> The Five Nations have such absolute Notions of Liberty, that they allow of no Kind of Superiority of one over another, and vanish all Servitude from their Territories. They never make any Prisoner a Slave; but it is customary among them to make a Compliment of Naturalization into the Five Nation; and considering how highly they value themselves above all others, this must be no small Compliment. This is not done by any general Act of the Nation, but every single Person has a Right to it, by a Kind of Adoption.
>
> *(1727/1922, pp. xxviii–xxix)*

Colden, who was the first in-depth European chronicler of the Haudenosaunee, often wrote about what he observed that was different from the English socio-cultural practices with which he was familiar. Although this resulted in some errors (e.g., misunderstanding gender roles, mistaking dream analysis and readings of the natural world as superstitions), Colden made many accurate observations corroborated by later scholars and the Great Law of Peace itself (Grinde, 1992; Lyons, 1992; Tehanetorens, 1970/1999; Van Doren & Boyd, 1938). For example, he wrote above about "absolute notions of liberty" and the absence of servitude and enslavement among the Haudenosaunee. He also wrote that the authority of Haudenosaunee leaders is based on their wisdom, integrity, and the esteem of their people—not on force; that leaders receive no salary or profit from their office and forfeit that office if their actions are unworthy; that their hospitality is unbounded and that theft is abhorrent; that Europeans escaping debtor's prison are sheltered and their debts paid by the Haudenosaunee due to their disdain of servitude; that they have perfected the art of persuasion through elegant oratory that accompanies all public gatherings, and that sudden responses are avoided in favor of silence and lengthy reflection during treaty and other important negotiations. These are the first-hand observations of a man with colonial interests, which makes his reporting all the more poignant in that he could discern numerous Haudenosaunee values and practices in ways that are consistent with knowledge documented by Haudenosaunee and other scholars. What is missing, of course, is a cultural framework for what Colden observed. By knowing about and locating the Haudenosaunee within their cultural framework, the practices listed above can be understood as outcomes of communal and interdependent cultural orientations—a worldview that makes freedom, equanimity, and collective concern and responsibility normative (Cajete, 1994; Dumont, 2002; Grande, 2004; McCarty, Wallace, Hadley Lynch, & Benally, 1991; Shenandoah, 1988). Thus Colden's scholarship is useful when combined with scholarship that connects his observations to the cultural platform that carries Haudenosaunee knowledge, beliefs, values, and ways of being, knowing, and doing.

Identifying and Comparing Themes

The third phase in the "re-membering" process takes us closer to producing democratized knowledge for children. At this phase, we identify and compare themes from the identity-group narratives in Appendix A. Through an iterative process of multiple re-readings, the salient themes in each of the four identity-group narratives related to the development of freedom and democracy were identified and refined to reflect the main ideas in these narratives and to remove thematic redundancy. Thus, narrative themes provide concise views of engagement with the ideas and practices of freedom and democracy—views informed by Indigenous, African, and European cultural contexts. This iterative process resulted in 6–11 themes for each identity group, with a total of 32 themes that were then examined to determine what relationships existed among them. Three overarching categories were identified into which the 32 themes could be organized. These thematic categories are (a) knowledge of and experience with freedom and democracy (9 themes), (b) claims related to maintaining culture (11 themes), and (c) actions and practices related to freedom and democracy (12 themes). Table 3.1 shows these three overarching categories and themes for each of the four identity-groups.

Table 3.1 allows us to compare the main themes in the four identity-group narratives, yet the four sets of narrative themes are still separate. To write a "re-membered" student text about freedom and democracy, the narrative themes of the four identity-groups must be joined. In other words, not only do we need to write the group narratives from Appendix A to grade level, we need to connect them. This is where the narrative themes in Table 3.1 and the power relations they exhibit become relevant.

Themes and Power Relations

In societal contexts that are inequitable, such as those established and maintained by Europeans during the colonial period, the position of a culture or group as dominant or dominated means that the themes in its group narrative reflect those power relations. Thus, we refer to themes in the narratives of dominant groups as "dominant themes." The narratives of cultures and groups that are dominated are also supported by the historical record, even though the content in these narratives is omitted or distorted in PK–12 social studies curricula. We have identified two categories of dominated groups in the colonial period. The first category includes Indigenous and African Peoples. Based on the dominant group's establishment of a White supremacy/racism cultural model, these liminal cultural groups have a perspective advantage of alterity (Wynter, 1992, 1997). We call the themes in identity-group narratives related to Indigenous and African Peoples "alterity themes." The second category in the dominated group includes a sub-group of White colonists. Members of this group had increasing privileges as the idea of whiteness (White supremacy) evolved in the colonies, but based on their socioeconomic status and political positions—contesting the dominant practices of their racial group—were socially, politically, and/or economically marginalized. We call the theme related to this sub-group of White colonists a "marginalized theme." Some Quaker Friends groups and individuals such as Elijah H. Burritt, Judith Sargent Murray, James Hall Mumford, and Benjamin Rush represent this sub-group of White colonists (Aptheker, 1993; Drake, 1950; Runes, 1947; Sargent Murray, 1994). (See the European/White colonists Narrative in Appendix A for more details about this sub-group.)

In either dominant or dominated locations, as discussed in the previous chapter, *all* group narratives are framed with Afrocentric metatheory and concepts and written with principles of culturally informed curricular practice. Thus, *all* group narratives (and the themes within them), *are not the hegemonic versions of knowledge found in standard accounts*. Instead, the dominant group themes of European/White colonists and European Enlightenment philosophers as seen in Table 3.1 describe what these groups knew, experienced, claimed, and did, but without the euro-spin that communicates the sole rightness and inevitability of their knowledge and actions. In Table 3.1 the alterity themes of Haudenosaunee and African Peoples in the Diaspora (in italic bold), and the

TABLE 3.1 Narrative Themes *

Thematic Categories	1) Haudenosaunee	2) Africans in the Diaspora
1 **Knowledge of and experience with freedom and democracy**	• *Experienced centuries of freedom understood as an inherent right and shared responsibility* • *Set up a democracy to bring about unity and protect freedom* • *Knew that a democracy required participation, justice, equity, the right to speak, and consensus*	• *Experienced centuries of freedom (prior to enslavement in the Americas), which was understood as a natural right and shared responsibility to bring goodness and justice into the world* • *When in the Americas, knowing that freedom was an inherent right that they had never given up*
2 **Claims related to maintaining culture**	• *Maintaining culture is the common right of all Peoples.* • *Agreement, unity, and peace among people preserve community and culture.* • *Serving and being accountable to the people preserve community and culture.* • *Negotiation is an initial strategy for resisting colonial expansion and maintaining culture.*	• *Maintaining culture is the common right of all Peoples.* • *Having freedom for all, not just for some, preserves all cultures.* • *Self-determination and community building (e.g., establishing institutions such as newspapers, churches, schools, and mutual aid societies) maintains culture.*
3 **Actions and practices related to freedom and democracy**	• *Lived by the Great Law of Peace that included protocols and practices modeling democracy* • *Leaders existed by the consent of the people.* • *Women were central to the continuity of leadership, the sacredness of life, and the well-being of families.* • *Modeled democratic practices and taught colonial leaders about the value of unity and confederation*	• Leaders were elders who made decisions by agreement and were publicly accountable for just treatment of people. African people brought such ideas about freedom from their homelands. • Resisted and revolted against enslavement, restrictions of freedom, and the denial of democracy in North America • Expressed the logic of freedom for all groups of people in speeches, petitions, and writing

★ Alterity themes on this chart are italicized and bold, dominant themes are in regular type, and a marginalized theme is in italics.

3) European/White Colonists	4) Enlightenment Philosophers
• Experienced subjugation to monarchy and tyranny by rulers and landed aristocracy prior to arrival in North America • Learned about the practices of freedom and democracy from the Haudenosaunee, and experienced African people's logical arguments for freedom and resistance to its denial	• Experienced social and political environments defined by monarchy and oligarchy • Knew about the freedoms and egalitarian practices of Indigenous Americans and used some aspects of Indigenous practices to support their natural law theories
• Maintaining culture is the singular right of Europeans and their White descendants. • Preserving European cultures and power in North America depends upon imposing colonization, subjugation, and exploitation onto the cultures of Indigenous Americans and African Peoples in the Diaspora.	• European cultures are more advanced and therefore more worthy of continuance than Indigenous and African cultures. • Promoting European land-use policies and practices preserves European communities and cultures in North America.
• Provided rights and freedom for only wealthy White landowning men • Wrote a Constitution including some aspects of the Great Law of Peace, but the document excluded African and Indigenous people, poor White men, and all women • *A White sub-group acted as allies and advocates of freedom and justice—some for their own disenfranchised men and women and others for African and Indigenous Americans.*	• Constructed the exclusionary and therefore contradictory framework that guided democracy's development in the West • Used natural law theories and pseudo-scientific rationalizations to deny freedom and democracy to "others" and to maintain a privileged class through structured inequalities

marginalized theme of a sub-group of White colonists (in italic) describe what these groups knew, experienced, claimed, and did from locations that offer both liminal and marginalized historical content not available in grand narratives and master scripts. As such, liminality—an originally imposed location of "otherness" established by White supremacy—is transformed into a location that unearths the narratives heretofore kept silenced by "agreed-upon versions of knowledge." Marginality—as seen in a sub-group of White colonists—is another location from which knowledge about national development can be gained.

Using Alterity, Marginalized, and Dominant Themes

Of the final 32 themes there are 19 alterity themes, 1 marginalized theme, and 12 dominant themes (see Table 3.1). It is important to reiterate that using Afrocentric metatheory and concepts and the principles of culturally informed curricular practice to produce content about *both* dominant and dominated groups reduces the omissions and distortions that occur when history is viewed through only one lens or location. Thus, in this third phase of the "re-membering" process, dominant groups are located in a more nuanced relationship to those with whom they interacted. Dominance remains to be told, but does not continue its reign in the telling.

At times, a liminal identity-group's perspective advantage of alterity uncovers and clarifies its influence on or centrality in a particular event, topic, or era, as seen in the well-documented case of Haudenosaunee influence on colonial thought and actions. At other times this perspective advantage provides access to different ontological and epistemological orientations that recover aspects of history that dominant historical interpretations have obfuscated. For example, the African perspective advantage of alterity locates the advocacy for human freedom of figures such as Prince Hall, Mum Bett, and Crispus Attucks in their ontological and epistemological orientations of interdependence, collective responsibility, and relational and group-based knowing. While standard social studies materials inform students that Attucks—and more recently Hall and Mum Bett are African American, it is the perspective advantage of alterity that recovers the history surrounding them and reveals how *being* African informed who they were and what they did.

The ideas and actions of a sub-group of White colonists also influenced events in the colonial period. For example, after the Revolutionary War, small groups of mostly White farmers in Massachusetts and several other states—many who had just fought in the war—armed themselves and took various actions to stop the courts from repossessing their small farms and sentencing them to debtor's prison (Szatmary, 1980; Zinn, 1980/2003). It was a time of economic crisis, and these disenfranchised farmers revolted against the professional class of merchants, land speculators, lawyers, large landowners, and public officials who benefit financially from the seizures of their property. States supported the professional and land owning classes and crushed these rebellions. This account of how a sub-group of White colonists fought against the injustices they were experiencing points to the colonial roots of power relations that still exist within the White class hierarchy. That said we do not equate this sub-group's marginalized status with the status of liminal cultural groups due to the overshadowing White supremacy/racism cultural model from which all White people benefit then and now (Mills, 1997; Robinson, 200; Wynter, 1992).

The following three sub-sections describe, in narrative form, the themes in each of the three overarching thematic categories presented in Table 3.1, including what they offer, when connected, to the writing of a "re-membered" student text. While some of the scholarship used in the writing of these sub-sections is cited below, scholarship that supports the content in these sections is more fully cited in Appendix A.

Thematic Category 1: Knowledge of and Experience with Freedom and Democracy

When comparing the themes that emerged for each of the four groups in the first thematic category, it is Haudenosaunee and African Peoples who experienced centuries of freedom and democracy prior to their interactions with European/White colonists in North America. During the same period, the themes of European/White colonists and European/Enlightenment philosophers show centuries of experience with monarchy and oligarchy, albeit in different ways depending on class. Despite this absence of knowledge and experience with freedom and democracy, it is only the actions and ideas of White colonial leaders and Enlightenment philosophers that have shaped standard social studies knowledge about this topic. However, when we view this topic from Haudenosaunee and African locations of alterity, different knowledge emerges. To the Haudenosaunee, freedom is understood as an inherent right and shared responsibility; and having a democracy that includes the whole community requires participation and practices that result in justice, equity, the right to speak, and the consent of the governed, which protect freedom and unity. For Africans in the Diaspora, freedom is also understood as an inherent right and shared responsibility to bring goodness, justice, and rightness into the world.

Dominant themes show how European/White colonists learned about practices of freedom and democracy from the Haudenosaunee and experienced African people's arguments for freedom and resistance to its denial; and how Enlightenment philosophers knew about the freedom and egalitarian practices of Indigenous Americans based on reports they read from European explorers and travelers to the Americas. A "re-remembered" text on freedom and democracy connects both alterity and dominant themes to teach students which cultural groups had knowledge of and centuries of experiences with freedom and democracy, which did not, and why. Combining themes that represent these two positions connects the scholarship related to the topic of freedom and democracy, making it possible for all students to see which cultural groups brought leadership to modeling and sustaining these practices. As for Indigenous and African students, they can now see the normative presence of their ancestors in shaping freedom and democracy prior to and during the colonial period.

Thematic Category 2: Claims Related to Maintaining Culture

In thematic category 2, the claims that were identified are assertions about maintaining culture and how that can be accomplished. During the colonial period, these assertions differed across identity groups. Haudenosaunee and Africans in the Diaspora represent communally oriented cultures that view freedom and cultural maintenance as inseparable. Denials or restrictions of freedom to some contradict the cultural tenets (e.g., oneness/unity, sanctity of all life, right action within community and with nature, equanimity) that underpin the traditions and practices of these communal cultures (Cajete, 1994; Karenga, 2006; McCarty et al., 1991; Sindima, 1995; Witherspoon, 1983). Due to these cultural tenets, communally oriented cultures were and are inclined to assert that maintaining culture is a common right, attached to sustaining freedom for all, and linked to serving community needs.

Europeans and their White descendants represent individually oriented cultures that define freedom as individual rights and choices—with those who are the most powerful being the main beneficiaries of those rights and choices. Denials or restrictions of freedom to some are in sync with the cultural tenets (e.g., duality, a hierarchy of human worth, might makes right, social isolation and fragmentation) that underpin European/White traditions and practices (Durkheim, 1949; Hobbes, 1977/1651; Spencer, 1897). Due to these cultural tenets, individually oriented cultures were and are inclined to make exclusionary claims about maintaining culture, with the conservation of the dominant culture viewed as achievable only by separation from and subjugation and exploitation of other cultures.

The claims of both Haudenosaunee and African Peoples are alterity themes, with both groups making similar assertions about maintaining community and culture. Their common ontological orientations of collectivity, interdependence, and survival of the group mean that they view the group as the source of everyone's strength and that reliance on others and reciprocity informed their understanding of and experiences with freedom and democracy.

Living by the Great Law of Peace, Haudenosaunee people understood that cultural and community preservation depended upon agreement, unity, and peace among people, and upon serving and being accountable to each other. This resulted in efforts to treat and negotiate with Europeans as a form of resistance to colonial expansion and domination. African Peoples at home and in the Diaspora knew that cultural preservation was related to human freedom for all. They also acted on the claim that establishing social, economic, and spiritual institutions to support, care for, and inform each other are forms of self-determination that maintain culture.

European/White colonists asserted that it was only their right to maintain culture in North America, and that this depended upon imposing colonization, subjugation, and exploitation on Indigenous and African Peoples. Enlightenment philosophers claimed that European cultures were more advanced and therefore more worthy of continuance than Indigenous and African cultures; and that promoting European land-use policies and practices would preserve European communities and cultures in North America. The claims of European/White colonists and Enlightenment philosophers are dominant themes. Their common ontological orientations of independence, separation, and survival of the fittest mean that they viewed the strongest individuals and cultures as the ones that should survive. Non-reliance on and disconnection from "others" informed their understanding of and experiences with freedom and democracy. Standard social studies materials cloak the claims advanced by European/White colonists and Enlightenment philosophers by portraying land theft and enslavement—with all the cultural disruptions they entailed—as inevitabilities of colonial settlement, expansion, and economic development. However, when the claims of the four identity groups are compared, it becomes clear that there was nothing inevitable about land theft and enslavement. They were outcomes of the European assertion that only they had the right to maintain culture. A "re-remembered" text on freedom and democracy connects alterity and dominant themes, and in so doing, shifts the study of freedom and democracy from sole assertions of supremacist inevitability to examining both sets of assertions. When this occurs, the Haudenosaunee and African claims that cultural self-determination is normative can be considered, and both sets of claims can be critically examined by teachers and students.

Thematic Category 3: Actions and Practices Related to Freedom and Democracy

When comparing the four groups' themes in the third thematic category, we see a range of actions and practices related to freedom and democracy. The Haudenosaunee lived (and still do) by the Great Law of Peace—their founding document of governance. It provides the protocols and practices for a participatory democracy, including government by the consent of the people and the essential role of women in maintaining the continuity of leadership, the sacredness of life, and the well-being of families. These practices and actions represent positions of alterity as they provide a pre-colonial democratic model based on this 12th-century document that verifies the anteriority of democracy and gender equity in Indigenous America (Grinde, 1992; Johansen, 1995). Colonists' early and well-documented observations of Haudenosaunee freedoms exposed them to a society with an absence of coercion; and their interactions with Haudenosaunee leaders taught them about unity and confederation. The practices and actions of the Haudenosaunee positioned them not only as legitimate leaders in freedom and democracy, but as one source of influence, albeit rarely acknowledged, on the thinking of White colonial leaders as they established a structure of governance for themselves in the new United States.

For millennia, the cultural orientations of harmony, collectivity, and interdependence, and cultural tenets such as the oneness of being and the sanctity of all life framed the socio-political and spiritual practices of African Nations (Dixon, 1971; Karenga, 2006; Sindima, 1995). The central tendency was for decision-making to be viewed as a shared responsibility among the living (e.g., elders, experts) and the ancestors, with leaders being held publicly accountable and evaluated based on their just treatment of people (J. E. King, personal communication, June 2, 2011; Maiga, 2010). Examples such as the right to practice more than one religion, the right to maintain local traditions, and the absence of prisons that took away individuals' freedom are evidence of this understanding. During the *Maafa* (European enslavement of African people), African people brought their knowledge of and experiences with the natural and shared right of freedom to the Americas. These experiences were translated into immediate and ongoing resistance to both enslavement and the restrictions placed on free Africans in the Diaspora (Bennett, 1975). Scholarship on African people's prior experiences with freedom—which are congruent with their written and spoken position that they had never given up their right to be free—are themes of alterity that can be used in "re-membered" texts to highlight the cultural continuity between Africa and the Diaspora (Aptheker, 1951/1969; Hart, 1985/2002). This is a major departure from standard textbooks that contain no content that connects African people's experiences of just governance and freedom at home to their pursuit of freedom in the Americas. While the European slave trade severed millions of African people from their families, communities, and Nations, it did not sever them from the knowledge, experiences, values, and cultural orientations that they brought with them and passed on from generation to generation (Bennett, 1975; Carney, 2001; Hall, 2005; Holloway, 1990; Littlefield, 1981; Piersen, 1993; Walker, 2001).

European/White colonists wrote a Constitution that included some ideas from the Haudenosaunee Great Law of Peace *that did not exist in any European governments of that time* (e.g., the right to speak freely, the idea that leaders should serve not rule people, a process for the orderly removal of leaders who are not serving people well, the right to practice any religion), but did not include the Haudenosaunee and other liminal or marginal groups in its benefits. The document's central focus was on individual rights and freedom for wealthy,

White, male landowners, not for poor and working White men, African and Indigenous people, and all women. The exclusionary character of this document contradicted the natural rights discourse of White colonists, who lived in a milieu informed by European/Enlightenment philosophers and their theoretical underpinning for the colonial project and its "right" to proceed. Their use of natural law theories and pseudo-scientific rationalizations denied freedom and democracy to "others" and worked to maintain a privileged class through structured inequalities. The actions and practices of these two European identity-groups provide dominant group themes, which are included in "re-membered" texts in order to describe the development and maintenance of an inequitable system and the resistance that took place in response to it.

Dominant groups are often challenged from within, as seen in a sub-group of White colonists who acted as allies and advocates of freedom and justice—some for their own disenfranchised and politically marginalized men and women and others for African and Indigenous Peoples. Knowledge of this sub-group's various actions against the system of slavery, unfair treaties with Indigenous Peoples, and the disenfranchisement and exploitation of "common" White men and women comes from its marginalized location. As individuals and in small groups this sub-group made attempts to counteract oppressive practices. It is important to note here why these White colonists are not a separate identity-group, even though some of their practices differed from the majority of their White counterparts. There are three reasons: (a) they were not a coherent group in colonial North America; (b) while their resistance to oppression is an important outlier on the White colonial spectrum, their impact on the development of freedom and democracy in North America was small in comparison to the four main identity-groups; and (c) they increasingly received the race and class benefits of the dominant group due to their changing status over time. The forebears of most poor rural farmers and urban workers in this sub-group were indentured servants who, along with African indentured servants, were not free. When colonial laws enslaved African people for life in the mid-1600s, disenfranchised people of European origin increasingly received the benefits of whiteness (White supremacy), even though their economic status placed them at the low end of the class hierarchy. That said the actions of a sub-group of colonial men and women who resisted injustice ran counter to dominance, meaning that content about them—which is omitted or distorted in standard curricula—reflects a marginalized perspective worth knowing about. (See the European/White colonists Narrative in Appendix A for specific details about this sub-group.) By using alterity, marginalized, and dominant themes, the distinctive actions and practices of the four identity-groups can be brought together to reveal the complexities involved in shaping freedom and democracy in colonial North America.

Connecting Knowledge Bases and Experiences

We have arrived at the fourth phase of the "re-membering" process. After using this process to (a) select the identity groups that shaped freedom and democracy, (b) research and write identity-group narratives, and (c) identify and compare identity-group themes, we are ready to (d) write a heterarchal macro-narrative and a "re-membered" student text that reconnect the knowledge bases and experiences of the four identity-groups that shaped freedom and democracy in the colonial period. Figure 3.1 illustrates how this connection occurs. The four boxes at the top of the diagram represent the separate narratives of each identity-group. Each narrative is framed with Afrocentric metatheory and concepts and written with the principles of culturally informed curricular practice. The themes in these narratives are identified by arrows pointing to alterity, marginalized, or dominant theme boxes. These three sets of themes are then joined to write a heterarchal macro-narrative and student text.

Writing a Heterarchal Macro-Narrative

As depicted in Figure 3.1, constructing a heterarchal macro-narrative precedes writing a "re-membered" text. The macro-narrative serves to focus writers of

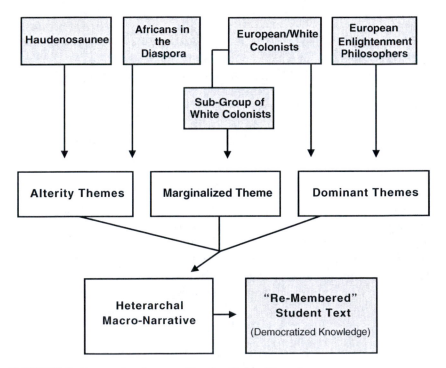

FIGURE 3.1 Connecting Separate Identity-Group Narratives

"re-membered" texts on the themes that explain the topic about which they are writing so that the texts they produce can convey those themes. As discussed in chapter 2, master scripts in social studies convey the themes of hierarchal grand narratives, reflecting monocultural knowledge and experiences that remain fixed over time. In contrast, "re-membered" texts convey the themes of heterarchal macro-narratives, which reflect multiple knowledge bases, experiences, and shifting leadership—themes that are continually open to change based on new scholarship. In chapter 2, we exemplified these two types of explanatory narratives in Tables 2.1 and 2.2. By rereading the heterarchal macro-narrative in Table 2.2, you will see how it includes themes from the four identity-group narratives. Connecting these themes in a concise macro-narrative explains, in broad strokes, the development of freedom and democracy in colonial North America through the combined knowledge, experiences, assertions, and actions of the Haudenosaunee, Africans in the Diaspora, European/White colonists, and European Enlightenment philosophers. In this way, heterarchal macro-narratives sketch the contours of "re-membered" student texts.

Organizing the "Re-Membered" Student Text

Before writing a "re-membered" student text, we need to make decisions about its grade level, content, and format. We begin by deciding at which grade level to write about a particular topic, and then identify the age-appropriate content themes to be used. At the elementary level, a text about freedom and democracy would incorporate themes for Haudenosaunee, African, and European cultural groups. Themes about Enlightenment philosophers would be added to this foundation for older students so that by high school, a "re-membered" student text on this topic could incorporate all 32 themes related to the four identity groups. We decided to use our praxis of historical recovery to enact a process of "re-membering" at the fourth grade, where democracy as a structure of government related to the concept of freedom is typically introduced. Our "re-membered" text follows this precedent, making student content available on these combined concepts at the fourth grade.

Our format for demonstrating the "re-membering" process is a stand-alone book entitled *Freedom and Democracy: A Story Remembered* (Swartz, 2013). This text has six lessons, including tables, charts, biographies, maps, highlighted vocabulary related to a glossary, and end of lesson questions for students. *Freedom and Democracy* can be used instead of standard social studies materials on this topic or as an elementary informational reading text. (For information regarding how to obtain copies of *Freedom and Democracy,* readers may contact omnicentricpress@gmail.com.)

All Themes Are Not Equal

The themes produced in the Afrocentric culturally informed praxis of historical recovery do not reproduce hegemony, yet all themes are not equal. One example will suffice. The claim that culture is a singular right of one group of people is not equal to the claim that culture is the common right of all people (see Table 3.1, category 2). Both are cultural assertions, both shaped history, and both need to be included, but that is where their equableness ends. The destructive and genocidal outcomes of the European/White exclusionary claim about maintaining culture clarify the ethical differences between it and an inclusionary claim about maintaining culture. These two claims are not just different; they are not alternative standpoints to be equally considered. The value of life is not a matter of perspective. History does not raise ethical questions for us to ignore them and the truths their answers may reveal. "Remembered" texts respond to ethical questions, which explains why alterity themes that raise these questions are aligned with core values in the American Historical Association's *Standards of Professional Conduct* that include "navigating ethical dilemmas" (AHA, 2011, p. 2).

Decades of challenging the corporate gatekeepers of social studies knowledge has shown their steadfast resistance to engaging with ethical standards. What can explain this anti-ethical stance? Where did it originate? Sylvia Wynter (2000, 2006) would likely suggest that we begin by looking at the medieval period when the European Christian Church viewed non-Christians as "others" —as a negation or opposite of their perceived humanness as Christians. She explains how this continued in the colonial and imperial projects of Europe's Renaissance and modern era that positioned Indigenous and African Peoples as non-cultural beings in a liminal status defined by a biological, somatotypical conception of being human—all resulting in the West's racist metaphor of itself as the "true self" and all others as the "untrue self" (Pandian ,1985; Wynter, 2000). In this racially coded construction, the European/White "true self" becomes the arbiter of ethics, since non-cultural beings are presumed to have no set of governing principles or ethics. So what's White is right and, conveniently, there is nothing else to think or talk about. In the land of textbook history, this eliding of ethical questions is re-framed as avoiding judgment and holding the line on objectivity. Locations of alterity and the themes that represent them, however, belie the unstated supremacist assumptions beneath this euro-arbitration of ethics, revealing its animus in the light of the normative cultural productions, in this case, of Indigenous and African Peoples.

Writing a "Re-Membered" Text

As explained above, writers of "re-membered" texts use a heterarchal macro-narrative to identify the important themes that outline the topic about which they are writing. However, it is the writing of student texts that brings together separate identity-group narratives into one detailed account for children. This bringing together of knowledge is what occurs in the six lessons of *Freedom and Democracy* (Swartz, 2013).

The general focus of each lesson comes from the three thematic categories in Table 3.1. Thus, there are lessons about knowledge of and experience with freedom and democracy, claims related to maintaining culture, and actions and practices related to freedom and democracy. Together, the six lessons include all themes related to the Haudenosaunee, Africans in the Diaspora, and European/White colonists (a total of 26 themes). The content details needed to develop each lesson were taken from identity-group narratives, with some additional details needed for biographies, charts, maps, and images. As Afrocentric concepts and principles of culturally informed curricular practice framed and wrote the content in identity-group narratives, these concepts and principles were "carried" into the "re-membered" student text. However, while writing group narrative content to grade level, care must be taken to preserve these Afrocentric concepts and culturally informed principles. In Appendix B you will find summaries of the six lessons in *Freedom and Democracy*. These summaries include how Afrocentric concepts and the principles of culturally informed curricular practice were preserved in the framing and writing of each lesson.

References

AHA (American Historical Association). (2011). *Statement on standards of professional conduct*. Washington, DC: American Historical Association.

Aptheker, H. (1951/1969). *A documentary history of the Negro people in the United States: From colonial times through the Civil War* (Vol. I). New York, NY: The Citadel Press.

Aptheker, H. (1976/1990). *Early years of the republic: From the end of the Revolution to the first administration of Washington (1783–1793)*. New York, NY: International Publishers.

Aptheker, H. (1993). *Anti-racism in U.S. history: The first two hundred years*. Westport, CT: Praeger.

Arneil, B. (1996). *John Locke and America: The defence of English colonialism*. New York, NY: Oxford University Press.

Asante, M. K. (1987/1998). *The Afrocentric idea*. Philadelphia, PA: Temple University Press.

Asante, M. K. (2007a). *The history of Africa: The quest for eternal harmony*. New York, NY: Routledge.

Asante, M. K. (2007b). *An Afrocentric manifesto*. Malden, MA: Polity Press.

Barreiro, J. (1992) (Ed.). *Indian roots of American democracy*. Ithaca, NY: Akwe:Kon Press.

Beard, C. (1914). *An economic interpretation of the Constitution of the United States*. New York, NY: Macmillan.

Bennett, L., Jr. (1968). *Pioneers in protest*. Chicago, IL: Johnson Publishing Company.

Bennett, L., Jr. (1975). *The shaping of Black America*. Chicago, IL: Johnson Publishing Company.

Biddiss, M. D. (1966). Gobineau and the origins of European racism. *Race,* 7(3), 255–270.

Blakey, M. L. (1998). The New York African Burial Ground Project: An examination of enslaved lives, a construction of ancestral ties. *Transforming Anthropology, 7*(1). Retrieved from http://www.huarchivesnet.howard.edu/0008huarnet/blakey1.htm

Boyd, C. D., Gay, G., Geiger, R., Kracht, J. B., Ooka Pang, V., Risinger, C. F., & Sanchez, S. M. (2011). *The United States.* Boston, MA: Pearson.

Cajete, G. (1994). *Look to the mountain: An ecology of Indigenous education.* Durango, CO: Kivaki Press.

Carney, J. A. (2001). *Black rice: The African origins of rice cultivation in the Americas.* Cambridge, MA: Harvard University Press.

Cayton, A., Israels Perry, E., Reed, L., & Winkler, A. M. (2007). *America: Pathways to the present.* Boston, MA: Pearson Education/Prentice Hall.

Colden, C. (1727/1922). *The history of the Five Indian Nations of Canada, which are dependent on the Province of New York, and are a barrier between the English and the French in that part of the world* (Vols. 1-2). New York, NY: Allerton Book Co.

Deloria, V., Jr. (1992). The application of the Constitution to American Indians. In O. Lyons & J. Mohawk (Eds.), *Exiled in the land of the free: Democracy, Indian nations, and the U.S. Constitution* (pp. 281–315). Santa Fe, NM: Clear Light Publishers.

Deloria, V., Jr. (2004). Promises made, promises broken. In G. McMaster & C. E. Trafzer (Eds.), *Native universe: Voices of Indian America* (pp. 143–159). Washington, DC: National Museum of the American Indian, Smithsonian Institution/National Geographic Society.

Di Nunzio, M. R. (1987). *American democracy and the authoritarian tradition of the West.* Lanham, MD: University Press of America.

Dixon, V. J. (1971). African-oriented and Euro-American-oriented world views: Research methodologies and economics. *The Review of Black Political Economy, 7*(2), 119–156.

Drake, T. E. (1950). *Quakers and slavery in America.* New Haven, CT: Yale University Press.

Drinnon, R. (1980/1997). *Facing west: The metaphysics of Indian-hating & empire-building.* Norman: University of Oklahoma Press.

Dumont, J. (2002). Indigenous intelligence. *Native Americas, XIV*(3 & 4), 15–16.

Durkheim, E. (1949). *The division of labor in society* (trans. G. Simpson). Glencoe, IL: The Free Press.

Fenton, W. N. (1998). *The Great Law and the Longhouse: A political history of the Iroquois Confederacy.* Norman: University of Oklahoma Press.

Franklin, V. P. (1992). *Black self-determination: A cultural history of African American resistance.* Chicago, IL: Lawrence Hill Books.

Frohne, A. (2000). Commemorating the African Burial Ground in New York City: Spirituality of space in contemporary art works. *Ijele: Art eJournal of the ijele African world.* Retrieved from http://www.africaknowledgeproject.org/index.php/ijele/article/view/1292

Gould, S. J. (1981). *The mismeasure of man.* New York, NY: Norton.

Grande, S. (2004). *Red pedagogy: Native American social and political thought.* Lanham, MD: Rowman & Littlefield.

Grinde, D. A., Jr. (1992). Iroquois political theory and the roots of American democracy. In O. Lyons & J. Mohawk (Eds.), *Exiled in the land of the free: Democracy, Indian nations, and the U.S. Constitution* (pp. 228–280). Santa Fe, NM: Clear Light Publishers.

Grinde, D. A., Jr., & Johansen, B. E. (1991). *Exemplar of liberty: Native America and the evolution of democracy.* Los Angeles: American Indian Studies Center, University of California, Los Angeles.

Hall, G. M. (2005). Slavery and African ethnicities in the Americas: Restoring the links. Chapel Hill: University of North Carolina Press.

Harris, N. (2003). A philosophic basis for an Afrocentric orientation. In A. Mazama (Ed.), *The Afrocentric paradigm* (pp. 111–119). Trenton, NJ: Africa World Press.

Hart, R. (1985/2002). *Slaves who abolished slavery: Blacks in rebellion.* Kingston, Jamaica: University of the West Indies Press.

Hilliard, A. G., III (1997). *SBA: The reawakening of the African mind.* Gainesville, FL: Makare Publishingy.

Hobbes, T. (1977). *Leviathan, or the matter, forme, & power of a common-wealth ecclesiasticall and civill* (C. B. Macpherson, Ed.). New York, NY: Penguin Books. (Original work published 1651)

Hoff Wilson, J. (1976). The illusion of change: Women and the American Revolution. In A. F. Young (Ed.), *The American Revolution: Explorations in the history of American radicalism* (pp. 383–445). De Kalb: Northern Illinois University Press.

Holloway, J. E. (1990). The origins of African-American culture. In J. E. Holloway (Ed.), *Africanisms in American culture* (pp. 1–18). Bloomington: Indiana University Press.

Jennings, F. (1984). *The ambiguous Iroquois empire: The Covenant Chain Confederation of Indian tribes with English colonies from its beginnings to the Lancaster Treaty of 1744.* New York, NY: W. W. Norton & Company.

Johansen, B. E. (1982). *Forgotten founders: Benjamin Franklin, the Iroquois and the rationale for the American Revolution.* Ipswich, MA: Gambit.

Johansen, B. E. (1995). Dating the Iroquois Confederacy. *Akwesasne Notes New Series, 1*(3 & 4), 62–63.

Karenga, M. (2006). Philosophy in the African tradition of resistance: Issues of human freedom and human flourishing. In L. R. Gordon & J. A. Gordon (Eds.), *Not only the master's tools: African American studies in theory and practice* (pp. 243–271). Boulder, CO: Paradigm.

Keita, M. (2000). *Race and the writing of history: Riddling the Sphinx.* New York, NY: Oxford University Press.

Kershaw, T. (2003). The Black Studies paradigm: The making of scholar activists. In J. L. Conyers, Jr. (Ed.), *Afrocentricity and the academy: Essays on theory and practice* (pp. 27–36). Jefferson, NC: McFarland & Company.

King, J. E. (2004). Culture-centered knowledge: Black studies, curriculum transformation, and social action. In J. A. Banks & C. A. McGee Banks (Eds.), *Handbook of research on multicultural education* (2nd ed., pp. 349–378). San Francisco, CA: Jossey-Bass.

King, J. E. (2006). If justice is our objective": Diaspora literacy, heritage knowledge and the praxis of critical studyin' for human freedom. In A. Ball (Ed.), *With more deliberate speed: Achieving equity and excellence in education—realizing the full potential of Brown v. Board of Education* (pp. 337–360). National Society for the Study of Education, 105th Yearbook, Part 2. New York, NY: Ballenger.

King, J. E., & Goodwin, Susan (2006). *Criterion standards for contextualized teaching and learning about people of African descent.* Rochester, NY: Authors.

Kliewer, C., & Fitzgerald, L. M. (2001). Disability, schooling, and the artifacts of colonialism. *Teachers College Record, 103*(3), 450–470.

Littlefield, Daniel C. (1981). *Rice and slaves: Ethnicity and the slave trade in colonial South Carolina.* Baton Rouge: Louisiana State University Press.

Lyons, O. (1992). The American Indian in the past. In O. Lyons & J. Mohawk (Eds.), *Exiled in the land of the free: Democracy, Indian nations, and the U.S. Constitution* (pp. 14–42). Santa Fe, NM: Clear Light Publishers.

Lyons, O., & Mohawk, J. (Eds.) (1992). *Exiled in the land of the free: Democracy, Indian nations, and the U.S. Constitution.* Santa Fe, NM: Clear Light Publishers.

Maiga, H. O. (2010). *Balancing written history with oral tradition: The legacy of the Songhoy people.* New York, NY: Routledge.

Mankiller, W. (2004). A new path for the people. In G. McMaster & C. E. Trafzer (Eds.), *Native universe: Voices of Indian America* (pp. 248–25). Washington, DC: National Museum of the American Indian, Smithsonian Institution/National Geographic Society.

Martin, J. K. (1973). *Men in rebellion: Higher government leaders and the coming of the American Revolution.* New Brunswick, NJ: Rutgers University Press.

McCarty, T. L., Wallace, S., Hadley Lynch, R., & Benally, A. (1991). Classroom inquiry and Navajo Learning styles: A call for reassessment. *Anthropology & Education Quarterly, 22,* 42–59.

Millican, E. (1990). *One united people: The Federalist Papers and the national idea.* Lexington: The University Press of Kentucky.

Mills, C. W. (1997). *The racial contract.* Ithaca, NY: Cornell University Press.

Mohawk, J. (1992). Indians and democracy: No one ever told us. In O. Lyons & J. Mohawk (Eds.), *Exiled in the land of the free: Democracy, Indian nations, and the U.S. Constitution* (pp. 44–71). Santa Fe, NM: Clear Light Publishers.

Morrison T. (1992). *Playing in the dark, whiteness and the literary imagination.* Cambridge, MA: Harvard University Press.

Nash, G. B. (1976/1990). Social change and the growth of pre-Revolutionary urban radicalism. In A. F. Young (Ed.), *The American Revolution: Explorations in the history of American radicalism* (pp. 3–36). DeKalb: Northern Illinois University Press.

Nobles, W. W. (2005). Consciousness. In M. K. Asante & Ama Mazama (Eds.), *Encyclopedia of Black Studies* (pp. 197–200). Thousand Oaks, CA: Sage.

Norton, M. B. (1980). *Liberty's daughters: The Revolutionary experience of American women, 1750–1800.* Boston, MA: Little, Brown and Company.

Pandian, J. (1985). *Anthropology and the Western tradition: Toward an authentic anthropology.* Prospect Heights, IL: Waveland Press.

Piersen, W. D. (1993). *Black legacy: America's hidden heritage.* Amherst: University of Massachusetts Press.

Quarles, B. (1961). *Negro in the American Revolution.* Chapel Hill: University of North Carolina Press.

Robinson, R. (2000). *The debt: What America owes to Blacks.* New York, NY: Dutton.

Runes, D. D. (Ed.). (1947). *The selected writings of Benjamin Rush.* New York, NY: The Philosophical Library.

Sargent Murray, J. (1994). On the equality of the sexes. In P. Lauter (Ed.), *The Heath anthology of American literature* (2nd ed., pp. 1011–1016). Lexington, MA: D.C. Heath and Company. (Originally published in the *Massachusetts Magazine,* April and May, 1790)

Semmes, C. E. (1992). *Cultural hegemony and African American development.* Westport, CT: Praeger.

Shenandoah, A. (1988). Everything has to be in balance. *Northeast Indian Quarterly, IV*(4) & *V*(1), 4–7.

Sindima, H. (1995). *Africa's agenda: The legacy of liberalism and colonialism in the crisis of African values.* Westport, CT: Greenwood.

Somekawa, E., & Smith, E. (1988). Theorizing the writing of history or, "I can't think why it should be so dull, for a great deal of it must be invention." *Journal of Social History, 22*(1), 149–161.

Spencer, H. (1897). *The principles of sociology.* New York, NY: D. Appleton & Co.

Swartz, E. E. (2013). *Freedom and democracy: A Story Remembered.* Rochester, NY: Omnicentric Press.

Szatmary, D. P. (1980). *Shay's rebellion: The making of an agrarian insurrection.* Amherst: The University of Massachusetts Press.

Tayac, G. (2004). Keeping the original instructions. In G. McMaster & C. E. Trafzer (Eds.), *Native universe: Voices of Indian America* (pp. 72–83). Washington, DC: National Museum of the American Indian, Smithsonian Institution/National Geographic Society.

Tehanetorens (Fadden, R.). (1999). *Wampum belts of the Iroquois.* Summertown, TN: Book Publishing Company.

Thompson, V. B. (1987). *The making of the African diaspora in the Americas 1441–1900.* New York, NY: Longman.

Van Doren, C., & Boyd, J. P. (Eds.) (1938). *Indian treaties printed by Benjamin Frankl, in 1736–1762.* Philadelphia: Historical Society of Pennsylvania.

Walker, S. S. (Ed.). (2001). *African roots/American cultures: Africa in the creation of the Americas.* Lanham, MD: Rowman & Littlefield.

Williams, W. A. (1980/2007). *Empire as a way of life: An essay on the causes and character of America's present predicament along with a few thoughts about an alternative.* New York, NY: Ig Publishing.

Witherspoon, G. (1983). Navajo social organization. In W. C. Stuartevant & A. Ortiz (Eds.), *Handbook of North American Indians, Vol. X* (pp. 524–535). Washington, DC: Smithsonian Institution.

Wynter, S. (1992). *Do not call us "Negroes": How multicultural textbooks perpetuate racism.* San Francisco, CA: Aspire Books.

Wynter, S. (1997). Alterity. In C. Grant & G. Ladson-Billings (Eds.), *Dictionary of multicultural education* (pp. 13–14). New York, NY: Oryx.

Wynter, S. (2000). The re-enchantment of humanism: An interview with Sylvia Wynter by David Scott. *Small Axe 8,* 119–207.

Wynter, S. (2006). On how we mistook the map for the territory, and re-imprisoned ourselves in our unbearable wrongness of being, of Désêtre: Black studies toward the human project. In L. R., Gordon & J. A. Gordon (Eds.), *Not only the master's tools: African American studies in theory and practice* (pp. 107–169). Boulder, CO: Paradigm.

Young, A. F. (Ed.). (1976). *The American Revolution: Explorations in the history of American radicalism.* DeKalb: Northern Illinois University Press.

Zinn, H. (1980/2003). *A people's history of the United States: 1492–present.* New York, NY: Harper Collins.

4

STANDARDS "RE-MEMBERED"

Liminal and marginalized cultures and groups enter state standards through their experiences with domination—being victimized by it, in conflict with it, struggling to change it, or assimilated by it. How can a "re-membered" standards model alter this relationship?

What Do Standards Measure?

Now that we have described the four phases of the "re-membering" process and used it to produce democratized knowledge in *Freedom and Democracy: A Story Remembered* (Swartz, 2013), we examine and identify existing state and other standards that can guide teaching and measure student learning. While this examination is applicable to all grade levels, we use the fourth grade as an exemplar because this is the grade level at which the "re-membering" process produced *Freedom and Democracy*. As we have shown, an Afrocentric culturally informed praxis of historical recovery can democratize knowledge by reconnecting or "re-membering" it. Likewise, standards for the social studies can provide curricular guidance if they too are informed by a range of diverse knowledge bases and experiences that shaped the past and present. Current state standards, by themselves, fail to provide such a foundation.

States produce standards that delineate the content and skills students need to know and be able to do; and given that PK–12 education funding is mostly a state responsibility, their standards—which are tied to student and teacher assessments—bear strong influence on curricular frameworks and course content generated at the local level. As we will show throughout this chapter, "official" knowledge in the form of grand narratives is embedded in state-sanctioned social studies standards, and by disseminating these explanatory accounts of national development in the form of standards, states take the lead in reproducing a hegemonic translation of U.S. history year after year and generation after generation. They do this by omitting and misrepresenting knowledge about both historically oppressed and dominant cultures and groups. For example, at Grade 4 in the *New York State Common Core K-8 Social Studies Framework*, the focus is Local History and Local Government. Key Idea 4.10 states: "New York State has faced economic, political, and social challenges as the diversity of its population has changed and its settlement patterns shifted" (NYSED, 2012a). One of the Conceptual Understandings (4.10.c) related to Key Idea 4.10 states: "At times, the cultural, racial, and ethnic diversity of the state has led to conflict, prejudice, and discrimination." It is not "diversity" that leads to economic, political, and social challenges, conflicts, prejudice, and discrimination; it is practices of domination, exploitation, and oppression that do. This standard obfuscates the injustices and inequalities that dominant groups have enacted and perpetuated (e.g., land theft, genocide, disenfranchisement) by omitting any reference to them. Standards such as 4.10 are a foundation for a number of grand narratives, such as colonization, manifest destiny, and civil rights. States with "diversity" standards such as this typically position the very presence of diverse "others" as responsible for the unjust practices they experience, leaving practices of dominance unquestioned (Swartz, 2012).

With grand narratives firmly ensconced in state social studies standards—as well as in the corporate products that mirror those standards—curricula and assessments written and/or adopted at the state and local levels and taught by the majority of teachers follow suit. This means that student learning in the social studies is typically guided and measured by standards that omit, distort, and misrepresent knowledge about the past. That said there are state standards that can be used if they are accompanied by culturally informed standards. In this chapter we propose such a "re-membered" model—one that teachers can use as a guide to select standards that provide a democratized foundation for teaching and learning.

The State of State Standards

Educational standards are not new, but what is referred to as standards-based education has grown exponentially since the alarm sounded by the 1983 report, *A Nation at Risk* (National Commission on Excellence in Education). Over the past three decades, the neo-reformist push for management-driven accountability has led to the development of a common set of standards called the *Common Core State Standards* (typically written as *Common Core Standards*) in English Language Arts (NGA & CCSSO, 2010). There is also a *Common Core State Standards Initiative in Mathematics* (NGA & CCSSO, 2012). The K-12 literacy standards state that their focus is to prepare students for college and careers by the end of high school. While it is too soon to tell what effects these *Common*

Core Standards for literacy are having on teaching and learning, we do know that these standards have already enhanced the capacity of publishers, consortia of foundations, institutes, and for-profit and not-for-profit assessment providers to develop and market new products aligned with the *Common Core Standards;* and this is often done with the support of federal funds (Education Northwest, 2012; ETS, 2010).

As for social studies, there are no common state standards. We conducted an online review of fourth-grade standards in the 48 states that have state-sanctioned social studies standards, and the variation is evident. Unfortunately, what is uniform about these state standards is that they fail to locate all cultures and groups at the center of knowledge that describes and defines them. They do, however, require students to know something about such concepts as diversity, equality of opportunity, tolerance, respect for the rights of others, and/or value for the common good. Notice that the inverse of each of these concepts references the oppressive actions of the individuals and groups (who go unnamed in state social studies standards) with enough power to produce systemic inequality of opportunity, to foster intolerance and disrespect for the rights of others, and to devalue the common good. The cultures and groups targeted by these inversions enter state standards only to exemplify these experiences, meaning their experiences with domination—being victimized by it, in conflict with it, struggling to change it, or assimilated by it. Their presence, albeit limited and controlled, is required in order to unfold grand narratives such as European exploration and colonization, slavery, freedom and democracy, manifest destiny, industrialization, and civil rights. For example, people of African ancestry are first presented as "slaves" and then as second-class citizens who struggle for equal opportunity with some advances over time. These "gains"—typically presented through the contributions of exceptional (to the rule) African Americans—serve to confirm the existence of national ideals such as equal opportunity and meritocracy. Likewise, women had few rights and opportunities in colonial America and have since struggled to gain more. Achieving what men achieve is supposed to signal progress, which also confirms national ideals of equal opportunity and meritocracy, even though wage differentials and other socio-economic indicators exemplify entrenched inequalities. Indigenous Americans first appear in state social studies standards in relation to climate, land features, and settlement patterns, with the securing of food, clothing, and shelter defining their existence and eclipsing other aspects of culture. While they help European colonizers survive through "cooperation," differences between them cause (seemingly inevitable) "conflict." Poor and working-class White people have also been disenfranchised and socio-economically marginalized since the colonial period. They are virtually invisible in state standards as are their documented alliances with people of color.

Of course, liminal cultures and groups were and are heavily impacted by oppression and disenfranchisement. In state social studies standards, however, they are wholly defined by this impact. While living their lives in the thick of oppression, dominated groups concurrently contribute to their communities, country, and the world by producing knowledge in all disciplines, maintaining traditions, developing socio-political and economic structures to maintain sovereignty, and advancing the idea of a collective humanity (King & Goodwin, 2006; RTC, 2007). Yet, there is no sense of this—that is, their humanity—in state social studies standards. Given the melting pot theory that still lingers in these standards, the inclusion of these groups shows what is being done to them in their state-assigned struggle to assimilate, not what they have been and are doing for themselves in their indigenously assigned journey of liberation.

A Democratized Standards Model

The model we propose in this chapter combines current state standards with a set of culturally informed standards called *Criterion Standards for Contextualized Teaching and Learning about People of African Descent* (King & Goodwin, 2006). These standards include alterity themes that open up access to the knowledge bases of liminal groups—including their critical analysis of and engagement with the worldview and practices of dominant groups. *Criterion Standards,* which are for all groups, uncover connections between liminal and dominant groups that more fully represent the past and therefore the present compared to state standards. The need for culturally informed standards is widespread yet particular, and such standards have been created in various locations. For example, if you teach in Alaska or Hawaii, you can access standards authored by Indigenous organizations in those states (Alaska Native Knowledge Network, 1998, 1999; Native Hawaiian Education Council, 2002).

The three sub-sections below describe the three sets of standards used in a democratized standards model. Along with analysis of their content, we discuss what each can contribute to guiding the teaching of *Freedom and Democracy: A Story Remembered* (Swartz, 2013). While one fully integrated set of social studies standards would be optimal, the current effects of state standards on local districts—particularly with regard to student and teacher assessments—suggests that we consciously develop a way to complement state standards that, by themselves, support a limited euro-spun version of the past.

Common Core State Standards

Educational policies and practices vary from state to state, but by 2013 all but four U.S. states had adopted the *Common Core State Standards for English Language Arts* (ELA) developed by the National Governors Association and the Council of Chief State School Officers (NGA & CCSSO, 2010). While these standards are called state standards, they are more accurately national standards written by consultants for the NGA, with funds from the Gates Foundation, and with most states experiencing pressure to adopt them, since their adoption was linked to receiving federal Race to the Top grants (Au et al., 2013). In ELA, *Common Core Standards* guide teaching and measure learning in four strands: reading (literature, informational texts, and foundational skills), writing, speaking and listening, and language. While *Common Core Standards* provide no content standards for the social studies or other disciplines, the interdisciplinary expectation is that the literacy skills they require are necessary for learning in other disciplines. Thus, *Common Core Standards* in all four strands can be met when using social studies materials.

The *Common Core Standards* for literacy are quite extensive and seemingly applicable to all students. But in their assumption of student sameness, their consideration of culture is nil. This is evident in the authorship and content of suggested illustrative texts and in the admission that it is beyond the scope of *Common Core Standards* to provide support appropriate for English Language Learners (ELL; see NGA & CCSSO, 2010, p. 6, #5). While all literature—including fiction, poetry, drama, speeches, myths, fables, fantasies, and legends—is culturally situated, the illustrative texts provided in the *Common Core Standards* for grades K–5 suggest that the dominant culture is the location where literature is to be found (see NGA & CCSSO, 2010, p. 32). There is only one African American author and one Asian American author—a total of 4% of the 46 authors and illustrators, with the rest being European or White American. The document's disclaimer about space limitations and individual titles being "representative of a wide range of topics and genres" (p. 32), does not "fix" this *Common Core* presentation of literature—one with so few exceptions as to suggest that literature is only a European/White enterprise. Conflating Whiteness with generic-ness teaches disregard for the cultures of "others" (Shujaa, 1994). Furthermore, while the National Council for the Social Studies (NCSS, 2010a) calls for social studies classrooms to be "laboratories of democracy," none of the suggested titles in the K–5 *Common Core Standards* invite students to explore the contradictions of systemic sociocultural inequalities in a democracy. This misses an opportunity for teachers and students to critically explore ways in which to either relinquish or resist race, gender, and cultural supremacies and the inequalities they continue to produce (Smith & Anderson, 2012). These problems with the *Common Core* might have been avoided if teachers and parents had been a central part of the process. In fact, mostly academics and assessment experts—many with ties to testing companies—wrote the standards; and there were very few classroom teachers and no parents on the review panels (Au et al., 2013).

Examining Conventions of Standard English Grammar and Usage

A requirement of standard English as the normative yardstick against which all students are measured is embedded in the *Common Core Standards,* which require "conventions of standard English grammar and usage" when writing, speaking, reading, or listening (see NGA & CCSSO, 2010, pp. 28-29). There are, however, millions of students whose discourse styles and grammar and usage practices stem from their first language being one other than standard English. This applies to students who are in bilingual, ELL, and ESOL programs and students who speak African American Language. These groups of students have language practices that are conventional in their cultures. While we are not suggesting that other language conventions be taught in school, we are suggesting that these conventions be viewed as a bridge to learning standard English conventions, especially when the *Common Core Standards* state that English Language Learners "must meet the same high standards" even though it is beyond the scope of the *Standards* to support this outcome (see p. 6, #5). To exemplify what is missing, consider how adding the following standards to the *Common Core Standards* would serve as guidance in teaching fourth-grade students whose first language is other than standard English:

Grade 4 Students Whose First Language Is Other Than Standard English

1. hear and identify differences between their first language and standard English by listening to language;
2. translate oral and written first-language conventions into standard English conventions;
3. identify and explain the meaning of similar words and phrases in first-language literature and standard English literature; and
4. compare first-language and standard English discourse practices (e.g., metaphors, alliteration, structured repetition, analogies, aphorisms/ adages) in both oral and written language

(Delpit, 1998; Duncan, 1997; Secret, 1998; RTC, 2007).

Effectively teaching the conventions of standard English does not begin with ignoring the language platforms students bring with them to school or refusing to incorporate the strengths of language practices that represent the conventions of "others" (Kynard, 2013; Lee, 2000, 2007; Lessow-Hurley, 2009; Nieto, 1996, 2002; Smitherman, 2000; Soto, 1993). That said most teachers would need to acquire the knowledge base underneath the above four standards in order to effectively use them. To begin, we suggest readings by the following authors: Theresa Perry and Lisa Delpit (1998), Garrett Duncan (1997), Carmen Kynard (2013), Kris Gutierrez and Joanne Larson (1994), Carol D. Lee (1995, 2007), Sonia Nieto (2002), Carrie Secret (1998), and Geneva Smitherman (1977/1986, 1994, 2000).

While the *Common Core Standards* are seen by some educators as having the potential to raise expectations for all students, we have seen the undesirable and even punitive outcomes of such top-down mandates before, with the most recent example being No Child Left Behind. Given the heavy presence of corporate hands—not the least of which are the assessment providers that stand to make huge profits; given the absence of cultural considerations and the rush to implement more high stakes testing that early indications suggest will result in disproportionate failure in urban schools and negative outcomes for teachers' assessments; and given the virtual absence of classroom teachers and parents in the process, we are concerned that the *Common Core* is another in a long line of neo-reforms designed to set up urban schools for failure. If the outcomes of assessments related to *Common Core Standards* are used as one more indication that urban public schools should be shuttered, charter schools—for the most part another corporate venture with the potential to turn public schools into private spaces—will gain more traction in government policy and public perception.

Social Studies State Standards

Partly in response to the variation of state-sanctioned social studies standards, the National Council for the Social Studies (NCSS) recently updated its standards to encourage states to align their standards with its *National Curriculum Standards for Social Studies: A Framework for Teaching, Learning, and Assessment* (NCSS, 2010a & b). These standards are not content standards; they are curriculum standards with a thematic focus on "big ideas" and "enduring understandings" (Herczog, 2010). The NCSS suggests that curriculum developers select content standards from the National History Standards (NCHS, 1994) and from their state's social studies standards (NCSS, 2010b, p. 12). This suggestion actually contradicts this organization's call—referred to above—for social studies classrooms to be "laboratories of democracy" (NCSS, 2010a). Whether curriculum developers select content from their state's standards or National History Standards, our review of these standards reveals an abundant presence of grand narratives. Without standards that reflect the worldview and knowledge bases of those cultures and groups that participated in any topic, event, or movement, the NCSS call for social studies classrooms to be "laboratories of democracy" is a pretense.

New York and Virginia

We chose Lesson 3 (African People in North America) from *Freedom and Democracy* (Swartz, 2013) as the exemplar for our "re-membered" standards model (see Appendix B for a summary of this lesson). To examine state standards, we created a pool of states that once were the 13 colonies. This North American region and colonial time period (17th and 18th centuries) relate to content in Lesson 3. We then randomly selected two states from this pool: New York and Virginia. New York's *Common Core K-8 Social Studies Framework* (NYSED, 2012a) integrates 1996 Social Studies Learning Standards and slightly revised versions of NCSS themes, with an emphasis on Key Ideas, Conceptual

Understandings, and Themes (NYSED, 2012a & b). Sets of Social Studies Practices (social science and historical thinking skills) are enumerated in the same document at three grade bands (i.e., K-4, 5-8, 9-12). In addition to using NCSS and NCHS standards, New York lists five other state standards and the NAEP (National Assessment of Educational Progress) *U.S. History Framework* among its reference documents. While the *Core K-8 Social Studies Framework* is in draft form as this volume goes to publication, we have decided to use them in our "re-membered" standards model. While changes in form and language exist from one approved set of state standards to the other, the grand narratives of national development and the central ideas and concepts students are to learn stay remarkably the same.

Virginia's History and Social Science Standards of Learning (VDOE, 2012) enumerates specific skills for analyzing, interpreting, and demonstrating knowledge of historical events and ideas, with content objectives listed under broad topic headings that describe a chronologically sequenced history of Virginia and the United States. In 2012 the Virginia Department of Education reviewed and updated their standards in consultation with several organizations, such as the Colonial Williamsburg Foundation, United States Slavery Museum, Virginia Council on Indians, Virginia Historical Society, and Library of Virginia. In the following section we examine a number of New York and Virginia fourth-grade state social studies standards.

Worldview and State Social Studies Standards

State standards are cultural productions, and at the foundation of any cultural production is the worldview of its producers. Let us be clear at the outset that a worldview refers to complexes of cultural patterns and meanings, with divergent worldviews best understood as a placement of cultural attributes across a continuum rather than as opposites that ignore intragroup variations (Boykin, 1986; Dixon, 1976). As state standards are the cultural productions of dominant groups with the power to shape and disseminate knowledge about the past, social studies standards are weighted in the direction of representing euro-informed cultural patterns and meaning making (Nobles, 1976, 1991; Myers, 1988/1993). For example, the worldview at the foundation of New York State fourth-grade social studies standards is shaped by the cultural orientation of difference. This orientation values practices that show the ways in which people and groups differ from each other, which positions historically oppressed groups, vis-à-vis dominant groups, under the concept of "diversity." In these standards "diversity" means the presence of people of color, women, immigrants, and any groups other than White people—particularly wealthy, White men who are considered the norm. In other words, diversity is a code word for difference; it occurs when "others"—whose identities make them different than the dominant group—are present.

To set this discussion in historical context, Europe's colonial project—and the worldview from which it emerged—viewed Indigenous and African Peoples as not having culture and as uncivil beings compared to Europeans who considered themselves as having culture and being civil(ized) (Deloria, 2004; Mills, 1997; Wynter, 1992). The racist metaphor of the West was itself as the "true self" and all others as the "untrue self" (Pandian, 1985). In this environment of cultural supremacy—which has only changed somewhat in form over the centuries—difference from the "true self" is viewed as a deficit (Boardman, 2013; Boykin, 1986; Dixon, 1971; Mills, 1997; Nobles, 1976). Those who are "different" are constructed as deviations from the norms of Whiteness, maleness, and upper-classness and placed lower on the hierarchy of human worth (Fox Keller, 1985; Wynter, 1992, 2005). When different groups interact in New York State fourth-grade standards, "diversity" is presented as the reason for the challenges, conflicts, and discrimination that exist (see NYSED, 2012a, Standards 4.6, 4.10, 4.10c). By omitting European colonial practices, such as land theft, cultural assault, removal, and genocide, state standards sanitize the historical record of the colonial period through misrepresentation of both Europeans and Indigenous Americans (see NYSED, 2012a, Standards 4.2a, 4.6a, 4.6b, c, & d). Fitting oppressed groups into the dominant worldview of diversity perpetuates the grand narrative of colonization by cloaking the motivations, interests, and oppressive practices that actually produced the problems that "others" experienced (Swartz, 2012).

The worldview at the foundation of Virginia's fourth-grade social studies standards is also informed by the dominant cultural orientation of difference. In an extreme example of this orientation, Indigenous cultures are presented as more akin to geography than to humanity. These standards direct teachers to introduce "American Indians" to students under a broad topic heading entitled, "Virginia: The Physical Geography and Native Peoples" (VDOE 2012, Standards VS.2a–g). Other than locating "American Indian language groups" on maps (along with mountains, water features, and the state itself), the other fourth-grade standards that refer to Indigenous Peoples are only about their interactions with Europeans. In addition to lumping Indigenous Peoples under Columbus's misnomer ("American Indians"), thereby failing to call Peoples by the names they call themselves (e.g., Monacan, Pamunkey, Catawba), there are no standards that refer to Indigenous cultural knowledge and values, political structures, and socio-cultural practices in the area colonists called Virginia. The absence of such standards obscures the knowledge bases of Indigenous people who only exist in these state standards to play a "role" in European American history (see VDOE 2012, Standards VS.3g, VS.5b, VS.7c). Omitting Indigenous knowledge and cultural practices paves the way to present history standards that reproduce the grand narrative of European exploration and colonization, even though these grand narratives include faulty assumptions about sovereignty, legitimacy, choice, right of conquest, difference, and development (see chapter 1 for a discussion of these assumptions; Grande, 2004; Lomawaima & McCarty, 2006; Lyons, 2000).

Fourth-grade social studies standards in New York and Virginia also foster distortions and false assumptions about African Peoples who are first introduced as enslaved (with no mention of by whom; see NYSED 2012a, Standards 4.6, 4.6e). No connections are made between enslaved or free African people and their homelands, including the knowledge, traditions, values, and skills they brought with them to the Americas (Carney, 2001; Hall, 2005; Holloway, 1990; Karenga, 2006; Littlefield, 1981; Walker, 2001). This is a missed opportunity to connect African people in the Diaspora to their ancestral heritage (Aptheker, 1951/1969; Bennett, 1975; Hart, 1985/2002). Another standard states that there were free African people who—along with Native Americans, European settlers, and enslaved African people—interacted in the New York colony, but their presence is only related to bringing about "a culturally diverse state" (NYSED 2012a, Standard 4.6a). What were free African people doing? What did they contribute to the development of the colony and state, not only to its diversity? And another New York standard suggests that African Americans and women were part of bringing about social change through struggling for rights (see NYSED 2012a, Standard 4.11d), which supports the civil rights grand narrative that valorizes the struggle for rights while failing to identify the racism/White supremacy and sexist policies and hegemonic practices that dominant groups cyclically manufacture—and against which people of African ancestry and women continue to struggle (Sizemore, 2008). Failing to identify hegemony cloaks the institutional practices and people who benefit in the past and present from systemic injustice. While inequalities are not inevitable, failing to identify their sources makes them appear so.

In a final example, one Virginia standard states, "The student will demonstrate knowledge of life in the Virginia colony by explaining the importance of agriculture and its influence on the institution of slavery" (VDOE, 2012, VS.4a). So, was it agriculture or the White plantocracy and its control of agriculture that influenced the institution of slavery? This is some version of "The cotton gin caused slavery to grow," as if machines and farming systems, not people, are responsible for practices that benefit some people at the expense of others. It is standards such as this one that support and maintain the grand narrative of slavery—a distorted narrative that ignores extant scholarship and obstructs critical thinking.

We offer the foregoing analysis to raise consciousness about the content of these state standards, and to invite teachers to consider using a "re-membered" model that includes selected state standards as well as culturally informed standards. In this standards model, teachers have access to the worldviews and knowledge bases of liminal, marginalized, and dominant groups, meaning that all groups are located in standards as subjects with agency, not as objects described and defined by others. (See chapter 3 for an explanation of how we distinguish between liminal and marginalized groups.) Ultimately, this means that the selection of standards that define the past, guide teaching, and measure learning in the social studies is in the hands of teachers. In the next section we describe a set of culturally informed standards that provide more accurate and comprehensive content than what New York State and Virginia have heretofore produced.

Criterion Standards for Contextualized Teaching and Learning about People of African Descent

Criterion Standards for Contextualized Teaching and Learning about People of African Descent provide concepts and content related to African and Diasporan experiences (King & Goodwin, 2006). These 19 standards include cultural knowledge, which teachers need, and heritage knowledge, which is the repository of retentions and experiences of people in the Diaspora that reflect African knowledge, skills, and worldview (Hall, 2005; King, 2006). (See the Preface of this volume for descriptions of both "heritage knowledge" and "cultural knowledge.) *Criterion Standards* can also guide teaching and learning for other cultures and groups who represent "co-existing/concurrent civilizations, events, social and political movements, and human endeavors in multiple geopolitical locations" (King & Goodwin, 2006, Standard 6, p. 2). In other words, standards that guide learning about African people also guide learning about their interactions with others.

Criterion Standards are compatible with the Afrocentric culturally informed praxis of historical recovery that we used to develop the process of "re-membering" and to conceptualize and write "re-membered" student texts. For example, in *Freedom and Democracy* (Swartz, 2013), students learn about various forms of resistance to enslavement. This content is framed by Afrocentric concepts such as Centrality/Location, Self-Determination, Subjects with Agency, and Reclamation of Cultural Heritage; and it is written using principles of culturally informed curricular practice, such as representation, accurate scholarship, and indigenous voice. Criterion Standard 9 (below) reflects these concepts and principles, thereby correcting distortions and false assumptions that occur, such as when fourth-grade social studies state standards omit any reference to immediate and ongoing individual and collective resistance to enslavement by free and enslaved African people:

> *Criterion Standard* 9: African people have resisted domination and oppression from the earliest period of enslavement. Resistance by African descent people to racism and oppression continues and has taken many social, political, economic and cultural forms, including self-determination, spiritual resilience, and agency in education, cultural expression, and community building (e.g., mutual aid societies, benevolent associa-

tions, social movements, fraternal lodges, Freedom schools, Kwanzaa, Rites of Passage).

(King & Goodwin, 2006, p. 2)

The following three *Criterion Standards* include concepts and content that describe the African Continental/Diasporan connection. Having access to these standards informs teachers about the normative connections across time and place that are visible when you consider chronology, the extant cultural unity across African cultures and communities, and African retentions in the form of cultural orientations, traditions, values, and socioeconomic practices. These connections are severed in state standards that first mention African people as "enslaved Africans" (NYSED 2012a, standard 4.6) without any connecting information about their homelands, as if being kidnapped and brought to the Americas obliterated the worldview, traditions, cultural practices, knowledge, skills, values, and beliefs—in effect the heritage knowledge and humanity of African Peoples:

> *Criterion Standard* 2: African Diasporan histories begin in Africa with human history, not with the period of enslavement.
>
> *(King & Goodwin, 2006, p. 2).*

> *Criterion Standard* 5: African descent people are one people, Continental and Diasporic. There is a cultural unity across Diasporan communities as well as a common experience of domination, disenfranchisement, and social/political/economic inequalities.
>
> *(King & Goodwin, 2006, p. 2),*

> *Criterion Standard* 10: African retentions form the basis of African American and other Diasporan cultures. African descent people's cultures, both Continental and Diasporic, share ontological, epistemological, and axiological orientations—a worldview foundation that is ultimately based on the idea and experience of the oneness and interconnectedness of all in creation. Life, Nature, and Creator are thought of and experienced as allies to engage rather than control. There is a perceived relationship of complementarity rather than an assumed hostility among them.
>
> *(King & Goodwin, 2006, p. 3).*

The above three standards cut through false assumptions and inaccurate information still found in state standards, textbooks, and local curricula that position Africans in the Western hemisphere as coming here with nothing more than their labor, and retaining nothing of significance from their homelands in the form of knowledge or cultural practices. It is as if an enclosed wall has been erected around African people in the Diaspora beginning with enslavement, blocking access to the thousands of years of civilization, heritage knowledge, and cultural memory that people carried with them to the Americas. Even though community protests and scholarly work have caused a few visible cracks in this wall of obfuscation, state standards safeguard the wall by making it invisible. *Criterion Standards* bring the wall down.

Criterion Standard 13 identifies those responsible for the enslavement of African people and how they profited from Africans' knowledge, skills, and cultural practices. In state social studies standards, Europeans and their White descendants are never named, as if enslavement—which the state calls an institution—developed on its own, unlike any other institution. Significantly, this standard acknowledges African people's human capacity to live life despite this system of dehumanization.

> *Criterion Standard* 13: Europeans and their descendants in the Americas targeted, enslaved, and dehumanized African peoples in order to exploit and profit from African technical knowledge, skills, expertise, and cultural assets. People of African descent not only survived enslavement but lived life in the midst of it, creating and inventing new cultural forms, variations, and representations of Black life.
>
> *(King & Goodwin, 2006, p. 3)*

This standard also opens the door to well-documented accounts of the period of enslavement that locate free and enslaved African people as having agency, self-determination, and verve (Asante, 2007; Bennett, 1975; Boykin, 1983, 1994; Franklin, 1992). (See the Africans in the Diaspora narrative in Appendix A.) Yet, these African characteristics of agency, self-determination, and verve are nowhere to be found in New York State and Virginia State social studies standards.

Criterion Standard 16 guides instruction and student learning about some of the earliest African achievements and demonstrations of excellence in the decades preceding (and of course following) the legalization of slavery in the American colonies:

> *Criterion Standard* 16: People of African descent have distinguished themselves in every field from agriculture, academics, and art to medicine, law, science and invention, math, and space travel. These achievements and demonstrations of excellence have occurred despite systemic patterns and processes of racism, segregation, and other barriers to education, adequate income, health, and full civil and human rights.
>
> *(King & Goodwin, 2006, p. 3)*

For example, in 1619 a Dutch crew brought 20 African men and women to the Virginia colony and sold them as indentured servants to landowners in Jamestown. The importance of this event is that from 1620 to 1661 African people were mostly indentured, not enslaved, in Virginia. They worked out their terms of indenture as did Europeans, acquired land, testified in courts, interacted with European indentured servants on equal terms, and contributed to the development of the colony (Bennett, 1982; Horton & Horton, 2001). A gradual shift from indenture to enslavement began in the 1640s, and in 1661 Virginia passed a law that targeted African people for enslavement. Current Virginia state standards identify (but do not explain) "the importance of the arrival of Africans and English women to the Jamestown settlement" (VDOE, 2012, Standard VS.3e). Without a standard about the ways in which African people distinguished themselves before 1661, to what is this "importance" likely to refer? The next standard that mentions African people is VS.4a ("The student will demonstrate knowledge of life in the Virginia colony by explaining the importance of agriculture and its influence on the institution of slavery"). Given this standard—and in the absence of any mention of indenture—Standard VS.3e (about the "importance of the arrival of Africans") refers by default to slavery, thereby eclipsing the four decades in which Africans were indentured servants and free men and women who contributed to the development of the Virginia colony. By excluding indenture, these two Virginia social studies standards direct teachers to post-1661, which positions African people as a semiotic signifier of slavery before slavery existed in that colony.

Existing records from the earliest 40-year period of Virginia history attest to the contributions of African people as indentured servants and free men and women. In 1648 Sir William Berkeley, the governor of Virginia, sent a letter to England in which he wrote about ordering the planting of rice. He stated that the planting of rice was affirmed by "African farmers" who pointed out the similarities of the soil and climate in Virginia to their own countries (Carney, 2001; Littlefield, 1981). Depending on their contracts, both European and African indentured servants in Virginia received some acres of land, food, clothing, and tobacco when their terms of indenture ended (Bennett, 1882). It is quite likely that the "farmers" Governor Berkeley wrote about were African men who had worked out their terms of indenture, were free, and owned their own farms—as did a number of Africans in the Virginia colony during this early period.

Like the six standards we have presented above, all 19 *Criterion Standards* reference liminal concepts and content not found in New York's or Virginia's fourth-grade social studies standards. While *Criterion Standards* could be used to revise these and other state social studies standards, the ubiquitous presence of grand narratives in state standards and National History Standards suggests that such revisions are not immanent. In the meantime, by using *Criterion Standards* with selected state standards, teachers can expand historical knowledge for themselves and their students. (See Appendix A for content and citations of readings that can increase knowledge of many topics in the *Criterion Standards*).

Teacher-Determined Standards

A "re-membered" standards model encourages teachers to define the standards of their discipline, rather than allow standards to be defined for them by the state. Taking this professional stance engages teachers in critically questioning standards and making decisions about how to connect state standards and culturally informed standards. When teachers (both PK-12 teachers and teacher educators) make these connections—when we "re-member" the worldviews and knowledge bases of liminal, marginal, and dominant groups in the form of standards—we open ourselves and our students to a more critical and comprehensive view of the past and therefore the present. This democratizing process presents us with the opportunity to loosen the hegemonic hold of grand narratives and master scripts on the telling of history. In fact, teachers are in a prime position to disrupt hegemony in the current state and corporate-driven educational system. If we act collectively and with agency, we are the Achilles heel of an entrenched and recalcitrant system that depends on teacher obedience and compliance to serve state and corporate interests (Buras, 2008; Gatto, 2003; Swartz, 2009). This state-corporate alliance makes and imposes decisions on teachers about what to teach, how to teach, and when and how to test, which positions PK-12 teachers near the bottom of the education hierarchy.

The same state-corporate alliance relies on teacher educators to validate and normalize state standards as a given and immutable component of teachers' lives. By accepting our assigned roles and doing the bidding of the state, we have become complicit with practices that are harmful to students. However, it is this proximal relationship and natural alliance among teachers, students, and families—as well as the influential relationship of teacher educators as potential elders and mentors of pre-service teachers—that creates vulnerability for a system designed to reproduce itself based on the compliance of its workers. If PK-12 teachers and teacher educators identify more with the families of their students and the communities their students will be serving than with the hierarchy above them, the system can be interrupted. When we become conscious of our collective power, both in-service teachers and teacher educators can select standards for achieving academic and cultural excellence.

Constructing a "Re-Membered" Model

Teachers construct "re-membered" standards by selecting standards that complement and supplement each other based on the lessons they design and on students' needs. Table 4.1 shows what this might look like. Three topics from Lesson 3 (African People in North America) in *Freedom and Democracy* (Swartz, 2013) are connected with selected social studies state standards and *Criterion Standards* (King & Goodwin, 2006). While we include possible *Common Core Standards* in reading, writing, speaking and listening, and language, we view these as place holders, since the selection of these standards is logically done when each lesson is written and in consideration of students' literacy needs at that time.

The first selected topic from Lesson 3 in *Freedom and Democracy* (Swartz, 2013; see Table 4.1, column 1) refers to African people bringing ideas about freedom and justice with them from their homelands to the Americas, including how they viewed freedom as a natural right of all people that they had never given up. At the fourth grade there are no social studies standards in New York or Virginia—or in any other states for that matter—that acknowledge the retention of these African traditions of freedom and value for justice. Thus, we supplement New York's Standard 4.6.e in column 3 about the transatlantic slave trade impacting life and culture in New York, and Virginia's Standard VS.3e in the same column about students identifying the importance of the arrival of Africans and English women in Jamestown with *Criterion Standards* 2 and 10 in column 2. These two standards remove the objectification of African people that was instituted by the system of slavery and maintained educationally in state standards and curricula that define and teach about that system. Describing the continuity of African heritage and the significance of retentions that continue the ideas and practices brought by African people into the Diaspora removes this objectification.

The second selected topic from Lesson 3 in *Freedom and Democracy* (Swartz, 2013; see Table 4.1, column 1) refers to the ongoing and varied forms of resistance to enslavement and the oral and written advocacy for freedom by enslaved and free African people. At the fourth grade, neither New York nor Virginia includes any standards that refer to resistance and advocacy for freedom. Thus, we supplement New York's 4.6.e ("The transatlantic slave trade impacted life and culture in New York.") with *Criterion Standard* 9 (column 2). One impact on life in New York was revolts against enslavement, such as the 1712 revolt of enslaved African men and women and the Conspiracy of 1741 in which free and enslaved African people and poor and indentured White people joined together in rebellion (Berlin & Harris, 2005; Katz, 1997). These revolts in New York City led to brutal reprisals by White authorities, including participants being burned at the stake, hung, gibbetted, and broken on the wheel; and the New York Assembly passed severely restrictive laws designed to control free and enslaved African people. While we do not recommend the gruesome details of these reprisals for fourth graders, they do need to know that African people risked their lives to resist domination and oppression.

We also supplement Virginia's Standard VS.7.c (in column 3) that refers to the "roles played by whites, enslaved African Americans, free African Americans, and American Indians" in "issues that divided our nation and led to the Civil War" with *Criterion Standard* 9 (column 2), which provides information about what are some of these "roles." With access to this standard, teachers are guided to identify and include content about free and enslaved Africans who resisted enslavement and advocated for human freedom. For example, within a

TABLE 4.1 "Re-Membered" Standards Model for Lesson 3 ("African People in North America") in *Freedom and Democracy, A Story Remembered*

(1) Selected Topics	(2) Criterion Standards
1. African people brought ideas about freedom and justice from their homelands to the Americas as exemplified by the governance practices of the Songhoy Nation. African people knew that freedom was the natural right of all people, and stated and wrote that they had never given up their right to be free.	2. African diasporan histories begin in Africa with human history, not with the period of enslavement. 10. African retentions form the basis of African American and other Diasporan cultures. African descent people's cultures, both continental and Diasporic, share ontological, epistemological, and axiological orientations—a worldview foundation that is ultimately based on the idea and experience of the oneness and interconnectedness of all in creation. Life, Nature, and Creator are thought of and experienced as allies to engage rather than control. There is a perceived relationship of complementarity rather than an assumed hostility among them.
2. Various forms of individual and collective resistance to enslavement were immediate and ongoing, including revolts, escape, and setting up Maroon communities. Other forms of resistance can be seen in speeches, petitions, and the writings of free and enslaved African people who advocated for freedom.	9. African people have resisted domination and oppression from the earliest period of enslavement. Resistance by African descent people to racism and oppression continues and has taken many social, political, economic and cultural forms, including self-determination, spiritual resilience, and agency in education, cultural expression, and community building (e.g., mutual aid societies, benevolent associations, social movements, fraternal lodges, Freedom schools, Kwanzaa, Rites of Passage).
3. European/White colonists enslaved African men, women and children. Along with exploiting African labor, colonists made great wealth by using the knowledge and skills African people brought with them from their homelands.	13. Europeans and their descendants in the Americas targeted, enslaved, and dehumanized African peoples in order to exploit and profit from African technical knowledge, skills, expertise, and cultural assets. People of African descent not only survived enslavement but *lived* life in the midst of it, creating and inventing new cultural forms, variations, and representations of Black life.

(3) *Social Studies State Standards (Grade 4)* *(see VDOE, 2012 & NYSED, 2012a)*	*(4)* *Common Core* *State Standards (Grade 4)* *(see NGA & CCSSO, 2010)*
New York State	**Reading for Informational Text**
(Content) 4.6.e The transatlantic slave trade impacted life and culture in New York.	1., 3., 4., 7.
(Social Studies Practices/Skills)	**Reading: Foundational skills** 4., 4.a. & c.
Comparison and Contextualization	**Writing**
Describe historical developments with specific circumstances including time and place.	2., 2.a., b., & e, 5.
Virginia State	**Speaking and Listening**
(Content and Skills)	1., 1.a., b., c., & d., 4.
VS.1 The student will demonstrate skills for historical and geographical analysis and responsible citizenship, including the ability to:	**Language** 3., 3.a., b., & c., 4., 4.a. & c.
b) determine cause-and-effect relationships;	
d) draw conclusions and make generalizations;	
VS. 3 The student will demonstrate knowledge of the first permanent settlement in America by	
e) identifying the importance of the arrival of Africans and English women to the Jamestown settlement	
VS.7 The student will demonstrate knowledge of the issues that divided our nation and led to the Civil War by	
c) describing the roles played by whites, enslaved African Americans, free African Americans, and American Indians.	

few years of the legalization of slavery in 1661, there were rebellions in Virginia that increased in frequency during the 1700s and 1800s, with the most noted being the rebellions of Gabriel Prosser (1800) and Nat Turner (1831) (Aptheker, 1957, 1974).

Speeches and written work by liberationists are also examples of "the roles played" by African and White people in Virginia and slavery's impact on "life and culture" in New York. For example, the 1861 published account by Osborne P. Anderson (1974/1861)—a free Black man and only surviving participant in John Brown's 1859 raid on Harper's Ferry in West Virginia—describes how free and enslaved Africans and White people resisted enslavement. (West Virginia was part of Virginia in 1859. It became a state in 1863.) Anderson wrote this text within a year after the military attack on Harper's Ferry in an effort to provide an accurate account of John Brown's effort to invade the South and engage enslaved people in taking their own freedom.

In New York City, numerous graduates of the early 19th-century African Free Schools later participated in abolition efforts and the securing of civil rights for free Africans (Andrews, 1830; Franklin, 1995; Mabee, 1979). For example, Henry Highland Garnett—who became an educator and minister in Troy, New York—steadily advocated for an end to the system of slavery. In 1843 he made a speech at the Negro Convention in Buffalo, New York, that called for enslaved people to revolt—to "rather die free men, than live to be slaves" (Franklin, 1992). He opposed the passive resistance and gradualist approaches of other abolitionists, such as William Lloyd Garrison and Frederick Douglass, advocating instead open rebellion by the enslaved (Bennett, 1968). *Criterion Standard* 9 guides teachers to identify examples such as these that demonstrate the agency and self-determination of African people's resistance to domination and oppression. Rather than being objects in the grand narrative of slavery, *Criterion Standards* (King & Goodwin, 2006) present African people as subjects who speak and act, in this case, in the interests of defining and achieving freedom.

The third selected topic from Lesson 3 in Freedom and Democracy (Swartz, 2013; see Table 4.1, column 1) names European/White colonists as those who enslaved African men, women, and children, and describes how they exploited African knowledge, skills, and labor. While New York standards refer to "enslaved Africans" and "the transatlantic slave trade," and Virginia standards refer to "the institution of slavery" and "enslaved African Americans," neither state names the group responsible for this "trade" and "institution." Virginia has a standard that refers to the "role played by whites" in "issues that divided our nation and led to the Civil War" (VS.7.c in column 3). We supplement this general standard with *Criterion Standard* 13 that identifies the role White people played in targeting, enslaving, exploiting, and dehumanizing African people. As stated earlier in this chapter, this standard also shows the agency and self-determination of African people who lived life and created new cultural forms during enslavement. Neither New York nor Virginia standards guide teachers to provide instruction about African agency and self-determination. In these state standards, African people are only the victims of unnamed perpetrators.

Toward Congruency

State standards have long been compatible with standard school knowledge, as both are cut from the same cloth. From one generation to the next, these euro-bound state standards—which are designed to direct what is taught and tested in U.S. schools—sustain grand narratives and the master scripts that teach them. As a result, state standards are located at the core of maintaining a hierarchy of whose knowledge is worth knowing, with "core" and "common core" foreseeably appearing in the names of numerous standards and curricular documents today. To counter this meme of "common core," whose moniker belies the hierarchy it fosters, the "re-membered" standards model we have proposed seeks a different kind of congruency—one in which teachers as professionals select standards that are compatible with the teaching of democratized knowledge and with the needs of their students.

As shown in this chapter, state standards by themselves are not accordant with the Afrocentric culturally informed praxis of historical recovery that produces democratized knowledge. In fact, using some of these state standards represents harmful practice due to the inaccuracies, distortions, and assumptions they foster about all groups of people. To circumvent this harmful practice, teachers need access to culturally informed standards when planning lessons. We have proposed using *Criterion Standards* (King & Goodwin, 2006), which are compatible with "re-membered" student materials, since both are framed with Afrocentric concepts that build upon the cultural platforms of African people and those with whom they interact. Rather than comply with standards designed to serve state and corporate interests, we invite teachers and teacher educators to democratize the very process of using standards by making conscious choices of standards that are compatible with democratized knowledge and with the communities they are serving.

References

Alaska Native Knowledge Network (ANKN). (1998). Alaska standards for culturally-responsive schools. Retrieved from http://ankn.uaf.edu/publications/culturalstandards.pdf

Alaska Native Knowledge Network (ANKN). (1999). Guidelines for preparing culturally responsive teachers for Alaska's schools. Retrieved from http://www.ankn.uaf.edu/publications/teachers.html

Anderson, O. P. (1974/1861). *A voice from Harper's Ferry, 1859: A narrative of events at Harper's Ferry, with incidents prior and subsequent to its capture by Captain Brown and his men.* New York, NY: World View Publishers.

Andrews, C. C. (1830). *The history of the New York African Free Schools, from their establishment in 1787, to the present time; embracing a period of more than forty years: Also a brief account of the successful labors of the New York Manumission Society.* New York, NY: Mahlon Day.

Aptheker, H. (1951/1969). *A documentary history of the Negro people in the United States: From colonial times through the Civil War* (Vol. I). New York, NY: The Citadel Press.

Aptheker, H. (1957). *Nat Turner's slave rebellion.* New York, NY: International Publishers.

Aptheker, H. (1974). *American Negro slave revolts.* New York, NY: International Publishers.

Asante, M. K. (2007). *An Afrocentric manifesto.* Malden, MA: Polity Press.

Au, W., Bigelow, B., Christensen, L., Gym, H., Levine, D., Karp, S., … Walters, S. (2013). The trouble with the Common Core. *Rethinking Schools, 27*(4), 4–6.

Bennett, L., Jr. (1982). *Before the Mayflower: A history of Black America.* Chicago, IL: Johnson Publishing Company.

Bennett, L., Jr. (1968). *Pioneers in protest.* Chicago, IL: Johnson Publishing Company.

Bennett, L., Jr. (1975). *The shaping of Black America.* Chicago, IL: Johnson Publishing Company.

Berlin, I., & Harris, L. (2005). *Slavery in New York.* New York, NY: New Press.

Boardman, W. (2013). United States of Zimmerman. Retrieved from http://readersup portednews.org/opinion2/304-justice/18427-united-states-of-zimmerman

Boykin, W. (1983). The academic performance of Afro-American children. In J. Spence (Ed.), *Achievement and achievement motives* (pp. 321–371). San Francisco, CA: W. Freeman.

Boykin, W. A. (1986). The triple quandary and the schooling of Afro-American children. In U. Neisser (Ed.), *The school achievement of minority children* (pp. 57–92). Hillsdale, NJ: Erlbaum.

Boykin, W. A. (1994). Afrocultural expression and its implications for schooling. In E. R. Hollins, J. E. King, & W. C. Hayman (Eds.), *Teaching diverse populations: Formulating a knowledge base* (pp. 243–273). Albany: State University of New York Press.

Buras, K. L. (2008). *Rightist multiculturalism: Core lessons on neoconservative school reform.* New York, NY: Routledge.

Carney, J. A. (2001). *Black rice: The African origins of rice cultivation in the Americas.* Cambridge, MA: Harvard University Press.

Deloria, V., Jr. (2004). Promises made, promises broken. In G. McMaster & C. E. Trafzer (Eds.), *Native universe: Voices of Indian America* (pp. 143–159). Washington, DC: National Museum of the American Indian, Smithsonian Institution/National Geographic Society.

Delpit, L. D. (1998). What should teachers do? Ebonics and culturally responsive instruction. In T. Perry & L. Delpit (Eds.), *The real Ebonics debate: Power, language, and the education of African American children* (pp. 17–26). Boston, MA: Beacon Press in collaboration with Rethinking Schools.

Dixon, V. J. (1971). African-oriented and Euro-American-oriented world views: Research methodologies and economics. *The Review of Black Political Economy, 7*(2), 119–156.

Dixon, V. J. (1976). World views and research methodology. In L. M. King, V. J. Dixon, & W. W. Nobles (Eds.), *African philosophy: Assumptions and paradigms for research on Black persons* (pp. 51–102). Los Angeles, CA: Fanon Research and Development Center.

Duncan, G. A. (1997). African American language in the classroom: Some political and pedagogical considerations. *Raising Standards: Journal of the Rochester Teachers Association,* 5(1), 10–18.

Education Northwest (2012). Common Core State Standards assessment resources. Retrieved at http://educationnorthwest.org/resource/1331

ETS (Educational Testing Service) (2010). Thoughts on an assessment of common core standards. Retrieved from http://www.pearsonassessments.com/NR/rdonlyres/6063DE04-2372-4EC4-9642-7B8A584F942F/0/ThoughtonaCommonCoreAssessmentSystem.pdf

Fox Keller, E. (1985). *Reflections on gender and science.* New Haven, CT: Yale University Press.

Franklin, V. P. (1992). *Black self-determination: A cultural history of African American resistance.* Chicago, IL: Lawrence Hill Books.

Franklin, V. P. (1995). *Living our stories, telling our truths.* New York, NY: Oxford University Press.

Gatto, J. T. (2003). *The underground history of American education: A schoolteacher's intimate investigation into the prison of modern schooling.* Oxford, NY: The Oxford Village Press.

Grande, S. (2004). *Red pedagogy: Native American social and political thought.* Lanham, MD: Rowman & Littlefield.

Gutierrez, K., & Larson, J. (1994). Language borders: Recitation as hegemonic discourse. *International Journal of Educational Reform,* 3(1), 22–36.

Hall, G. M. (2005). *Slavery and African ethnicities in the Americas: Restoring the links.* Chapel Hill: University of North Carolina Press.

Hart, R. (1985/2002). *Slaves who abolished slavery: Blacks in rebellion.* Kingston, Jamaica: University of the West Indies Press.

Herczog, M. M. (2010). Using the NCSS National curriculum standards for social studies: A framework for teaching, learning, and assessment to meet state social studies standards. *Social Education* 74(4), 217–222.

Holloway, J. E. (Ed.). (1990). *Africanisms in American culture.* Bloomington: Indiana University Press.

Horton, J. O., & Horton, L. E. (Eds.). (2001). *Hard road to freedom: The story of African America.* New Brunswick, NJ: Rutgers University Press.

Karenga, M. (2006). Philosophy in the African tradition of resistance: Issues of human freedom and human flourishing. In L. R. Gordon & J. A. Gordon (Eds.), *Not only the master's tools: African American studies in theory and practice* (pp. 243–271). Boulder, CO: Paradigm.

Katz, W. L. (1997). *Black legacy: A history of New York's African Americans.* New York, NY: Atheneum.

King, J. E. (2006). "If justice is our objective": Diaspora literacy, heritage knowledge and the praxis of critical studyin' for human freedom. *Yearbook of the National Society for the Study of Education,* 105(2), 337–360.

King, J. E., & Goodwin, S. (2006). *Criterion standards for contextualized teaching and learning about people of African descent.* Rochester, NY: Author.

Kynard, C. (2013). "I want to be African": Tracing Black radical traditions with "Students' rights to their own language." In C. Kynard (Ed.), *Vernacular insurrections: Race, Black protest, and the new century in composition-literacies studies* (pp. 73–105). Albany: State University of New York Press.

Lee, C. D. (1995). A culturally based cognitive apprenticeship: Teaching African American high school students skills in literary interpretation. *Reading Research Quarterly,* 30(4), 608–630.

Lee, C. D. (2000). Signifying in the zone of proximal development. In C. D. Lee & P. Smagorinsky (Eds.), *Vygotskian perspectives on literacy research* (pp. 191–125). New York, NY: Cambridge University Press.

Lee, C. D. (2007). *Culture, literacy, and learning: Taking bloom in the midst of the whirlwind.* New York, NY: Teachers College Press.

Lessow-Hurley, J. (2009). *The foundations of dual language instruction* (5th ed.). New York, NY: Pearson.

Littlefield, D. C. (1981). *Rice and slaves: Ethnicity and the slave trade in colonial South Carolina.* Baton Rouge: Louisiana State University Press.

Lomawaima K. T., & McCarty, T. L. (2006). *To remain an Indian: Lessons in democracy from a century of Native American education.* New York, NY: Teachers College Press.

Lyons, S. R. (2000). Rhetorical sovereignty: What do American Indians want from writing? *College, Composition and Communication, 51*(3), 447–468.

Mabee, C. (1979). *Black education in New York State: From colonial to modern times.* Syracuse, NY: Syracuse University Press.

Mills, C. W. (1997). *The racial contract.* Ithaca, NY: Cornell University Press.

Myers, L. J.(1988/1993). *Understanding an Afrocentric world view: Introduction to an optimal psychology.* Dubuque, IA: Kendal/Hunt Publishing.

Native Hawaiian Education Council (2002). Hawai'i guidelines for culturally healthy and responsive learning environments. Retrieved from http://www.olelo.hawaii.edu/pub/NHMO.pdf

NCHS (National Center for History in the Schools) at UCLA (1994). *National standards for history for grades K-4: Explaining children's world in time and space.* Los Angeles, CA: NCHS/UCLA.

NCSS (National Council for the Social Studies) (2010a). National curriculum standards for social studies: Introduction. Retrieved from http://www.socialstudies.org/standards/introduction

NCSS (National Council for the Social Studies) (2010b). *National curriculum standards for social studies: A framework for teaching, learning, and assessment.* Silver Spring, MD: Author.

NGA (National Governors Association) & CCSSO (Council of Chief State School Officers) (2010). *Common core state standards for English language arts & literacy in history/social studies, science, and technical subjects.* Washington, DC: Author.

NGA (National Governors Association) & CCSS (Council of Chief State School Officers) (2012). *Common core state standards initiative in mathematics.* Retrieved from http://www.corestandards.org/Math

Nieto, S. (1996). "I like making my mind work": Language minority students and the curriculum. In C. E. Walsh (Ed.), *Education reform and social change, multicultural voices, struggles, and visions* (pp. 147–163). Mahwah, NJ: Erlbaum.

Nieto, S. (2002). *Language, culture, and teaching: Critical perspectives for a new century.* Mahwah, NJ: Erlbaum.

Nobles, W. W. (1976). Extended self: Rethinking the so-called Negro self-concept. *The Journal of Black Psychology, 2*(2), 15–24.

Nobles, W. W. (1991). African philosophy: Foundations for Black psychology. In R. Jones (Ed.), *Black psychology* (3rd ed., pp. 47–63). Berkeley, CA: Cobb and Henry.

NYSED (New York State Education Department) (2012a). New York State common core K-8 social studies framework (Draft). Retrieved from http://engageny.org/sites/default/files/resource/attachments/ss-framework-k-8.pdf

NYSED (New York State Education Department) (2012b). Draft NYS common core K-8 social studies framework is now posted. Retrieved from http://engageny.org/content/nys-common-core-k-8-social-studies-framework-is-now-posted

Pandian, J. (1985). *Anthropology and the western tradition: Toward an authentic anthropology.* Prospect Heights, IL: Waveland Press.

Perry, T., & Delpit, L. (Eds.). (1998). *The real Ebonics debate: Power, language, and the education of African American children.* Boston, MA: Beacon Press in collaboration with Rethinking Schools.

RTC (Rochester Teacher Center). (2007). *Cultural learning standards: What students are expected to know, be able to do, and be like.* Rochester, NY: Author.

Secret, C. (1998). Embracing Ebonics and teaching standard English: An interview with Oakland teacher Carrie Secret. In T. Perry & L. Delpit (Eds.), *The real Ebonics debate: Power, language, and the education of African American children* (pp. 79–88). Boston, MA: Beacon Press, in collaboration with Rethinking Schools.

Shujaa, M. J. (Ed.). (1994). *Too much schooling, too little education: A paradox of Black life in white societies.* Trenton, NJ: Africa World Press.

Sizemore, B. (2008). *Walking in circles: The Black struggle to school reform.* Chicago, IL: Third World Press.

Smith, D. H., & Anderson, S. (2012). Principle criticisms of the common core state standards: On the road to educational genocide. Retrieved from http://blackeducationnow.org/id17.html

Smitherman, G. (1977/1986). *Talkin and testifyin: The language of Black America.* Detroit, MI: Wayne State University Press.

Smitherman, G. (1994). *Black talk.* Boston, MA: Houghton Mifflin.

Smitherman, G. (2000). *Talkin that talk: Language, culture, and education in African America.* New York, NY: Routledge.

Soto, L. D. (1993). Native language school success. *Bilingual Research Journal, 17*(1 & 2), 83–97.

Swartz, E. E. (2009). Diversity: Gatekeeping knowledge and maintaining inequalities. *Review of Educational Research, 79*(2), 1044–1083.

Swartz, E. E. (2012). Distinguishing themes of cultural responsiveness: A study of document-based learning. *The Journal of Social Studies Research, 36*(2), 179–211.

Swartz, E. E (2013). *Freedom and democracy: A Story Remembered.* Rochester, NY: Omnicentric Press.

VDOE (Virginia Department of Education) (2012). Standards of learning (SOL) and testing: History and social science. Retrieved from http://www.doe.virginia.gov/testing/sol/standards_docs/history_socialscience/index.shtml

Walker, S. S. (Ed.) (2001). *African roots/American cultures: Africa in the creation of the Americas.* Lanham, MD: Rowman & Littlefield.

Wynter, S. (1992). *Do not call us "Negroes": How multicultural textbooks perpetuate racism.* San Francisco, CA: Aspire Books.

Wynter, S. (2005). Race and our biocentric belief system: An interview with Sylvia Wynter. In J. King (Ed.), *Black education: A transformative research and action agenda for the new century* (pp. 361–366). Mahwah, NJ: Erlbaum for the American Educational Research Association.

SECTION II

Studying the Use of "Re-Membered" Texts

The four chapters in Section II present practitioner case studies that show how pre-service and in-service teachers and teacher educators use several "re-membered" texts to write lessons and to interact with students and families. While it is important to know that it is possible to produce democratized knowledge for students, and to learn about a process that can produce such knowledge, it is equally important to know what happens when these materials are used. As the third component of the Afrocentric culturally informed praxis of historical recovery, reflexive practitioner inquiry also aims to democratize knowledge in the social studies. Seeking knowledge from practitioners, students, and families—viewed as subjects not objects of research—democratizes the research process by altering the power differentials in who controls ideas about teaching and learning. It assumes that all participants have knowledge worth knowing. Findings of the four case studies in this volume indicate that using "re-membered" texts can bring about changes in classroom practices as well as in the educational system. Thus, recovering history is a chain of curricular and pedagogical events that incorporates "re-membered" texts as well as the voices of all case study participants whose ideas further expand the process of knowing about teaching and learning.

5

AUSTIN STEWARD

"Home-Style" Teaching, Planning, and Assessment

Linda Campbell

Below is a portion of a conversation between Joyce E. King (JEK) and Linda Campbell (LC) in the early stages of Ms. Campbell's research. As she describes what is happening to her, we can observe her shift from a teacher with "great management skills" valued by administrators to a teacher who has come to see that effective teaching depends upon building relationships with students and parents.

JEK: Your teacher research project focuses on how students respond when parents have an expanded role in culturally responsive curriculum and assessment. What are your thoughts about involving parents?

LC: As we learn about Austin Steward, I'm including parents in coming up with what they want their children to get out of this Austin Steward project. I want their ideas, so I am asking them to help me come up with some ways to assess students. I have pretty much figured out how to center students so that they feel that school is not a foreign place. I want them to feel that the school is a part of their community. I want parents to feel the same way.

JEK: Yes, typically, in order for you to be successful in school, you have to leave everything about yourself outside of school.

LC: Right, you are leaving home to go to somewhere foreign that is not even about you, and you go and learn things about everybody but you. I was raised up in a system where you teach a certain way and I am still being torn, fighting with myself about what to give up, what to keep, or should I keep anything? For example, I've thrown out rules. As you know, Kwanzaa is a cultural celebration that combines traditional African practices and beliefs with African American principles and ideals. We use the Seven Principles of Kwanzaa to guide our interactions with each other.

JEK: Now, say a little more about that.

LC: I don't punish my children through point systems based on following or breaking rules. I rarely send my children to the office. Instead, I endure the challenges that I face with my students as I teach them Kwanzaa Principles, such as Unity and Collective Work and Responsibility. Whatever they do, I tell them that I love them. I constantly tell them that, and it works. They come to see that I am genuine.

Students don't automatically trust teachers. For example, I had a little boy who never stayed in my classroom in the beginning of the year, Shyquan, beautiful little boy, very talented, witty. He is supposed to be in the fifth grade so he has some reasons to act out. I spent a lunch period with him one day and I told him, "You know, you are acting ugly toward me, but, I don't see that ugliness. All I see is Shyquan." I told him how wonderful he was and how much I loved him. "Whether you like me or not, I am going to love you." He looked at me as if to say, "What is she talking about?" But, he is coming around. He will sit at a table with me, he hasn't made it to a desk with his classmates, but he sits at a table with me and he stays in the classroom. He used to spend every other day in ISS [In School Suspension], and that is not happening anymore. We are building a relationship—as I try to do with all my students—and when they leave me, I am hoping that what I have done will give them the strength to hang in there.

Unfortunately, we have been teaching and treating our children as if they are objects, and not realizing they are extensions of our family. I was alienating my children and their parents from me because I had the rules in place; I had the good management.

JEK: And if it wasn't working, it was their fault.

LC: Right, exactly, and I was admired for that because I had such good management. Administrators would say, "She's got great management skills, talk to her." But then I realized I had no relationship with my students and none with their parents. I could get them in there, teach them what they told me to teach, and get them out of the door. Once I realized that these are my people—that I want to make a difference in my children's lives and in my families' lives—things began to change. I want to do whatever I can to not let my children be robbed of their history. We have a beautiful history, we are beautiful people, and we have been denied knowledge of that. By building a relationship with my students, I can teach them about this.

JEK: Yes, and through teacher research you will have an opportunity to understand more about what you are doing and why it produces the results you are getting. One of the larger purposes of teacher research is to be able to open up your process for someone else who may not be quite where you are, but coming along that path. So, we are learning with you and we're documenting this, almost as something to leave along the pathway for others who may be coming.

Introduction

As a result of my participation in the Rochester Teacher Center (RTC) annual Summer Institute on Teaching and Learning Informed by Cultural Knowledge, I have begun to question the system of teaching in which I was raised. As a result I have decided that a change is needed, one that considers the children and the parents who are represented in the school. For me that change begins with me, thus, the catapult for agreeing to participate in a teacher action research project. I also agreed because it is an organized approach to examining my teaching and my own learning, which has provided me with an opportunity to learn about my students, their parents, my teaching, and myself.

This research process has provided me with a way of making connections—between heritage knowledge [the repository of cultural memory, knowledge, experiences, and retentions that reflect African knowledge, skills, and worldview] and the core subject areas, between parents and the instructional program, and between several sets of standards (King, 2004). For example, connections were made between New York State (NYS) standards, the RTC *Cultural Learning Standards* (RTC, 2007), and *Criterion Standards for Contextualized Teaching and Learning about People of African Descent* (King & Goodwin, 2006). In terms of my prior practice over the last 5 years, I have been using the Kwanzaa Principles, historical knowledge, the idea of building classroom community, and the concept of cultural well-being in the past and present. I primarily use text that is representative of the Black students who are the majority population I am currently teaching.

When I began this teacher action research project, I only had a vague recollection of Austin Steward from an article I once read in a local newspaper many years ago, and I wondered why I hadn't been taught anything about him. Having been born, raised, and schooled in Rochester, New York, I found it quite unsettling that this man had not received even a notable mention—a man who left such a legacy of human dignity and progress to Rochester, to the USA, and to Canada. As I began to reflect on this, I realized that I had to educate myself about his life and the era in which he lived, the early to mid-1800s. I read the chapter titled "Austin Steward: Self Determination and Human Freedom" in *Document-Based Learning, Curriculum and Assessment* (Goodwin & Swartz, 2009). I also read Austin Steward's autobiography titled *Twenty-two Years a Slave and Forty Years a Freeman* (1857/2004), and I was very fortunate to be able to view a video titled *The Quiet Builder* (Ayorinde & Swartz, 1986) that was put together several years ago by a group of Rochester citizens who were trying to bring information about Austin Steward to light. Once I had enough background knowledge I was ready to begin.

A main component of this action research was to engage parents in the process of teaching about Austin Steward. How to engage parents took quite a bit of reflection. I finally looked at what it would take for me to be involved with my own child in a project about a person I had very little knowledge of, and a topic that I might find difficult and time consuming. As I was very busy as a parent, I knew that I should not ask for a long-term commitment from other parents. I also knew that I would like the project to be fun and satisfying. I would need to be invested to get me to follow through with my commitment. I realized that my child would have to be playing an important role in this project in order for me to encourage her to be engaged and committed. It would have to feel like a good investment for me to participate.

After this reflection, I developed a way for parents to help their child create a book that would be published about Austin Steward, a book they could keep. A parent/child reflection could be included in each book, along with a parent/child picture, something they could cherish over time. The book would include details learned about Steward's life, his business accomplishments, his efforts for human freedom, the character traits he had that led to his success, and how he met economic and social justice challenges of his day.

The project proceeded from the following research question: How do students respond when parents have an expanded role in culturally responsive curriculum and assessment? This question related to my interest in (a) engaging parents in curriculum and assessment, (b) learning more about what an expanded parent role might look like, and (c) grounding this research in my ongoing search to provide culturally responsive instructional content and pedagogy for my students.

Methods

The third-grade class in which this research was completed was located in an urban school district. There were 21 students in this regular education class, 11 girls and 10 boys. There were 15 Black children and 6 White children in the class. Eight of the 21 children were diagnosed with some form of attention deficit disorder. Six of these eight students were boys. All of the children received free breakfast, and 19 received free lunch. There was a wide reading range from first grade to eighth grade.

Several methods were used to explore this study's research question: (a) reviewing historical content and related curriculum; (b) collaboration; (c) classroom observations; (d) self-reflection; and (e) assessment of student work. In terms of the first method, text and curriculum about Austin Steward were reviewed. It was necessary for me to become very familiar with the seven documents in the chapter entitled "Austin Steward: Self-Determination and Human Freedom." This "re-membered" text reconnected knowledge about Austin Steward with events and people in the era in which he lived. I also read the autobiography of Austin Steward, *Twenty-two Years a Slave and Forty Years a Freeman* (1857/2004) and viewed the video *The Quiet Builder* (Ayorinole & Swartz, 1986) for their historical content.

Collaboration, the second method, occurred in a number of ways with parents. A parent letter was written to enlist participation in the form of a commitment to help children create a book that would be published about Austin Steward. Phone calls were a regular part of the process to encourage, remind, and to inform; and parents were invited to an orientation on the project. Collaboration was also used to jointly create a rubric to assess student work. Parents and teacher both assessed students' work utilizing this rubric.

Classroom observations, the third method, were made during instruction and conferences with students. Observations were made of levels of participation, follow-through on homework, level of students' knowledge beyond what was required, and levels of enthusiasm and excitement. All observations were regularly recorded in a journal.

Keeping a journal of self-reflections and personal thoughts throughout the project was the fourth method. Questions about my knowledge of history and my teaching practices surfaced early on in this study. These questions led to deeper questions about the system of education, and how it affected me as a person and as a teacher. Ideas for lessons were included as well as thoughts about how to engage parents in the instructional process. Observations and outcomes were also recorded in the journal.

The assessment of student work was the study's fifth method. Copies of student work were collected related to the Austin Steward Project. This included in-class assignments, homework, artwork, glossaries of vocabulary, and the final book project. The quality and quantity of student work as well as the level of participation and understanding that students showed when parents were or were not involved was compared.

Findings

This study's findings are described in sub-sections below. These sub-sections correspond to the study's five research methods.

Reviewing Historical Content and Related Curriculum

Reading the reconnected or "re-membered" knowledge about Austin Steward in *Document-Based Learning, Curriculum and Assessment* (Goodwin & Swartz, 2009) encouraged me to become more familiar with the historical background and the era of Austin Steward before beginning to plan. Reading Austin Stewards' autobiography provided the knowledge that I needed to feel comfortable in teaching about Steward, and at the same time, insure that the children would have a clear understanding of the era in which he lived. Once I reviewed the material, I felt better equipped to teach my students about Austin Steward and help them to have an authentic feel for his era and the influence it had on his life.

The autobiography was the bridge that was needed in order for me to have an understanding of what the system of slavery was like in a period about which I had a different perception. My understanding of the system of slavery was no longer left to the collection of bits and pieces that I had been given in an educational and social system that literally stole that knowledge from me. This system did not even give me the information or desire to search out information about my own background as a Black woman living in the United States. Steward's personal account of what he, his family, and other enslaved people endured became very emotional for me as I lived through the pages. This was an actual account of what slavery was like. My lenses have become much clearer as a result, and an awakening has occurred. I gained a better understanding of the pain, the forced degradation, the depravation, and injustice experienced by people who were enslaved. I admired and found hope in Steward's determination, his confidence, his compassion, and his intelligence, from which I drew examples of character traits that I discussed with my students. It was now personal, and I could share a renewed desire to learn more about my history as a Black person who is part of a family that was once enslaved and lived during the same era as Austin Steward.

Review of historical content brought clarity and reality to the lessons. It gave me a voice from the past, one that helped me to share with my students the magnitude of what Austin Steward had endured. In turn this knowledge helped them to understand that despite all that was against him and all that he had endured, he remained determined to get out of the system of slavery and to fight against it. And he did. I was now better equipped to share the pride I felt in Steward's character. I learned that Austin Steward is a model of empowerment. If he could accomplish all that he did with all that was against him, it is because of him that we can accomplish even more. Reviewing historical content and related curriculum became the foundation and motivation for being able to move forward.

Collaboration

The Table 5.1 Collaboration Chart provides specific data about collaboration with parents and some of its outcomes. The collaboration occurred in a number of ways. I sent a letter asking parents to participate in the Austin Steward project. There were phone calls that I initiated and phone calls that came from parents. I called parents to further inform them about the project. Only 2 of my 21 parents could not be reached this way, as they did not have telephones. I designed an orientation for the project to be held at school to inform parents about the project; and I wrote and sent a letter to parents encouraging them to attend. Seventeen parents (81%) responded to this letter, with 13 of these parents (76%) saying they would attend. This session was planned at a time selected by parents. It is unclear why only 3 (23%) of the 13 parents who agreed to attend actually attended. One reason might be that the project began late in the school year when activities were winding down and participation was less likely.

During the orientation, the agenda began with a question. The three parents were asked to write a note to me as to why they agreed to participate in the project. Those who wanted to share with the group did so. They all agreed that

TABLE 5.1 Collaboration Chart

Parents	1	2	3	4	5	6	7
	Calls	Returned Letters	Orientation	Other School Activities	Homework and Classwork	Provided Additional Information or Help	Final Project
1	√			√	√		√
2	√	√		√	√		
3	√				√		
4		√		√	√	√	√
5	√	√ n		√			
6	√	√		√	√		
7	√	√		√	√		
8	√	√	√	√	√	√	√
9	√	√	√	√	√	√	√
10	√	√			√		
11	√	√		√	√		
12	√						
13	√	√ n					
14	√	√		√	√	√	√
15	√	√					
16	√	√	√	√	√	√	√
17							
18	√	√ n					
19	√	√ n		√	√		
20	√	√		√	√		√
21	√	√					

Parents are listed and coded by numbers in the left column.

1. Phone conversations with parents during the project
2. Returned letters initiating participation and response to orientation (√ n refers to parents who agreed to assist with homework but not in other ways).
3. Attended orientation
4. Involved in other school activities (science fair, multicultural celebration, and flower planting)
5. Helped with homework and completion of class work
6. Provided additional information or help during the project
7. Assisted with final project

they wanted to not only help their child, but to help the class and the school. It was then shared how their expectations aligned with the *RTC Cultural Learning Standards* (RTC, 2007). For example, one standard states, "Students know and expect that families and community play a significant role in the educational process." I explained that we could meet this standard by working together on projects, which could become an expected occurrence in their child's education. As a result of their involvement, their children would know and expect their participation in helping to complete assignments and final projects. As seen in Table 5.1, 13 of my 21 parents (62%) became involved in other school activities such as a school-wide science fair, multicultural celebration, and flower planting at a local park *after* participating in the Austin Steward Project. Prior to the project there were no parents coming in to help out in the classroom or with school activities. Five participants (24%) provided unsolicited information and help. For example, two parents brought in literature and pictures related to Austin Steward and one father provided pizza and refreshments as a reward for children's hard work on the project. Fourteen (67%) of 21 parents regularly assisted their children with homework assignments throughout the study. Parents, grandparents, and a sibling who participated in the process supported the seven students (33%) who completed their final Austin Steward Project.

Another set of standards entitled *Criterion Standards for Contextualized Teaching and Learning about People of African Descent* (King & Goodwin, 2006) was also shared with the parents in the context of providing content about Austin Steward. *Criterion Standard 9* strongly supported this content about Steward's economic accomplishments and actions for justice:

> African people have resisted domination and oppression from the earliest period of enslavement. Resistance by African descent people to racism and oppression continues and has taken many social, political, economic and cultural forms, including self-determination, spiritual resilience, and agency in education, cultural expression, and community building (e.g., mutual aid societies, benevolent associations, social movements, fraternal lodges, Freedom Schools, Kwanzaa, Rites of Passage).
>
> *(King & Goodwin, 2006, p. 2)*

Information was also shared about lesson planning, and sample lessons were provided. I explained that each lesson would follow the same routine: reading of a document about Austin Steward, vocabulary identification and definition, and the development of an ongoing glossary. The vocabulary would be defined and reviewed with parents as part of their child's homework. A copy of a blank time line that would be completed while reading the documents and a list of character qualities that might be suited for use in their final projects was provided. Blank sample pages that could be used for their books were also provided.

Parents then viewed the video *The Quiet Builder* (Ayorinole & Swartz, 1986). Afterwards, we brainstormed what could be included in a rubric for assessing students' work. One of the parents suggested that the category for information on Steward's life up to his freedom, attaining his freedom, and information about his businesses be put into three categories instead of one. The other parents agreed. There were categories related to Steward's character and his work to end slavery; and categories related to neatness of writing and the required elements of the project. Parents also agreed to include a category for working cooperatively with parents. Although the rubric ended up with nine categories, the parents all agreed that it made assessing their child's work much easier.

Classroom Observations

During the 6 weeks of this project, I observed the 14 children whose parents were involved with helping them to complete their homework assignments and the 7 students whose parents were not involved. Children whose parents were involved were knowledgeable beyond my expectations. Not only had they completed the assignments, which was expected, they took care in what they produced. They were also able to effectively communicate information they had learned. Two students came with additional information that they discovered with their parents about Austin Steward. It was hard to contain the excitement. Students did not want to wait until the afternoon's lesson time to share their documents. Throughout the morning they often asked, "Is it time yet?" One child brought in a picture of Austin Steward's portrait and another brought a picture of a landmark of one of his former businesses. Three students whose parents were involved completed homework assignments on a regular basis, which was a new behavior for these children. Prior to this they were sporadic in their return of homework. One child came to a day's lesson with information on how Austin Steward was able to support himself while waiting for his freedom. This was information that was not required, but would be used in a future lesson. Two other children brought in documents that showed a hotel that is now built at the sight of one of Steward's businesses, and maps that showed areas where he once lived in Rochester, New York, and surrounding areas. I also observed that there was an increase in the number of hands raised to answer the review questions, as well as an increased readiness to use time-lines and glossaries to assist with answering questions. Prior to the increased parent involvement, I would usually have to answer the questions myself.

During this same period, I also observed the seven children who had no parent support during the project. They were usually unprepared for the lessons. Their assignments would be incomplete or not brought in at all. Those who had tried to complete the assignments on their own were less aware of the day's topic and lacked the readiness to participate in the day's discussion and review of the homework. They did not readily raise their hands to participate nor were they able to participate when called on or encouraged. They appeared to be less excited and ready to go with the lesson as compared to those whose parents were involved. Two of the boys and one of the girls were a challenge throughout the year as far as their behavior. Because they were unprepared, they became disruptive.

There was one exception that I feel is worth noting. One little boy, who typically did not complete his assignments or participate in discussions became interested in the Austin Steward Project. He began to make attempts at completing the homework assignments. He would make frequent comments that he wanted to complete his final project but that he was unable to get support at home. His mom told him that he had to do the homework himself. He did just that. He was not as prepared as the supported children but he would try. His motivation was his interest in Austin Steward and his desire to complete the book. He would make comments that he liked Austin Steward. He liked the way that he looked. He also liked the fact that Austin Steward ran a store and that he too wants to own a store. Near the conclusion of the project, he enlisted the help of an older brother. He did persevere and complete the project, attributing his motivation in completing the book to his relationship to Austin Steward as a Black man and a storeowner. He was also excited to be able to work with his brother, and he knew that this was one assignment that he could be successful at. He confirmed this for me in the many conversations that we had throughout the project. While his project was not as sophisticated as the other students and his illustrations were not always recognizable or compatible to his text, in my book, he did meet the important standards of commitment, engagement, and making a connection to his cultural heritage.

Self-Reflection

When asked to participate in this research project, I immediately became excited. I would now have an opportunity to participate in a project that could be shared with other educators, a project that might show how a change in teaching was made, and the results of that change. I also realized that I would have the support and company of others who believed in using authentic assessment to make connections between heritage knowledge and the core subject areas, connections between parents and the instructional program, and connections between the instructional program and the *RTC Cultural Learning Standards* (RTC, 2007) and the *Criterion Standards for Contextualized Teaching and Learning about People of African Descent* (King & Goodwin, 2006). It is also important to note that I was simultaneously involved in the RTC Summer Institute and an RTC Collegial Learning Circle. As a result, I became more aware of my own heritage and learned more about myself. I now wanted to teach in a way that made sense to the population of children I was teaching. It became very clear to me that the system that I had become thoroughly assimilated and raised in was no longer comfortable. It was not only a misfit for my students, but for me as well. A supported effort to change that was now at hand. I would no longer buy into this miseducation.

During this time I became aware of my own disconnect. I had to face the reality that as a Black woman I had no idea what slavery was really like, let alone what life was like for African people before slavery. Nor had I any sincere interest or realization of the necessity of knowing about it prior to my involvement with the RTC Summer Institute. I knew that in order for me to proceed

I would need to "Go Back and Fetch." I would need to find out what I did not know and not be embarrassed by it. It was not my fault. Once I understood and accepted the fact of my own reality, I was able to easily proceed. At this point I took the curriculum and the standards and began to write my lessons. Learning right along with the parents and the children would now come naturally. Education would take place for me as well.

I reflected on many personal thoughts before, during, and after the project. Most of these thoughts were recorded in a journal. This journal writing kept me and the project on track. I would reflect on what was happening in the class-room: Was I doing what I had intended to do and how were students respond-ing? Were parents involved in each aspect of the project? As I had been used to leaving parents out of the instructional process, the journal really helped me to stay in contact with them. I realized that school would need to be an extension of home. As I reflected on what was happening, it became clear when I needed to reach out—to send another letter or make some phone calls to reconnect.

During the project I noticed many things, which I wrote about in my jour-nal. I was excited, the students were excited, and the parents were excited. We were learning about an individual who against all odds persevered through self-determination. I wrote in my journal: "Austin Steward is a role model reaching forward in history, giving the gift of empowerment. If he could accomplish all that he did with all that was against him, I can accomplish even more with all that is against me." This kind of character had to be shared with my students. It was important for them to see this relatable role model, one that is not provided through the local curriculum or state standards.

I also noticed that this extension of the "home-style" teaching, planning, and assessment that included family members was helpful for me, informa-tive and desired by the parents, and acceptable and rewarding to my students. I found this type of collaboration with parents made the process of teaching easier. The children were more accepting of the assignments than usual and looked forward to their work and the support of parents and family members. Students' behavior indicated that they were so pleased to have their parents involved with them in this project, and the quality of the final projects was by far better than the quality of work I had received from students before. Overall the students were much more prepared, motivated, and willing to par-ticipate without the usual coercion that occurred with no parent involvement or no culturally responsive content and pedagogy. I also noticed that there was increased cooperation among the students. They encouraged one another in their efforts to complete their projects. It was fun to work together. I enjoyed it as much as they did. It was very natural.

After the projects were completed, I remember evaluating the work to make sure that many of the disciplines were included in the project. We included so many: reading, writing, mathematics, art, music, science, history, business, and technology to name some but not all. I also realized that I could easily do this again. I found that it was not difficult to include parents. The parents that I worked with wanted to know why this type of involvement was not the norm. It was so much fun for them and their children. They enjoyed learning along with the children and their teacher. They were excited to share the many talents that they possess with their child's class. I was glad to enlist the much-needed help of the parents. What a great motivator for the class.

Student Work

This section focuses on findings related to students' final projects. Other findings related to students' class work and homework (e.g., quality, participation, interest) are discussed in the Classroom Observations section above. The final project involved students in making a book about Austin Steward with parent or family support. Students knew about the book project from the beginning as did their families, and as the project neared completion, I informed parents by letter and through personal contacts about its elements and due date. Out of 21 students, seven (33%) completed a final project. This 33% far surpassed the percentage of students completing final projects in the past. In fact, the rate of project completion over the past several years was so low that I had stopped doing project-based work prior to the Austin Steward Project. All seven students who completed a final project had a parent, grandparent, or sibling providing them support.

Using the rubric co-developed with parents, my scores of the seven final projects ranged from 1.7 to 3.8 on a 4-point scale, with a mean score of 2.8. Four of the seven parents completed the rubric with scores ranging from 2.7 to 4.0, with a mean score of 3.4. My scores for these four students ranged from 2.4 to 3.8 with a mean score of 3.3. Together, the four parents who completed the rubric had only slightly higher assessments than mine in all but one case. The actual difference between parents' mean score and my mean score was only .1 point, with the differences between their scores and mine ranging from .2 points to .6 points.

While rubric scores tell a part of the story, students' actual work tells us much more. Looking at the work students produced, I can see the outcomes of many of the goals discussed with parents about their involvement. With family support, all seven students were able to produce a book about Austin Steward that chronologically followed major events in his life. Many recognized Steward's character qualities (e.g., bravery, determination, diligence, compassion, boldness, justice, patience, generosity) and the character qualities of others with whom he interacted. Some identified the location of the hotel in downtown Rochester that was built on land once owned by Steward. Most students wrote and drew pictures of abolitionists, orators, anti-slavery conventions, and emancipation celebrations, and identified Steward and his contemporaries who were involved in these activities. Some students used the images provided in the instructional materials, but many students drew pictures, added images they found, and drew maps that could go along with the text they wrote. Some students used current but related images, indicating connections they were making between a historical figure from almost 200 years ago and today. Students completed a glossary of terms and students and parents wrote reflections about the experience of working together on the book project.

Conclusion

For me, this teacher action research process was memorable. It became a demonstration of the Sankofan concept of "Go Back and Fetch"—an Akan proverb that reminds us to return to the source and retrieve knowledge that has been forgotten. Not only did I go back to find out about the history of my people, I went back to rethink my teaching and my relationship with parents. To be supported in a process of study that focused on change allowed me to reconsider significant aspects of my 25 years of teaching—in particular the role of parents and families in the educational process. I realized that changing the isolated and less successful way in which I was teaching was possible, and that two of the major keys to changing my teaching are to include parents and to use culturally responsive content and instruction. I shouldn't be teaching my students alone or using instructional materials that omit and distort content and are not relevant to my students. Unfortunately, this is exactly the result of the current system in which I work.

As I think about my research question (How do students respond when parents have an expanded role in culturally responsive curriculum and assessment?), the connections between parent engagement in curriculum and assessment, culturally responsive content, and cultural and state standards have become quite clear. As findings demonstrate, students were more engaged, completed assignments more thoroughly, were more cooperative with each other, and demonstrated more knowledge than usual—including content that was not requested, but was the result of their additional research with a family member. There is no doubt in my mind that framing the Austin Steward Project with three sets of standards was helpful to me as well as to parents. Austin Steward fits well as an example of a figure in American history who fostered major ideas and exemplified themes, developments, and turning points in the history of the United States and New York (NYS Social Studies Standard 1). Discussing the *RTC Cultural Learning Standard* ("Students know and expect that families and community play a significant role in the educational process") with parents (RTC, 2007, p. 2), gave us a way to see the naturalness of parents and family being a part of the instructional process. Once learning about this cultural standard, both parents and I wondered why this wasn't the norm, since it builds in accountability for students, parents, and teacher. Using the above quoted *Criterion Standard 9* set the Austin Steward Project in a historical context, making it clear that his story was one of many stories that demonstrate self-determination and resistance to injustice. Providing such culturally responsive content helped students to make connections with what they were learning—to see themselves in the history they were studying.

Most importantly, what I have called a "home-style" of teaching, planning, and assessment that includes parents and families, has changed my ideas and practices about their role in teaching and learning. Rather than just giving parents what I want them to have, I have learned that involving parents and family members in developing assessments makes the educational process more accessible to them. They better understand what is expected of their children and can assist them with their work, which have a positive influence on what students produce, as indicated by this study. And when I involve parents in instruction, I know they are there, and that I can rely on them to assist me because they have been informed and included in what is going on. We became partners. I no longer see parents and families as "out there," disconnected from me and what we do in the classroom. As a result of this project, I now have more communication with parents. I make ways for us to be in contact with each other, either in person or through phone conferencing. I know I need family support, and, as a result, I have become more approachable. It is a "we" thing now, not an "I" thing. In a sense, we—students, parents, and teacher—have been "re-membered" or put back together just like the Austin Steward text we used. It seems so logical, but it took me a long time to see the naturalness of this relationship. At first it means more work in planning and making connections, but later it is not only easier and less stressful, the quality of student work and student retention is much improved. As I stated earlier, I have begun to question the system of teaching in which I have been raised, and I know that change begins with me. This teacher research process has provided a context for this change—a context that has given me a way to know that change is possible and in the best interests of students, parents, families, and teachers.

References

Ayorinde, O., & Swartz, E. E. (1986). *Austin Steward, the quiet builder* [video]. Rochester, NY: Omobowale Productions.

Goodwin, S., & Swartz, E. E. (2009). *Document-based learning: Curriculum and assessment.* Rochester, NY: RTA Press.

King, J. E. (2004). Culture-centered knowledge: Black studies, curriculum transformation, and social action. In J. A. Banks & C. A. McGee Banks (Eds.), *Handbook of research on multicultural education* (2nd ed., pp. 349–378). San Francisco, CA: Jossey-Bass.

King, J. E., & Goodwin, S. (2006). *Criterion standards for contextualized teaching and learning about people of African descent.* Rochester, NY: Author.

RTC (Rochester Teacher Center). (2007). *Cultural learning standards: What students are expected to know, be able to do, and be like.* Rochester, NY: Author.

Steward, A. (2004). *Twenty-two years a slave, and forty years a freeman.* Mineola, NY: Dover Publications. (Original work published 1857)

6

USING "RE-MEMBERED" STUDENT TEXT AS A PEDAGOGICAL FRAME FOR URBAN PRE-SERVICE MATHEMATICS TEACHERS

Shonda Lemons-Smith

Below is a portion of an e-mail conversation between Ellen E. Swartz (EES) and Shonda Lemons-Smith (SLS) that took place after Dr. Lemons-Smith completed her chapter.

EES: You have said that your math methods course is a departure from traditional math methods courses. What prompted you to make these changes?

SLS: I approach the course from an equity-oriented stance. That's simply who I am and to teach in any other way would lack authenticity. In a math methods course it is not enough for pre-service teachers to espouse a belief in notions of equity and culturally responsive pedagogy. Those words must be coupled with purposeful instructional planning and implementation.

EES: What would be an example of this "purposeful instructional planning and implementation"?

SLS: Pre-service teachers are asked to create lessons that use aspects of students' backgrounds, families, communities, lived, or out-of-school experiences to anchor learning of a select mathematical concept (e.g., calculating hours spent at different activities in each student's daily schedule, predicting and calculating the time it will take to get from one location to the next using familiar sites in the community where students live, graphing milestones in the life of an historically well-known African American). This encourages pre-service teachers to use different avenues to engage students in the mathematics teaching and learning process—to go beyond the math textbook and physical boundaries of the school.

EES: For pre-service teachers who are unfamiliar with communities of color, how do you help them move beyond any misinformation and distorted perceptions they might have of children's families, communities, and experiences?

SLS: One approach is to engage in a number of math activities that are connected to historical content as well as to meeting Georgia Performance Standards. For example, prior to students being asked a series of computation questions based on Atlanta Life's 2008–2009 financial report, they were provided with historical content about the Sweet Auburn Historic District where the Black-owned insurance company originated in 1905. In the early 20th century, many African Americans established businesses, congregations, and social organizations along Auburn Avenue, which became a successful Black business district. Information about several historical Atlanta figures (e.g., John Wesley Dobbs, Alonzo Herndon, Maynard Jackson) is included. Thus, pre-service teachers are gaining information about the history of the community in which they will teach. Math is one way of knowing about the past and present, so it makes sense to use it as a context for learning about the community in which you are teaching.

Introduction

It is critical that teachers possess the knowledge, skills, and affirmative perspectives necessary to develop and implement instruction that takes into account the historical and cultural contexts of students of color. This chapter discusses a study that examined urban, elementary pre-service teachers' ability to create mathematics lessons using a "re-membered" social studies text for content. Specifically, in what ways does the text inform teachers' choices of math concepts, the ways in which they structure lessons, and their ideas about historical content? The study also underscores the significance of teacher preparation programs in which pre-service teachers explore issues of culture not only in the designated diversity course, but also in content methods and other courses.

In examining pre-service teachers' lesson planning, it is important to consider the broader context of the field of mathematics education. In its grounding document, *Principles and Standards for School Mathematics*, The National Council of Teachers of Mathematics (NCTM, 2000) calls for equity in mathematics education stating, "all students, regardless of their personal characteristics, backgrounds, or physical challenges, must have opportunities to study and support to learn mathematics." NCTM suggests that making equity a reality requires raising teacher expectations for students' learning, developing effective instructional strategies for supporting the mathematics learning of all students, and providing students and teachers the necessary resources to be effective. To realize NCTM's vision, teachers must function as agents of change and challenge the pervasive societal belief that only some students are capable of learning mathematics. They must hold high expectations for all students and challenge the implicit, often unspoken, belief that only the experiences of White middle-class students are valuable and reflect mathematical knowledge. Gergen (1995) refers to this deficiency stance as reflecting an exogenic perspective in which students are viewed as tabula rasas (i.e., blank slates) and treated as inactive participants in the teaching and learning process. Not valuing students' cultural and lived experiences (i.e., what students bring to the table) undermines the very notion of equity and implicitly encourages the silencing of historically marginalized learners. The heritage, lived experiences, prior knowledge, intellectual strengths, and personal interests of all students should be valued and utilized as a context for learning. Therefore, mathematics teachers must broaden their thinking about the nature of students' mathematical knowledge, bridging informal and formal mathematical experiences, and providing students opportunities to demonstrate their understanding of mathematics in a multitude of ways.

While content and pedagogy have historically privileged White students by reflecting their history and epistemology, gap rhetoric continues to drive the No Child Left Behind era. Leading the dialogue in mathematics education is the heavily posited "closing the gap," which is the descriptor dividing the mathematics academic achievement of White, African American, Asian, and Hispanic learners in K-12 and higher education communities. The intensity of this dialogue is evidenced by conducting a Google search on the topic and observing a staggering number of hits. Similarly, a plethora of articles on the topic have been written (e.g., Lubienski, 2008, 2002; Lubienski & Crockett, 2007; McGraw, Lubienski, & Strutchens, 2006; Tate, 1997). Inarguably, the mathematics education community should be concerned about the mathematics achievement of all students. However, it is the implicit message of the gap dialogue that is problematic. There are a number of concerns including the basic premise of upholding one racial group as the benchmark of success. That is, measuring the mathematics achievement of African American, Hispanic, and Asian students in relation to their White counterparts. Consider, however, a different perspective. Nearly all schools and school districts have identified standards and/or criteria that mark mathematics achievement/success. Rather than highlighting how various demographic groups perform in relationship to each other, why not look at how students perform in relationship to benchmarks? Little is required to make that shift, only the commitment to do so. Hilliard (1995) points out:

> Rarely do we hear of success in producing achievement for African American, Native American, and Hispanic students. When we do hear of such achievement, it is trumpeted as a miracle, as the exception that proves the rule, as the work that can only be done by teachers who have a special charisma, as outliers that have to be regarded as statistical errors or mere accidents.
>
> *(p. 102)*

Gutierrez (2008) echoes similar concerns about the prominence of the achievement-gap dialogue stating, "I see it as a moral imperative to move beyond this 'gap-gazing' fetish" (p. 357). Gutierrez further contends, "These dangers [of gap-gazing] include offering little more than a static picture of inequities, supporting deficit thinking and negative narratives about students of color and working-class students, perpetuating the myth that the problem (and therefore solution) is a technical one, and promoting a narrow definition of learning and equity" (p. 357). Similarly, Martin (2009) maintains that framing schooling outcomes in terms of racial achievement gaps inherently purports the intellectual inferiority of African American children.

Understanding the full magnitude of gap-oriented discourse requires stepping back and considering the unintended consequences. By unintended consequences I mean considering how the proliferation of deficit language impacts students of color and how they view themselves as learners of mathematics. Martin (2000) suggests that students' mathematical identities are influenced by social, cultural, historical, and political forces. Those identities are indeed powerful and play a pivotal role in students' mathematics experiences. How one sees mathematics and himself or herself as a learner of mathematics is salient for all students, particularly individuals who are members of historically oppressed groups. For these individuals issues of identity and power are of unique concern and consideration. Gap gazing, in effect, is counterintuitive to the very thing it purports to inform—the high level mathematics achievement of all students. This contradiction is at the heart of the well-intended policies and practices that are associated with promoting the mathematics success of all learners.

Gap gazing and other notions of deficiency are counterproductive to the development of teachers and must be challenged within teacher preparation programs. Not examining the long-held deficit paradigm and expecting a substantive change is tantamount to building a house with new state-of-the-art materials on a cracked foundation. The adoption of new curricula and instructional practices must include rethinking of the ideologies underpinning them. Ideologies that are oriented toward equity and social justice should be the norm rather than the exception. High expectation must transcend its current role as politically correct jargon to being operationalized and evidenced in all aspects of teacher education programs that educate pre-service teachers and in professional development offerings that serve practicing mathematics teachers.

Various scholars have suggested frameworks to facilitate teachers' use of students' personal and cultural capital as a foundation for teaching and learning. For example, Moll and González (2004) delineate a framework that teachers might draw upon to support the creation of an equitable mathematics learning community. This framework, Funds of Knowledge, is used to "refer to the knowledge base that underlies the productive and exchange activities of households" (p. 700). The basic tenet of the framework is that students' social (i.e., home) context can be utilized to document knowledge. For example, family-generated artifacts can be used to highlight students' out-of-school experiences and informal learning. Funds of Knowledge explicitly dismantles the notion that low-income households do not possess valuable knowledge and skills, and provides a backdrop for considering how children's knowledge might be accessed, identified, and documented.

Lemons-Smith (2009) describes "Mathematics Beyond the School Walls," a school-based family outreach project that applied the Funds of Knowledge concept in a high-poverty elementary school. The project consisted of two primary components: (a) collecting family visual and written artifacts, and (b) analyzing and using artifacts in the mathematics teaching and learning process. Students and their families were asked to document students' out-of-school mathematics experiences. They were asked to document the experiences by either (a) taking photographs of images that (they felt) reflected how their children experienced or interacted with mathematics in their home and/or community environment, or (b) cutting out images from magazines, newspapers, and other print media that (they felt) reflected how the student experienced or interacted with mathematics in his/her home and/or community environment. Families were also asked to jot down the reason(s) why they chose each artifact and why it was relevant to the mathematical learning of the student. After collecting the student- and family-generated artifacts, the teachers explored the mathematical content embedded in the artifacts, mapped them to state mathematics standards, and developed corresponding tasks. Nearly all of the artifacts could be utilized as a context for teaching multiple mathematics concepts. The created mathematical tasks were aligned with the district mathematics scope and sequence and subsequently implemented. The project afforded students opportunities to infuse their cultural presence in learning activities, something that is not commonplace in mathematics classrooms. The project said clearly to parents and students, we value you and the lived experiences you bring. Most importantly, that sentiment was not just rhetoric or empty words, but rather was explicitly reflected in the teachers' curriculum and instruction. Hilliard (1991) suggested that "powerful teachers" are those who reject the status quo and find ways to promote the academic excellence of all students regardless of circumstances. The "Mathematics Beyond the School Walls" project embodied Hilliard's conception of powerful teaching and facilitated the development of powerful teachers—teachers whose purposeful instructional planning, decision making, actions, and practices rejected notions of deficiency and were geared toward constructing an empowering mathematics learning community.

One theoretical framework that supports Hilliard's suggestion that teachers reject the status quo and find ways to promote the academic excellence of all students is Afrocentricity. This framework rethinks and reconstructs thousands of years of distortions and misinformation that underpin the notions of deficiency that we continue to see in mathematics and other fields (Asante, 2007; Karenga, 2003; Mazama, 2003). Afrocentric concepts such as Centrality/

Location, Self-Determination, and Subjects with Agency—which are discussed in Section I of this volume—guide educators to view African descent students and their ancestors as subjects with agency who make decisions that control their individual and collective lives. Like Moll's and González's (2004) Funds of Knowledge, Afrocentricity views all groups of students at the center of their present and past experiences.

Culturally Relevant Pedagogy (Ladson-Billings, 1995) is another theoretical framework that supports the development of a culturally engaged mathematics classroom. Ladson-Billings found that culturally relevant teachers fall into three categories: (a) Conceptions of Self and Others, which means that culturally relevant teachers hold high expectations for all students and believe all students are capable of achieving academic excellence; (b) Social Relations, which means that culturally relevant teachers establish and maintain positive teacher-student relationships and classroom learning communities, that they are passionate about teaching, and that they view teaching as a service to the community; and (c) Conceptions of Knowledge, which means that culturally relevant teachers view knowledge as fluid and facilitate students' ability to construct their own understanding.

Similarly, Leonard (2008) presents examples of culturally relevant teaching in her book Culturally Specific Pedagogy in the Mathematics Classroom. In it she highlights the instructional practices of several teachers including Ms. Cho and Ms. Baker. Leonard describes how their classrooms reflect a shared learning community, high expectations, and a valuing of students' contributions to the math teaching and learning process. She shares how Ms. Cho and Ms. Baker used the text Sweet Clara and the Freedom Quilt as a springboard for introducing the idea of quilting. The freedom quilt functioned as the cultural connection and spurred the learning of area, perimeter, symmetry, congruence, measurement, and geometric shapes.

The above examples reflect a cultural orientation to teaching mathematics. What, then, is the requisite development for teachers to engage in such instruction? What is needed of teacher education programs training pre-service teachers and professional development offerings serving inservice mathematics teachers? Howard and Aleman (2008) outline three elements comprising teacher capacity for teaching diverse populations: (a) subject matter and pedagogical content knowledge, (b) knowledge of effective practice about teaching in diverse settings, and (c) development of a critical consciousness. Often the conversation surrounding preparing teachers to work with diverse student populations centers more on interpersonal relations and less on curriculum and content; and teacher preparation programs often rely on a standalone multicultural course as a mechanism for addressing issues of diversity. Banks et al. (2005) argue that this is a cursory approach and advocate for integrated experiences throughout the professional preparation program. To develop mathematics teachers who are capable of enacting high quality, culturally responsive instruction, the traditional mathematics methods, mathematics content courses, and relevant pedagogy and other required courses must be revisited and reshaped to embrace an equity-oriented approach to teaching and learning. Notions of diversity, equity, and social justice would be central to and evident in all aspects of course readings, discussions, assignments, lesson plans, and field experiences. Typically, pre-service teachers draw on their own mathematics experiences and have distinct views of what constitutes "good" mathematics teaching, what counts as mathematical knowledge, and who is good at mathematics. Engaging in thought-provoking exercises that challenge those ideas, can encourage our students to adopt instructional content that includes and represents the students they teach, to use practices that reflect an asset perspective, and to explicitly focus on tapping into the mathematics capital that all students bring to the classroom.

Study Context

This qualitative study was conducted in a large urban city in the southeast United States. Participants were enrolled in a two-year alternative certification and master's program designed for career switchers who have an undergraduate degree in an area other than education. The post-baccalaureate program explicitly focuses on preparing teachers for urban, high-poverty elementary schools. Unlike many alternative certification programs, this program is not a "boot camp." Rather, during year 1 of the program individuals matriculate full-time, take coursework required for P-5 certification, and complete student teaching. Individuals spend over 900 hours in their assigned school over two semesters. During year 2, individuals hold a full-time teaching position and engage in induction and collaborative coaching.

The context for the study was a mathematics methods course in the first year of the program. The methods course takes the idea of cultural competence and links it directly to the teaching and learning of mathematics. As stated above, diversity, equity, and social justice are evident in most aspects of the course readings, discussions, assignments, lesson plans, and field experience. Pre-service teachers are challenged to utilize students' cultural backgrounds, families, communities, interests, and out-of-school experiences as an anchor for teaching mathematical concepts. Assignments explicitly focus on valuing the mathematics capital that all students bring to the classroom. It is fair to say the course is a significant departure from the traditional approach to teaching mathematics methods.

The study was conducted during the summer semester about midway through the mathematics methods course. The course was 6 weeks long and met once a week for a 5-hour class. Prior to participating in the study, pre-service teachers had engaged in class discussions related to using students' families, homes, communities, backgrounds, and out-of-school experiences as a springboard for mathematics teaching and learning.

Participants

The study consisted of 17 pre-service graduate students. Of those, 5 were Black and 12 were White. There were 5 males and 12 females, with ages ranging from 23 to 54.

Data Sources

Three data sources informed the study: (a) pre-service teachers' lesson plans; (b) responses to small group discussion questions; and (c) researcher's observations of small group discussions. During the study, the researcher introduced a culturally informed "re-membered" text, *Freedom and Democracy: A Story Remembered* (Swartz, 2013) and led a whole group discussion of the text's six Lessons. In the following class session, participants were divided into small groups and given a lesson-writing assignment related to *Freedom and Democracy*.

Research Question

The research question framing the study was: When pre-service teachers work collaboratively to create mathematics lessons using a "re-membered" social studies text for content, in what way does that text: (a) inform their choice of math concepts; (b) inform the ways they structure lessons; and (c) inform their ideas about historical content? To explore this question, participants were divided into five small groups and asked to write a lesson plan related to specific assignments listed in the section below.

Small Group Lesson Plan Assignments

Group A

According to the 1790 U.S. Census in the state of Georgia, there were 13,103 White males 16 years and older and 14,044 White males under 16 years of age. There were 25,730 White females. During the same year, there were 29,264 enslaved Black people and 393 "other free persons" (Black people).

Native Americans were not included in the 1790 U.S. Census. The Cherokee and the Creek were the two largest Native American Nations living in the general area that is called Georgia today. An estimate of the Cherokee population around that time is 20,000 people. An estimate of the Creek population around that time is 22,000.

Using the third-grade Math Georgia Performance Standards, consider the math concepts that can be taught using the data about the populations of Native Americans, Black Americans, and White Americans in Georgia in the late 1700s. Identify the standards and develop an appropriate math lesson that could be used as part of teaching *Freedom and Democracy: A Story Remembered* (Swartz, 2013).

Group B

After learning about Wampum Belts in *Freedom and Democracy* (Swartz, 2013), learn about how they were made of many shell beads strung on strings, with many strings woven together. For wampum history and how to make Wampum Belts, see Prindle (2013a & b). Discuss with students the meaning of the Ayonwatha Wampum Belt (see Swartz, 2013, p. 20). This belt is made of 38 horizontal rows and 173 vertical rows. The Ayonwatha Belt is made of white and purple shell beads, with 892 of the beads being white.

Using the third-grade Math Georgia Performance Standards, consider the math concepts that can be taught using the data about the Ayonwatha Wampum Belt. Identify the standards and develop an appropriate math lesson that could be used as part of teaching *Freedom and Democracy: A Story Remembered* (Swartz, 2013).

Group C

In the early 1800s, enslaved labor was used to grow indigo on plantations in Georgia. On one plantation, 25 enslaved workers each produced 500 bushels of indigo worth $25,000.

Using the third-grade Math Georgia Performance Standards, consider the math concepts that can be taught using the above data about the enslaved labor on a plantation in Georgia in the early 1800's. Identify the standards and develop an appropriate math lesson that could be used as part of teaching *Freedom and Democracy: A Story Remembered* (Swartz, 2013).

Group D

In this assignment, use a map with a scale of miles that shows the United States, Canada, and Mexico. Assume you took your freedom from being enslaved and traveled in secret from Atlanta, Georgia, to Rochester, New York, to Canada.

Using the third-grade Math Georgia Performance Standards, consider the math concepts that can be taught using the data about this journey to freedom. Identify the standards and develop an appropriate math lesson that could be used as part of teaching *Freedom and Democracy: A Story Remembered* (Swartz, 2013).

Group E

Benjamin Banneker built the first wooden clock in North America. The clock rang every hour for 50 years.

Using the third-grade Math Georgia Performance Standards, consider the math concepts that can be taught using the data about the first wooden clock built by Benjamin Banneker. Identify the standards and develop an appropriate math lesson that could be used as part of teaching *Freedom and Democracy: A Story Remembered* (Swartz, 2013).

Small Group Discussion Questions

Prior to the small groups working on their lesson plans, they engaged in discussions related to *Freedom and Democracy* (Swartz, 2013). Each group's discussion question was designed to bring students' attention to the historical and political aspects of their lesson-writing assignment. During these small group discussions, the researcher circulated among the groups, listening to and noting conversations, but not participating or attempting to influence student discussions. The discussion questions are listed below.

Group A

What does the lack of 1790 data for Native Americans and the ways in which Black Americans were characterized in the U. S. Census tell you about the ways in which White people viewed freedom and democracy at that time?

Group B

What were some of the uses of Wampum Belts by the Haudenosaunee? What does the Ayonwatha Belt communicate about the purpose of confederacy and what it sought to accomplish?

Group C

Today, one way to see the profits made from using unpaid labor is viewing the homes of plantation owners like George Washington (Mt. Vernon) and Thomas Jefferson (Monticello) that were built for them by enslaved people (Swartz, 2013, pp. 16–17). If African people had been paid for several hundred years of their stolen labor, what might you see today?

Group D

What meaning do you make from knowing thousands of people were willing to walk a thousand or more miles—among strangers, in unknown territory, and under the threat of being returned to enslavement and severely punished—in order to liberate themselves?

Group E

In addition to being an inventor, scientist, and surveyor, Benjamin Banneker was also an advocate for freedom. After reading *Freedom and Democracy* (Swartz, 2013), how do you think Banneker's demonstrated excellence and actions for human freedom are connected to his African heritage?

Findings/Discussion

To reiterate, the study examined the question: When pre-service teachers work collaboratively to create mathematics lessons using a "re-membered" social studies text for content, in what way does that text (a) inform their choice of math concepts, (b) inform the ways they structure lessons, and (c) inform their ideas about historical content? Table 6.1 highlights the math concept(s) selected by each small group.

Table 6.2 highlights the ways in which the small groups structured their lessons. The data in Tables 6.1 and 6.2 reveal that when pre-service teachers created math lessons using a "re-membered" social studies text for content,

TABLE 6.1 Selected Math Concepts

Groups	Selected Math Concept(s)	Math Content Strand
Group A	M3D1: Create and interpret simple tables and graphs	Data Analysis
	M3N5: Understand the meaning of decimal fractions and common fractions in simple cases and apply them in problem-solving situations.	Number & Operations
Group B	M3N3: Develop an understanding of multiplication of whole numbers and develop the ability to apply it in problem solving.	Number & Operations
	M3M1: Develop an understanding of the concept of time by determining elapsed time of a full, half, and quarter-hour.	Measurement
Group C	M3N4: Understand the meaning of division and develop the ability to apply it in the problem-solving situations.	Number & Operations
Group D	M3M2: Measure length choosing appropriate units and tools.	Measurement
Group E	M3N3: Develop an understanding of multiplication of whole numbers and develop the ability to apply it in problem solving.	Number & Operations

TABLE 6.2 Structure of Math Lessons

Group	Structure of Math Lessons
Group A	Lesson involved computation, and also analysis related to *Freedom and Democracy* text.
Group B	Lesson involved computation.
Group C	Lesson involved computation, and included home/school connection.
Group D	Lesson involved computation, and included home/school connection.
Group E	Lesson involved computation.

the lessons most often reflected mathematical computation, involving multiplication, division, fractions, and length. In two instances, Groups C and D, the lessons also included home/school connections. Group C related money generated by enslaved people from picking bushels of indigo to money students earn from doing household chores; and Group D related the distance enslaved people traveled to freedom to the distances students traveled in their day-to-day life. While Groups C and D attempted to make connections between the past and present, these two home/school connections minimize enslavement and liberation by comparing them to students' activities under far different circumstances. One way to respond to such minimizing comparisons would be to ask pre-service teachers thought-provoking questions. For example, a question for Group C could be, "While money is generated from both enslaved labor and from doing household chores, in what significant ways do these two contexts differ?" For Group D, a question could be, "While enslaved people journeying to freedom and students traveling in their daily lives both involve travel, in what ways are these two contexts very different? The intention of such critical questions would be for pre-service teachers to explore the comparisons they produced and to realize that making comparisons across vastly different contexts requires careful analysis. It would also be helpful to provide home/school connections that are comparable across time and place. For example, elementary students could be asked to identify current forms of injustice experienced by people of African ancestry in areas such as employment, voting, and housing by using mathematics to make comparisons across race. After using math to identify inequities in the past and present, students could be asked to think about how knowledge of mathematics is needed to solve social, economic, and political inequalities.

Only one math lesson engaged students in analysis related to *Freedom and Democracy* (Swartz, 2013). In Group A's lesson, students did computation related to fractions, but they also created bar graphs using the 1790 U.S. Census data. The lesson plan encouraged students to use the graphs to analyze the implications of the data and voting in terms of power and privilege. Students were asked to consider how enslaved Black people were counted due to the 1887 Three-Fifths Clause of the U.S. Constitution and who benefited from that.

They were also asked to consider how the political landscape may have shifted if Black people had the right to vote and if they had held political office.

The latter part of the research question relates to each group's ideas about historical content as evident in their lesson plans. The small–group lesson plans were categorized using the follow descriptors:

- **Historical/Political**: The lesson plan uses *Freedom and Democracy* (Swartz, 2013) as a context for teaching mathematics. Further, the lesson encourages students to consider other historical and/or political implications that are related to the lesson plan assignment.
- **Home/School**: The lesson plan uses *Freedom and Democracy* (Swartz, 2013) as a context for teaching mathematics. Further, the lesson makes connections between the mathematics and students' lived and out-of-school experiences.
- **Context**: The lesson plan uses *Freedom and Democracy* (Swartz, 2013) as a context for teaching mathematics. No other implications or connections are evident.

Of the five small group lessons, one was categorized as Historical/Political; two were categorized as Home/School; and two as Context (see Table 6.3).

The responses to small group discussion questions were categorized using the following descriptors:

- **Historical/Political**: The response raised thoughtful historical and/or political points and issues.
- **Factual**: The response (re)stated historical facts, but did not raise thoughtful historical and/or political points and issues.

Of the five small group responses, two were categorized as Historical/Political and three as factual by the researcher. Two groups reflected on historical/political issues, while the other three groups merely (re)stated facts related to the activity. Table 6.4 shows how each group's discussion was categorized.

Based on group discussions, students did not seem familiar with most of the content in *Freedom and Democracy* (Swartz, 2013). It is fair to say the text presented them with new ideas and information. Though the idea of using culturally

TABLE 6.3 Ideas about Historical Content in *Freedom and Democracy*

Group	Ideas about Historical Content in Freedom and Democracy
Group A	Historical/Political
Group B	Context
Group C	Home/School
Group D	Home/School
Group E	Context

TABLE 6.4 Discussion of Questions Related to *Freedom and Democracy*

Groups	Discussion of Questions Related to Freedom and Democracy
Group A	Historical/Political
Group B	Factual
Group C	Historical/Political
Group D	Factual
Group E	Factual

informed social studies text in math had been discussed, students seemed a little unsure of how to proceed. I would argue that students' lack of familiarity with the content, coupled with the interdisciplinary nature of the lesson, attributed to their initial tentativeness about engaging in the assignment. The collective data further suggest that when pre-service teachers worked collaboratively to create mathematics lessons using a "re-membered" social studies text for content, most gravitated to "safe" math instruction involving number and operations and computation. Their lessons were less likely to encourage students to use the math concepts to consider historical and/or political implications raised by the *Freedom and Democracy* content. This safeness was also reflected in small group discussions. Most teachers restated historical facts rather than raise thoughtful historical and/or political points and issues. These findings are consistent with much of the literature about how pre-service teachers engage issues of cultural diversity. Gay (2010) asserts:

> Many prospective teachers do not think deeply about their attitudes and beliefs toward ethnic, cultural, and racial diversity; some even deliberately resist doing so. When my students are asked about them, they make declarations about being "beyond race, ethnicity, and culture," colorblind, or advocates of racelessness. Yet they are hard pressed to articulate with any depth of thought what these ideologies mean, why they support them, and how they translate into teaching behaviors.
>
> (p. 45)

When you consider how most pre-service teachers chose to use the "re-membered" text, structure the lessons, and discuss questions related to their lesson plan assignment, it signals that they remained in their historical and political comfort zones and did not take full advantage of the culturally informed content. However, using such content affords pre-service teachers the opportunity to "go beyond" the math. They were given a space to use mathematics to venture into social realities and to consider the historical and/or political implications of the content. As discussed earlier, only Group A attempted to do that. The other groups could have also gone further with their lessons. For example, Group C's lesson plan could have encouraged students to use mathematics as a way to analyze the historical implications of enslaved labor on indigo plantations. Instead, this group chose only to have students engage in computation. In looking across the lessons of the five groups, it was striking that only Group A's lesson (i.e., choice of math concepts, lesson structure, ideas about historical content) and group discussion were consistently more thought provoking than the other groups. The composition of Group A may indicate why this was so. The group was comprised of two White males, a White female, and a Black female. One of the males was 54 years old, significantly older than the other group members, and functioned as the unofficial group leader. Based on my observations of their group discussions, I speculate that his open mindedness, confidence, and life experience influenced the conversations and design of this group's lesson.

Two additional points should be noted: (a) this stance of staying within familiar and comfortable historical and political spaces was not isolated to the *Freedom and Democracy* (Swartz, 2013) assignment, but was also the case with other assignments; and (b) as part of this study's design, the assignment was intentionally student-driven to better gauge how they might approach instructional planning. The findings, however, suggest that this (and other similar assignments) may need to be more instructor-driven. In this way, pre-service teachers can be guided to explore more than their familiar historical and political comfort zones; and they can be encouraged to structure lessons that go beyond computation, using math to consider the implications of content. Similarly, in small group discussions it appears that pre-service teachers need encouragement to go beyond merely stating facts to having more thought-provoking, critical dialogue related to the text. Also, given that this study was conducted midway in a 6-week summer course, it may have been a lot to expect participants to shift away from traditional and familiar thinking about how to teach math, what materials are appropriate, and how math can be used to include cultural knowledge. Such shifts in traditional thinking about mathematics are challenging for many students during a 15-week semester.

This study suggests that pre-service teachers need guidance and encouragement to engage in critical lesson planning, interdisciplinary learning, and the integration of cultural knowledge. Often teacher preparation programs rely solely on one culture course, which means that the integration of cultural knowledge is not shared and evident throughout the program. Preparing teachers who can engage in integrated, critical, and culturally and historically grounded content and pedagogy requires extending beyond the designated culture course to make connections through interdisciplinarity across content disciplines such as mathematics. If pre-service teachers are to develop the skills to critically engage with curriculum for all students, teacher preparation programs must rethink how they prepare teachers.

This study highlights the challenges and promise of developing teachers who are able to use culturally informed instructional materials as a foundation for teaching and learning. If teacher preparation programs are structured such that pre-service teachers are afforded this opportunity, then individual courses can support that work. Using "re-membered" content to teach mathematics does not seem to come naturally for most pre-service teachers. This study lends support to placing them in deliberate and directed learning situations where they have opportunities to collaborate, think through instructional planning, and engage in critical dialogue. Through these experiences, pre-service teachers' knowledge, skills, and dispositions related to culturally and historically engaged learning can be enhanced and add to their overall effectiveness as mathematics teacher. As a result, the children and communities they serve will be the beneficiaries of instruction geared toward academic and cultural excellence.

References

Asante, M. K. (2007). *An Afrocentric manifesto*. Malden, MA: Polity Press.

Banks, J., Cochran-Smith, M., Moll, L., Richert, A., Zeichner, K., LePage, P., ... with McDonald, M. (2005). Teaching diverse learners. In L. Darling-Hammond & J. Bransford (Eds.), *Preparing teachers for a changing world: What teachers should learn and be able to do* (pp. 232–274). San Francisco, CA: Jossey-Bass.

Gay, G. (2010). Acting on beliefs in teacher education for cultural diversity. *Journal of Teacher Education, 61,* 143–152.

Gergen, K. (1995). Social construction and the educational process. In L. Steffe & J. Gale (Eds.), *Constructivism in education* (pp. 17–39). Hillsdale, NJ: Erlbaum.

Gutierrez, R. (2008). On "gap gazing" fetish in mathematics education? Problematizing research on the achievement gap. *Journal for Research in Mathematics Education, 39*(4), 357–364.

Hilliard, A. G., III. (1991). Do we have the will to educate all children? *Educational Leadership, 49*(1), 31–36.

Hilliard, A. G., III. (1995). Mathematics excellence for cultural "minority" students: What is the problem? In I. M. Carl (Ed.), *Prospects for school mathematics* (pp. 99–113). Reston, VA: The National Council of Teachers of Mathematics.

Hopkinson, D. (1995). *Sweet Clara and the freedom quilt*. New York, NY: Alfred A. Kopf.

Howard, T. C., & Aleman, G. R. (2008). Teacher capacity for diverse learners: What do teachers need to know? In M. C. Smith, S. Feiman-Nemser, D. J. McIntyre, & K. E. Demers (Eds.), *Handbook of research on teacher education* (pp. 157–174). New York, NY: Routledge.

Karenga, M. (2003). Afrocentricity and multicultural education: Concept, challenge and contribution. In A. Mazama (Ed.), *The Afrocentric paradigm* (pp. 73–94). Trenton, NJ: Africa World Press.

Ladson-Billings, G. (1995). Toward a theory of culturally relevant pedagogy. *American Educational Research Journal, 32*(3), 465–491.

Lemons-Smith, S. (2009). Mathematics beyond the school walls project: Exploring the dynamic role of students' lived experiences. In C. E. Malloy (Series Ed.) & D. Y. White, & J. S. Spitzer (Vol. Eds.), *Mathematics for every student: Responding to diversity, grades Pre-K-5* (pp. 129–136). Reston, VA: National Council of Teachers of Mathematics.

Leonard, J. (2008). *Culturally specific pedagogy in the mathematics classroom*. New York, NY: Routledge.

Lubienski, S. T. (2002). A closer look at black-white mathematics gaps: Intersections of race and SES in NAEP achievement and instructional practices data. *Journal of Negro Education, 71,* 269–287.

Lubienski, S. T. (2008). On "gap gazing" in mathematics education: The need for gaps analyses. *Journal for Research in Mathematics Education, 39*(4), 350–356.

Lubienski, S. T., & Crockett, M. (2007). NAEP mathematics achievement and race/ethnicity. In P. Kloosterman & F. Lester (Eds.), *Results from the Ninth Mathematics Assessment of NAEP* (pp. 227–260). Reston, VA: National Council of Teachers of Mathematics.

Martin, D. B. (2000). *Mathematics success and failure among African American youth*. New York, NY: Routledge.

Martin, D. B. (2009). Liberating the production of knowledge about African American children and mathematics. In D. B. Martin (Ed.), *Mathematics teaching, learning, and liberation in the lives of Black children*. New York, NY: Routledge.

Mazama, A. (2003). *The Afrocentric paradigm*. Trenton, NJ: Africa World Press.

McGraw, R., Lubienski, S. T., & Strutchens, M. E. (2006). A closer look at gender in NAEP mathematics achievement and affect data: Intersections with achievement, race, and socio-economic status. *Journal for Research in Mathematics Education, 37,* 129–150.

Moll, L. C., & González, N. (2004). Engaging life: A funds-of-knowledge approach to multicultural education. In J. A. Banks & C. A. McGee Banks (Eds.), *Handbook of research on multicultural education* (2nd ed., pp. 699–715). San Francisco, CA: Jossey-Bass.

NCTM (National Council of Teachers of Mathematics) (2000). *Principles and standards for school mathematics*. Reston, VA: MCTM.

Prindle, T. (2013a). Woven wampum beadwork. Retrieved from http://www.nativetech.org/wampum/wamphist.htm

Prindle, T. (2013b). Single-strand square weave technique. Retrieved from http://www.nativetech.org/wampum/ssinstr.htm

Swartz, E. E. (2013). *Freedom and democracy: A story remembered*. Rochester, NY: Omnicentric Press.

Tate, W. F. (1997). Race-ethnicity, SES, gender, and language proficiency trends in mathematics achievement: An update. *Journal for Research in Mathematics Education, 28,* 652–679.

7

CULTURALLY INFORMED LESSON PLANNING

Ericka López

Below is a portion of a conversation between Ellen E. Swartz (EES) and Ericka López (EL) that took place after Ms. López completed her masters program. As Ms. López enters the field of teaching, you can observe the connections she is making between her practice, the process of historical recovery, Afrocentric concepts, and culturally informed principles.

EES: If the Afrocentric idea in education had been part of framing your masters in education program, how might this have affected your preparation for teaching?

EL: I think it would have created a shift in my ideas about the role of a teacher and the role of the student. I mean that without the idea of "centrality" the holders of knowledge are the teachers and those outside of student's communities. Teachers using this Eurocentric model are a bridge between the child's so-called deficits and the "education" that is "out there"—outside of a child's community. With exposure to the Afrocentric idea, I could have thought differently about lesson planning and how to educate children throughout my masters program, rather than only toward the end. Instead of thinking of myself as a cultural liaison, I could have been finding ways to access knowledge from students' cultures and communities and interweaving it into the larger body of human knowledge and ideas.

EES: You found inaccuracies and omissions in the way this body of knowledge was presented in standard instructional materials. How do such materials relate to Dr. Molefi Asante's idea that education is a process of socialization?

EL: If we as teachers of color do not recognize this socialization process, then what we do is socialize students to be part of a system that margin-

alizes and omits them from centers of power. We run the risk of leading students to believe that becoming educated and successful requires
cutting yourself off from your culture and background. Or worse yet,
by not showcasing and exposing students to the contributions of Africans and other groups we in essence say that no contributions are to be
spoken of. Omission in instructional materials is a way to send a message that African culture and people, along with other Peoples of color,
did little or nothing of great importance. This is perhaps something
that we do not explore enough: the idea that a lot is said when we say
little or nothing about the knowledge that comes from people outside
of Europe. The responsibility of educators is to socialize all children so
that they remain connected to their cultural identities.

EES: How does the lesson you wrote put the Afrocentric idea in education
into practice?

EL: My lesson does this by using more accurate scholarship about U. S. history. As Asante argues, Afrocentricity is not a supremacist approach to
education; rather it seeks to allow all students access to accurate historical content instead of feeding students a narrow view of the origins of
important intellectual ideas like freedom and democracy. In this way,
African history is human history. European history is also human history, but it is typically presented as universal. When all students are
taught the African roots of the ideas and values shared in our country,
we all discover an African heritage. It is no longer a "minority" or
"subculture," it is no longer the "other." The lesson further puts the
Afrocentric idea into practice by not disconnecting African or Native
American contributions through sidebars and asides, but by firmly placing them at the center of the historical narrative.

EES: In your chapter you write about the systematic marginalization of
ESOL [English for Speakers of Other Language] students. How do you
see the use of "re-membered" student content affecting this systematic
marginalization?

EL: Most importantly the "re-membered" student content presents the reality that many groups contributed to the development of human knowledge in general and American history in particular. ESOL students
are a diverse group of students from all over the world. By presenting
"re-membered" student content, students can see there has always been
space for many different peoples to contribute to the development of
knowledge. No one group owns the ability to innovate and discover.

Introduction

I became involved in writing a culturally informed lesson plan in the spring
of 2011 through the Teacher Opportunity Corps (TOC) program at Nazareth
College of Rochester. This is a program in which pre-service and in-service
teachers of color and other underrepresented groups participate in community

service, research, and other projects—along with their course work—to help them better prepare for a career in an urban district. I worked with Dr. Swartz, a consultant with the TOC program. We began with critiquing a social studies textbook series recently purchased for use in the area's urban school district. We specifically looked at the first- and fourth-grade textbooks, which focused on the United States in terms of neighborhoods, communities, and regions (Boyd et al., 2011a & b). This was important work for me, because as a pre-service teacher in the English for Speakers of Other Languages (ESOL) program, the school district in my community—with a majority population of students of color—is a major potential employer. The experience of looking through the textbooks was eye-opening to say the least.

The textbooks were critiqued within the context of a set of six culturally informed principles. The principles—put together by Dr. Swartz and her colleagues—are inclusion, representation, indigenous voice, accurate scholarship, critical thinking, and a collective humanity (Goodwin & Swartz, 2009; Swartz, 2009, 2011; Swartz & Bakari, 2005). These principles (described and exemplified in chapter 2 of this volume) call for practices that are often omitted in social studies texts that use grand narratives. I learned that grand narratives are large concepts that explain historical development in ways that support the interests of the dominant group(s) in our society and that these narratives are used to shape national identity and maintain the status quo (Appleby, Hunt, & Jacob, 1994; Epstein, 2009). As I became familiar with culturally informed principles, they seemed to be the opposite of a grand narrative approach to writing history. These principles bring forward the contributions of various groups and their experiences in the telling of events. This is not an artificial or disingenuous approach to inclusion. People are not anachronistically placed in time, and inclusion goes beyond placing more photographs of people of color in textbooks. Culturally informed principles are about taking the scholarship that is out there about all the different groups who participated in an historical era and giving them each voice in the matter of the history they created (Asante, 2003; Banks, 2001, 2004; Grant & Sleeter, 2007).

What we found in the textbooks gave me a new understanding of the role of the books in shaping what children think about the history of their country. I think that not having examples of how various groups have participated sends a false message to students of color that their ancestors were not agents of change—that they did not play a significant role in shaping our country (Asante, 2005). As an ESOL teacher who will work primarily with children of color, both native and foreign born, these texts communicate that only people of European descent contributed in important ways to the development of the United States, which in effect disengages students from thinking they can be active citizens and agents of change. Jim Cummins (1994) views curricula that primarily reflect the experiences of dominant groups as one of the systematic ways schools discriminate against students of color, including ESOL students.

As discussed below, we found many examples of systemic discrimination in the textbooks we examined.

We observed that textbook language subtly, and not so subtly, serves to promulgate the dominance of the White mainstream. Its heroes, events, and accomplishments are presented with definitive language. For example, in the fourth-grade textbook, the colonists' fight for freedom from England is presented as a warranted and unquestioned event, not as a debatable issue (Boyd et al., 2011b). Students are not told that some people agreed that they should be free while others did not. This is in contrast to the way slavery is presented in the same text. Students are told that some people agreed with the enslavement of African people and others did not. This is problematic on several levels. First, it disallows the categorical condemnation of an institution like slavery. Nowhere does the book say slavery is unethical and wrong. Talking about slavery as debatable also fails to accurately represent the agency of enslaved and free African people in their quest for freedom and equality. Their freedom, as written in the textbook, was debated by some (White people) and given to them later by others (White people).

In the first-grade textbook we reviewed, the discussion of law and governance is first introduced with the arrival of Europeans to North America (Boyd et al., 2011a). This ignores scholarship that exists about the governments and social structures of Native American Nations (Grande, 2004; Grinde & Johansen, 1991; Lyons & Mohawk, 1992). It also serves to present the false notion that the structures of civilization and society began with Europeans. These are only a few examples that show how these textbooks present history related to the White mainstream as compared to people of color.

A student text called *Freedom and Democracy: A Story Remembered* (Swartz, 2013) was written as a way to provide a culturally informed and more comprehensive view of how freedom and democracy came about in the colonial period. As described in chapter 3 and Appendix B in this volume, this text is written to bring to the foreground the historical relationships among different groups and the ways in which these interactions contributed to shaping the United States. After reading *Freedom and Democracy,* I thought about the informational holes in my own public school education and about the holes in educational texts that students are still using. Students are not getting anywhere close to a comprehensive account. In *Freedom and Democracy,* students can see how the United States was shaped by various groups, both privileged and oppressed. For example, in the first chapter of *Freedom and Democracy* the concept of freedom is discussed within the context of what Haudenosaunee and African people knew about these concepts. It presents both the societal structures of African people before their enslavement in North America and the existing government of the Haudenosaunee. This is in contrast to the above textbook example in which law, governance, and freedom in North America are shown as beginning with the arrival of Europeans.

Many of the teacher preparation courses I have taken in the past year and a half include lesson planning that focuses on engaging students, meeting their academic needs, differentiation, and adaptation. The lesson plan templates we were given guided us to look at the best ways to ensure students are accessing the content of a lesson. A culturally informed lesson plan places less emphasis on the activities that guide students to access information. Rather, the emphasis is placed on helping students use critical thinking skills to produce their own knowledge, individually and collectively. This requires creating a plan where students have more time to hash out ideas. Planning means more than getting students to understand and memorize facts. In a culturally informed lesson, students are encouraged to think critically about how various forces contribute to large, abstract concepts like community, freedom, and democracy. This means that along with student materials encouraging critical thinking, the pedagogy of teachers needs to do this as well. Thus, a culturally informed lesson plan involves emancipatory pedagogy that encourages both teachers and students to create knowledge together, rather than to accept knowledge given to them through textbooks and other materials (Goodwin, 2004; Swartz, 1996).

The rigor of a culturally informed lesson is critical for all teachers, but especially for ESOL teachers and other teachers of children of color. ESOL students are often placed in lower ability classes or special education. This group also experiences high drop-out rates (Cummins, 1994; Nieto & Bode, 2010). Jim Cummins (1994) sees this as the beginning of a systematic marginalization of ESOL students. Relegating students to these classes excludes them from a track that would lead to higher education and then, further down the line, participation in the workforce that can provide greater access to financial privileges. Nieto and Bode, who write about the relevance of culture in education, believe that a more rigorous curriculum that develops critical thinking skills is good for the development of engaged citizens:

> ... supporters of multicultural education assume that a curriculum that is multicultural is also more complicated and truthful and will, in the long run, help develop citizens who think critically, expansively, and creatively.
>
> *(p. 56)*

After we completed the process of textbook critique, Dr. Swartz asked me to write a culturally informed lesson plan for the first lesson in *Freedom and Democracy* (Swartz, 2013). This led me to study the process of writing the lesson. A typical objective of traditional lesson plans is to transmit knowledge to students. However, writing a culturally informed lesson plan, including the emancipatory pedagogy used to teach it, encourages students to construct knowledge, not only receive it (Goodwin, 2004). Thus, I knew that I wanted a plan that would engage teachers and students in critical thought with each other. This led to the following research question that guided my study: What does a lesson plan look like that uses culturally informed instructional materials and emancipatory pedagogy to encourage critical thinking?

Methods

The lesson plan I wrote was created for a fourth-grade ESOL classroom in an urban bilingual program in upstate New York. ESOL classrooms in elementary schools usually pull out students from mainstream classrooms or if all students require services, the ESOL teacher will push into the mainstream classroom. I created a lesson that could be used in a push-in setting. ESOL classes are usually small to optimize language learning.

Writing this lesson plan was part of my experience in the TOC program, which brings an increased number of underrepresented teachers into the profession and prepares these teachers to work effectively with students considered to be at risk for truancy, academic failure, or dropping out. The lesson plan I wrote uses culturally informed instructional materials and emancipatory pedagogy in classroom teaching to encourage critical thinking. I began this study with the assumption that this approach has the potential to increase academic success and reduce other at risk factors.

Best practices for the ESOL classroom suggest that students will effectively learn English through content (Díaz-Rico, 2007). While students traditionally learn basic interpersonal communication skills (BICS) within a year or two of exposure to a second language, attaining cognitive academic language proficiency (CALP) can take anywhere between 3 to 7 years (Collier & Thomas, 2002). The less the availability of first language maintenance programs, the more time it will take to develop CALP. By teaching language through content, students are developing their CALP skills, which in turn increase the possibility of success in their academic lives. Furthermore, you will see in the lesson plan at the end of this chapter that because this is an ESOL lesson plan, I used an overtly stated language objective, modified writing output in the form of an experience learning project, and homogeneous groupings based on social language proficiency. An experience learning writing project involves the teacher in writing what students orally tell the teacher to write. Each student contributes and editing takes place as a group. This approach is for emerging writers.

Three methods were used to explore this study's research question: reviewing historical content, collaboration, and self-reflection. Reviewing historical content included the study and critique of two textbooks in a series adopted for district-wide use (discussed above) and *Freedom and Democracy* (Swartz, 2013), including several of the texts referenced for teachers and families in this text. The purpose of examining these student materials and references was to compare them in relation to content about freedom and democracy in North America. The second method used was collaboration—between Dr. Swartz and myself—in which I was given feedback and articles about emancipatory pedagogy and Afrocentric theory that helped shape the lesson plan into one that was culturally informed. The third method was self-reflection. This refers to what was going on in my thinking throughout the whole process of writing the lesson plan. Self-reflection helped shape what I would be doing in my lesson plan to encourage critical thinking skills. This method also kept me mindful of writing a lesson plan that reflected the culturally informed student text I was using.

Findings

My research findings are described in three sub-sections below, which correspond to the study's three research methods. These findings refer to sections of the lesson that this study examined.

Reviewing Historical Content

Examining *Freedom and Democracy* (Swartz, 2013), and several references used in writing this text, indicated that its content was more comprehensive than the textbooks about who contributed to developing freedom and democracy in North America. This process also clarified that *Freedom and Democracy* lent itself to using emancipatory pedagogical practices, particularly those designed to generate a classroom environment where students are encouraged to think critically and generate their own knowledge. For example, in *Freedom and Democracy* "freedom" is not defined one way. Haudenosaunee and African people describe freedom as a natural right, as living and acting based on beliefs and values that show care for self and others, as related to peace, and as a responsibility to protect each other. Not giving one definitive answer or definition for this concept lets the teacher direct the lesson in ways that helps students explore and engage in dialogue about freedom.

I found the major difference between the current social studies textbooks I reviewed and *Freedom and Democracy* (Swartz, 2013) to be in the quality of the historical content. The first-grade social studies textbook promulgated the myth that governance, social structures, and other concepts like freedom, liberty, and justice were begun and developed by Europeans upon their arrival to the Americas (Boyd et al., 2011a). As discussed above, this is not only historically inaccurate, but it serves to reinforce and maintain the grand narrative of freedom and democracy (see chapter 2, Table 2.1 in this volume) that omits knowledge about Haudenosaunee and African involvement in developing freedom and democracy in North America.

In *Freedom and Democracy* (Swartz, 2013), the content includes and represents the voices of all those groups that were present, which makes it a more inclusive and representational account of the era portrayed. For example, the contributions to the concepts of both freedom and democracy by Haudenosaunee and

African people are explored. Furthermore, each group's historical participation is treated in its own right rather than only vis-à-vis the European experience, the experience of slavery, or the colonization and genocide of millions of Indigenous people. *Freedom and Democracy* recognizes that the concepts of freedom, democracy, and community existed prior to European contact. This demonstrates to students that the development of these concepts and their subsequent evolution throughout U. S. history were created, not by one group, but through the relationship of several groups. Thus, my review of historical content expanded my knowledge of history, which informed the lesson plan I wrote. This can be seen in my "Framing Question," "Essential Question," "Lesson Objectives," "Procedures/Processes" #2, #3, and #4c, and the "Authentic Assessment" of the lesson plan (see Table 7.1)—all which intend to engage the teacher and students with this expanded, culturally responsive knowledge in ways that can encourage their critical thought.

Collaboration

As a result of working with Dr. Swartz, my prior thinking and the process I would usually follow in creating a lesson plan was continuously challenged. Just as I wanted to develop a lesson plan that included the generation of knowledge by students, I too went through a process of generating knowledge. I had someone giving me feedback when my lesson plan became too activity-centered or teacher-centered. I also learned that teaching does not have to be a solo endeavor. The benefit of working in collaboration is that one gets to apply critical thinking skills to the lesson planning process, because through dialogue with a mentor one has to articulate one's ideas. I could not arbitrarily include activities that did not promote critical thinking or that involved the teacher in telling students what or how to think. The various revisions undertaken with the feedback of a mentor made the lesson much more deliberate. Nothing was rushed, and the process of choosing objectives became much more thoughtful with each revision.

In terms of my research question (What does a lesson plan look like that uses culturally informed instructional materials and emancipatory pedagogy to encourage critical thinking?), I saw how the elements that Dr. Swartz asked me to use produced a lesson plan in which the questions for students were open-ended. These types of questions are more likely to encourage students to make their own conclusions and arrive at their own knowledge. See #2 and #3 under "Procedures/Processes" in my lesson plan in Table 7.1 for examples of open-ended questions. A lesson that asks such questions plans more time for students to think about what they want to say. The role of the teacher becomes one of a guide who challenges students' thinking and thereby promotes higher levels of thinking. Using a lesson plan that requires the specific emancipatory pedagogies that will be used also means that students are given more time to process information rather than pushing them to quickly memorize facts. The lesson plan also asks for the use of authentic assessments, which are student-centered. Rather than being assessed on retention of lesson content, students demonstrate what they know and teachers guide the process of helping them to synthesize the information and create their own knowledge.

Self-Reflection

What stands out the most in reflecting about the process of constructing a culturally informed lesson plan is how I began to rethink the role of teacher. Most lesson plans are built on the premise that the teacher knows and tells the students the information she or he has. This is not in line with an emancipatory approach in which students generate their own knowledge; with this approach it is understood that students are not coming into the classroom empty of knowledge. Thus, the teacher must use the background knowledge of the student as a starting point. This is especially important with ESOL students because their cultural background is typically not seen by teachers as a resource for constructing knowledge. Historically, their cultural and linguistic background has been seen as a barrier to learning in U.S. classrooms (Lessow-Hurley, 2009).

One unique element of the culturally informed lesson plan I used is the framing question. The framing question in my lesson plan is: "How is a community's definition of freedom related to the knowledge and experiences of people in that community?" This question made me reflect throughout the writing of the lesson on how best to guide students to higher levels of thinking and knowledge production. What I included in the lesson plan was designed to help them connect abstract concepts like "freedom" to how different people create their societies. Keeping this framing question in mind as I was writing the lesson helped me to think of ways to guide students toward increased understanding. For example, in #2 and #3 under "Procedures/Processes" in my lesson plan (see Table 7.1), students are asked to develop a class list of their ideas about what freedom means, and what it might be like living in a community that saw freedom in the way they defined it. As these questions can be answered many different ways, the teacher's role is to encourage students to articulate their own ideas about the reciprocal relationship between definitions of freedom and community experiences, using their own classroom community as a context. In this way, a critically self-reflective framing question helps to maintain a focus on students thinking critically to produce knowledge. Importantly, I realized that a lesson plan that engages students as a class in answering critical questions can create a communal and collaborative learning experience. It changes the traditional way that teachers relate to students (i.e., transmitting information to them); it also changes the way students relate to each other (i.e., competing for "right" answers).

The essential question of the lesson plan is: "Why do you think that sharing freedom causes people to act in ways that are caring and right?" This question does not have a predetermined answer. In thinking about a question for students to answer, I wanted a critical question that could not be found in the text or answered with a "yes" or "no." To answer the essential question, students need to go through a process of synthesizing the knowledge presented in the text. This question becomes the lesson's authentic assessment in which students collaboratively determine how best to answer it and thus allows students to demonstrate their ideas and to use language to express their thoughts. They negotiate meaning with the group and apply the vocabulary and other language features of the chapter in an authentic setting.

The use of four sets of standards was new to me and stimulated much self-reflection. As a pre-service ESOL teacher, we learn to incorporate both ESOL and New York State content standards into lesson plans. I chose ESOL Standards 1 and 3 about using English to understand information and to evaluate it, and New York State Social Studies Standard 1 about teaching the history of the United States and New York. Adding the *Rochester Teacher Center (RTC) Cultural Learning Standards* (RTC, 2007) and the *Criterion Standards for Contextualized Teaching and Learning about People of African Descent* (King & Goodwin, 2006) brought some additional dimensions to the standards I had been using. As I reflected on incorporating them into the lesson planning process, I began to see that while teachers in public schools are increasingly bound by state standards and the performance of students on standardized tests, meeting these demands can occur alongside multicultural and culturally informed content and standards. I selected *Criterion Standard* 2 to guide the teaching of this lesson plan:

- African Diasporan histories begin in Africa with human history, not with the period of enslavement (p. 2).

The idea in this standard is absent in current curricula and textbooks, suggesting that history for African American people began with enslavement. *Criterion Standard* 2 is met in my lesson because it is built around content in *Freedom and Democracy* (Swartz, 2012) that lays a foundation for a much longer history of African people in North America—one that is connected to what African people brought with them from their homelands. I also used the following *RTC Cultural Learning Standards* (RTC, 2007):

- Students can think and act for themselves—producing their own answers, solutions, and meanings in the form of quality work (p. 3).
- Students listen for meaning, communicate, and produce knowledge with others in the classroom (p. 4).

These two standards aligned with the goal of giving students the opportunity to construct their own knowledge and collaborate with other students during the learning process, which are both seen in the "Procedures/Processes" and "Authentic Assessment" sections of my lesson. My plan considered these two standards by connecting critical thinking to collaboration—by putting critical thinking in a collaborative context rather than in an individualistic context. This can be seen in #2, #3, #4a, b, and c, and #5 under "Procedures/Processes" and in the "Authentic Assessment" section of Table 7.1. I also used another RTC standard that challenges the systematic marginalization that standard instructional content creates:

• Students know about their origins, history, and culture and the history and culture of others (p. 2).

RTC Cultural Learning Standards (RTC, 2007) and *Criterion Standards* (King & Goodwin, 2006) stimulated self-reflection for me, which allowed me to focus the flow and activities of the lesson to give time for students to also reflect and think about the information. Taking time to chart students' ideas about what they think freedom means (#2 under "Processes/Procedures" in Table 7.1) allows them time for reflection. This is in contrast to other lesson plans I had written where the focus was on disseminating information to students, which caused the flow to have a faster pace, since the teacher had to "get out" all of her or his ideas in a short and often predetermined amount of time.

As you will see in the lesson plan, I used the following three emancipatory pedagogies to stimulate critical thinking on the part of students:

1. Question Driven Pedagogy—Students arrive at answers as opposed to being told answers. Teachers and students do this together by co-producing knowledge.
2. Inclusion, Representation, and Indigenous Voice—Students need to experience curriculum that includes and represents diverse cultures and groups, including the use of indigenous accounts, beliefs, and values.
3. Authentic Assessment—Students are evaluated based on demonstrations of their understanding through projects, portfolios, products, and exhibitions. Authentic assessments do not compare students to each other as do standardized tests and other numbers-based assessments.

These three pedagogies change the role of the teacher from a keeper of knowledge to a participant in knowledge creation. In particular, question-driven pedagogy encourages group interaction and guides the teacher to avoid telling students answers and instead encourages critical thought (see questions in "Procedures/Processes" #3 and #4c in Table 7.1). Furthermore, having a more inclusive approach to history can help students come to the understanding that different people have different ideas and that, much like in the lesson, the exchange of ideas in a group setting can create new knowledge.

As I was studying the process of lesson plan writing, I became more conscious of the need for rigorous content objectives and goals for students, standards that encourage self-reflection on the part of the teacher, and the need to encourage critical thinking in group contexts, and at the same time foster the development of language skills for ESOL students. I learned that various standards and emancipatory pedagogies can create a lesson plan that encourages the collaborative construction of knowledge by students and teacher; and that students' role in helping their peers develop thinking skills is just as important as their role in helping their peers develop English language skills. This study demonstrated to me personally that just because students have not developed high levels of English language proficiency it does not mean they are to be removed from challenging content and challenging lesson plans.

Conclusion

As a result of what I found in this study, I am thinking differently about writing lesson plans. Mainly, I am rethinking the role I will have as a teacher. As lesson planning is a central part of teaching, this speaks directly to my research question: What does a lesson plan look like that uses culturally informed instructional materials and emancipatory pedagogy to encourage critical thinking? I learned that basing a lesson plan around culturally informed student materials produces a culturally informed lesson plan and that the use of emancipatory pedagogies has the potential to change the role of teachers by "asking" them to interact differently, that is, more collaboratively with their students. Instead of professing the information and being the sole holder of knowledge, the role is one of a teacher as a guide. The lesson plan under study encourages a teacher to create an environment through questioning in which students construct their own knowledge through collaborative and communal interactions. In this way a lesson plan that uses culturally informed instructional materials and emancipatory pedagogy to encourage critical thinking can foster collaboration, as students are asked to work together to generate new knowledge and reach conclusions. This is in contrast to traditional classroom environments where students are individually responsible for their own learning and thereby an environment of competition is created. Using culturally informed instructional materials and emancipatory pedagogy to stimulate critical thinking can also change the goal of learning from one of getting a good grade or the highest grade to one where students are agents of understanding and developing life-long thinking skills. I learned that this requires a lesson plan built around challenging content. And I also learned that standards such as *RTC Cultural Learning Standards* (RTC, 2007) and *Criterion Standards* (King & Goodwin, 2006) stimulated my self-reflection, which resulted in designing a lesson plan that would give students the time to think and work together.

Culturally informed lesson plans align with the goals of ESOL education, which recognizes that language learners are often placed in low ability and special education classes because of their lack of English language proficiency, resulting in a high drop-out rate among these students. As seen in the lesson plan in Table 7.1, culturally informed lesson planning attempts to change the classroom dynamic between teachers and students that has traditionally alienated and marginalized ESOL students. Instead, lesson planning that depends on culturally informed content and emancipatory pedagogy to encourage critical thinking can challenge students and allow them to develop the collaborative skills that prepare them for engagement in the larger society. This engagement comes in the form of academically rigorous content that prepares students for higher education.

TABLE 7.1 Lesson Plan

Lesson Plan
Chapter 1: Freedom and Democracy: A Story Remembered
by Ericka López

Framing Question

How is a community's definition of freedom related to the knowledge and experiences of people in that community?

Essential Question

Why do you think that sharing freedom causes people to act in ways that are caring and right?

Lesson objectives

1) Students will know how African and Haudenosaunee Peoples define freedom.
2) Students will be able to express how sharing freedom causes people to act in caring and right ways.
3) Students can identify the homelands of African, Haudenosaunee, and European Peoples.
4) Students will be able to explain Haudenosaunee, African, and European experiences with freedom prior to these groups meeting in North America.
5) Language objective: Students will learn to use language that expresses abstract concepts (freedom, caring, belonging, etc.) with the help of sentence models.

Standards

New York State Standards

ESL Standard 1: Students will listen, speak, read, and write in English for information and understanding.

ESL Standard 3: Students will listen, speak, read, and write in English for critical analysis and evaluation.

Social Studies Standard 1: History of the United States and New York

Criterion Standard for Contextualized Teaching and Learning about People of African Descent

Criterion Standard 2: African Diasporan histories begin in Africa with human history, not with the period of enslavement.

Rochester Teacher Center (RTC) Cultural Learning Standards

RTC Cultural Learning Standard 5: (What students know)	Students know about their origins, history, and culture and the history and culture of others.
RTC Cultural Learning Standard 11: (What students are able to do)	Students can think and act for themselves— producing their own answers, solutions, and meanings in the form of quality work.
RTC Cultural Learning Standard 10: (What students are like)	Students listen for meaning, communicate, and produce knowledge with others in the classroom.

Student Materials

Chart paper
Magic Marker
Freedom and Democracy book
Dictionaries (at each table for students)

Emancipatory Pedagogies

1) Question Driven Pedagogy – Students arrive at answers as opposed to being told answers. Teachers and students do this together by co-producing knowledge.
2) Inclusion, Representation, and Indigenous Voice – Students need to experience curriculum that includes them as well as represents diverse cultures and groups, including the use of indigenous accounts, beliefs, and values.
3) Authentic Assessment – Students are evaluated based on demonstrations of their understanding, analysis, and synthesis of the content, skills, and concepts they are learning through projects, portfolios, products, and exhibitions. Authentic assessments do not compare students to each other through standardized tests and other numbers-based assessments.

Procedures/Processes

1) Conduct a mini-lesson that provides content to answer these questions: Who are Haudenosaunee people? Who are African people? Who are European people? Where are their homelands? Where did they come together?

   a) Explain the term "homelands." On a wall map show where are the homelands of the Haudenosaunee, Africans, and Europeans.
   b) Explain that a "homeland" is a group's native land. It is where they first lived.
   c) Then explain that the three groups came together in what is now the United States, but that this land was then solely the homeland of various Native American Nations.
   d) Then tell students that when these three groups came together each one had different experiences with freedom and that we are going to learn about what were those different experiences with freedom.

2) What is freedom? Ask students what they think "freedom" means. For example: "When you hear the word 'freedom,' what comes to mind? What do you think this

(*continued*)

TABLE 7.1 Continued

word means? Let's all give our ideas about what freedom means and I'll write them down. Write student responses on chart paper. Check to see if anyone wants to add anything to the final list.

As part of helping students to clarify their thinking about freedom, assist them in rephrasing their responses to be the "best" version of what they are trying to express.

3) Ask students questions about the list they produced. For example: "As we look at the chart of ideas we produced about freedom, what do you think it would be like living in a community that saw freedom in the way we do? What do you think people would be doing or acting like? What might people be like with each other?" Put students' responses on another piece of chart paper to be used in the next activity.

4) Whole class will read lesson 1 of *Freedom and Democracy* together.

   a) As an entire class we will read about and discuss content related to the three groups (Haudenosaunee, African, and European).

   b) Rather than breaking into small groups, I will model the process of answering the questions for the Haudenosaunee group. Because this is an ESOL classroom, it may be necessary to stay together as a whole class for all three groups depending on the English language proficiency of students.

   ★ English language learners might need sentence models to answer the questions. Examples are: "The Haudenosaunee knew that freedom was…." "African people thought freedom was…." "African and Haudenosaunee people acted ……. because they defined freedom as…." "European people did not know about ….." etc.

   c) As a class we will answer the following questions: 1) "What did this group know about freedom? 2) Based on what this group knew about freedom, what do you think people would be doing or acting like? 3) What might people be like with each other?" Responses will be written on a chart paper for each group.
   ★ If there are similarities between the class' ideas of freedom and the ideas of freedom for any one of the cultural groups, then it can be pointed out to the students.

5) Check for understanding and appropriate use of sentence models:

   a) While the students are answering the questions, each member of the class is responsible for the other members understanding the reading. They will help each other look up words in the dictionary if they do not know a word or there is a sentence that does not make sense. (This is one way to create a classroom community.)

Authentic Assessment

Synthesizing information: Students answer the lesson's essential question (which is also question #4 at the end of Lesson 1 in *Freedom and Democracy*: "Why do you think that sharing freedom causes people to act in ways that are caring and right?" This question will be answered as a class. Students will have time to edit and refine what they write and then present to the class. It will be the basis for a class discussion.

★ Learning experience approach: In ESL, students who are not yet writing proficient can still "write." Each group answers question #4. The teacher jots down what everyone says (each person contributes a sentence). At first the goal is production. Editing each other's sentences comes later.

References

Appleby, J., Hunt, L., & Jacob, M. (1994). *Telling the truth about history*. New York, NY: W.W. Norton & Company.

Asante, M. K. (2003). The Afrocentric idea. In A. Mazama (Ed.), *The Afrocentric paradigm* (pp. 37–53). Trenton, NJ: Africa World Press.

Asante, M. K. (2005). *Race, rhetoric, and identity: The architecton of soul*. Amherst, NY: Humanity Books.

Banks, J. A. (2001). Multicultural education: Goals, possibilities, and challenges. In C. F. Diaz (Ed.), *Multicultural education for the 21st century* (pp. 11–22). New York, NY: Longman.

Banks, J. A. (2004). Multicultural education: Historical development, dimension, and practice. In J. A. Banks & C. A. McGee Banks (Eds.), *Handbook of research on multicultural education* (2nd ed., pp. 3–29). San Francisco, CA: Jossey-Bass.

Boyd, C. D., Gay, G., Geiger, R., Kracht, J. B., Ooka Pang, V., Risinger, C. F., Sanchez, S. M. (2011a). *All together*. Boston, MA: Pearson.

Boyd, C. D., Gay, G., Geiger, R., Kracht, J. B., Ooka Pang, V., Risinger, C. F., Sanchez, S. M. (2011b). *Regions*. Boston, MA: Pearson.

Collier, V., & Thomas, W. (2002). *A national study of school effectiveness for language minority students' long-term academic achievement*. Center for research on education, diversity, and excellence. Retrieved from: http://www.eric.ed.gov/ERICWebPortal/search/detailmini.jsp?_nfpb=true&_&ERICExtSearch_SearchValue_0=ED475048&ERICExtSearch_SearchType_0=no&accno=ED475048

Cummins, J. (1994). Knowledge, power, and identity in teaching English as a second language. In Genesee, F. (Ed.), *Educating second language children: The whole child, the whole curriculum, the whole community* (pp. 33–58). Cambridge, England: Cambridge University Press.

Díaz-Rico, L. (2007). *Strategies for teaching English language learners*. New York, NY: Allyn & Bacon.

Epstein, T. (2009). *Interpreting national history: Race, identity, and pedagogy in classrooms and communities*. New York, NY: Routledge.

Goodwin, S. (2004). Emancipatory pedagogy. In S. Goodwin & E. E. Swartz (Eds.), *Teaching children of color: Seven constructs of effective teaching in urban schools* (pp. 37–48). Rochester, NY: RTA Press.

Goodwin, S., & Swartz, E. E. (2009). *Document-based learning: Curriculum and assessment*. Rochester, NY: RTA Press.

Grande, S. (2004). *Red pedagogy: Native American social and political thought*. Lanham, MD: Rowman & Littlefield.

Grant, C. A., & Sleeter, C. E. (2007). *Doing multicultural education for achievement and equity*. New York, NY: Taylor & Francis Group, Routledge.

Grinde Jr., D. A., & Johansen, B. E. (1991). *Exemplar of liberty: Native America and the evolution of democracy*. Los Angeles: American Indian Studies Center, University of California, Los Angeles.

King, J. E., & Goodwin, S. (2006). *Criterion standards for contextualized teaching and learning about people of African descent*. Rochester, NY: Author.

Lessow-Hurley, J. (2009). *The foundations of dual language instruction* (5th ed.). New York, NY: Pearson.

Lyons, O., & Mohawk, J. (Eds.) (1992). *Exiled in the land of the free: Democracy, Indian nations, and the U.S. Constitution*. Santa Fe, NM: Clear Light Publishers.

Nieto, S., & Bode, P. (2010). Multicultural education in a sociopolitical context. In Nieto, S. (Ed.), *Language, culture, and teaching: critical perspectives* (pp. 38–65). New York, NY: Routledge.

RTC (Rochester Teacher Center) (2007). *Cultural learning standards: What students are expected to know, be able to do, and be like.* Rochester, NY: Author.

Swartz, E. E. (1996). Emancipatory pedagogy: A postcritical response to "standard" school knowledge. *Journal of Curriculum Studies, 28*(4), 397–418.

Swartz, E. E. (2009). Diversity: Gatekeeping knowledge and maintaining inequalities. *Review of Educational Research, 79*(2), 1044–1083.

Swartz, E. E. (2011). *Remembering our ancestors.* Rochester, NY: Rochester City School District.

Swartz, E. E. (2013). *Freedom and democracy: A story remembered.* Rochester, NY: Omni-centric Press.

Swartz, E. E., & Bakari, R. (2005). Development of the teaching in urban schools scale. *Teaching and Teacher Education, 21*(7), 829–841.

8

RECOVERING HISTORY AND THE "PARENT PIECE" FOR CULTURAL WELL-BEING AND BELONGING

Joyce E. King, Adrienne C. Goss, and Sherell A. McArthur

Joyce E. King conducted this case study in collaboration with two doctoral students. In the following excerpt, she sets their research apprenticeship in an historical context:

> I mention scholarship on "demonic grounds" at the end of this chapter. This term refers to historical spaces where people of African ancestry have been dehumanized—where our humanity has been erased. When I think of how the Dixie Hills [Atlanta, Georgia] neighborhood looks [where this case study took place]—certainly not the people who live there and their struggles for respect and to raise their children with dignity—but the blight, the abandoned homes and buildings that are literally falling down all around the school, then I think of "demonic grounds" where our heritage is not visible, especially to us.
>
> Only by digging deep beyond appearances were we able to discover the community's proud history. As we got to know students in the neighborhood from three-generation families, we gained insight from elders into what had happened to produce such devastation all around, and what Dixie Hills used to be like. It was a thriving Black community that exhibited cultural excellence as reflected in all that is left visibly—the streets named after Black colleges like Spelman and Morehouse and famous people like Joe Louis, George Washington Carver, and Tiger Flowers. It wasn't long before we realized that students didn't know about this local history or its connection to African history and culture. Even though the school walls were covered with Black History Month projects, there was nothing visible about our African heritage. The Songhoy Club was an anomaly, and apparently some teachers and parents did not welcome our emphasis on Africa. Dehumanization and subjugation leave wounds.

My doctoral students learned that Afrocentric curriculum and pedagogy can heal these wounds, and they learned to fully expect that parents and teachers can partner to elevate students' learning and identity development—even when there were efforts to make us invisible. For example, our Songhoy Club students learned to sing a song in Songhoy-senni—"Come, Let's Go to School" (*Wa K'ir Ma Koy Caw*) in preparation for performing at the holiday "extravaganza." While students did sing the song and were so proud of themselves, someone decided to leave the Songhoy Club's performance off the program. Then, at the next PTA meeting, when parents were choosing afterschool clubs for the next semester, the Songhoy Club was replaced by an International Club, with the image of a globe in place of a map of Africa that was part of our logo. That's when all these "erasures" started to make sense, including why the booklet a teacher gave me about Tiger Flowers was wrapped in brown paper—like contraband.

Fortunately, we had already proven our mettle to parents. One of the parents came over to where I was sitting with our Songhoy Club display—colorful artifacts and student work. She asked me why the Songhoy Club was not listed on the afterschool brochure. I assured her that I didn't know. She was concerned because she had come out to make sure her younger child would get into the Songhoy Club. I asked her if she would speak for us when the clubs were announced. She said she just wasn't sure she could do that—stand up and talk in front of an auditorium full of people. To my surprise, she did just that and she gave an eloquent testimony explaining why children need to know about their African heritage. Bingo!! We were back in business!

Introduction

This chapter documents and describes the Afrocentric curriculum and pedagogy a teacher educator (Joyce E. King) modeled in a collaborative study group in which doctoral students (Adrienne C. Goss and Sherell A. McArthur) prepared to teach and recursively analyzed—with parent input—the Afrocentric curriculum and pedagogy they implemented in an afterschool culture and heritage program for Black middle school students. Thus, the case study we present here is a collaborative practitioner investigation of Afrocentric curriculum and teaching practice in three embedded "research-as-pedagogy" contexts: (a) a pedagogical *Study Group* in which doctoral students as practitioner researchers prepare to teach and recursively examine their curriculum and pedagogy teaching middle school students, (b) the *Songhoy Club* (an afterschool program), and (c) a series of *Parent Workshops* where the researchers invited parents to participate in critical collaborative discussions about the Afrocentric curriculum and pedagogy used in the Songhoy Club. (Songhai, Songhay, Sonrai, Soŋay are other spelling variations.) Research-as-pedagogy is an inquiry practice in which data gathering takes place within a teaching context.

This study examines: What happens when a teacher educator models the use of Afrocentric curriculum and pedagogy to support doctoral students teaching middle school students? This study also asks: What happens when parents are engaged with practitioner researchers in reviewing and discussing Afrocentric curriculum and pedagogy that their middle school children experienced?

Each research-as-pedagogy context was a space for iterative inquiry, with each generatively linking to the next one that was implemented, and each doubling as a site for both teaching practice and practitioner inquiry. The Study Group doubled as a learning experience for doctoral students studying Afrocentric curriculum and pedagogy guided by a teacher educator, and as a space for collaborative reflection with this teacher educator on Afrocentric teaching practice. The Songhoy Club, the second research-as-pedagogy context, was a pedagogical lab that doubled as a practice space for the doctoral students to teach middle schools students and a research apprenticeship for these doctoral students/practitioner researchers to study their own practice. The Parent Workshops, the third research-as-pedagogy teaching context, doubled as a space for the teacher educator to observe her doctoral students (the Songhoy Club teachers) demonstrate lessons that engaged parents in reciprocal learning and a space for the parents to examine and co-reflect on the curriculum and pedagogy their children experienced in the Songhoy Club. The collaborative practitioner inquiry that resulted is a co-constructed analysis of the impact of Afrocentric curriculum and pedagogy on doctoral students, including input from parents whose children were taught this curriculum.

This case study can be described as an "inquiry on inquiry" *within* a broader collaborative practitioner inquiry. Teacher education researchers, Cochran-Smith, Barnatt, Friedman, and Pine (2009) describe their research on student teacher learning as a double-layered inquiry on inquiry that involved holding themselves to the same expectations for learning from reflection and analysis of data (on their own practice) that they held for the students whom they taught to use practitioner inquiry. In our case study's triple-layered "inquiry on inquiry" within inquiry, practitioner researchers' and parents' collaborative investigation of the Afrocentric curriculum and pedagogy used in the Songhoy Club takes place as part of the larger inquiry examining how doctoral students in the Study Group prepared to teach using Afrocentric curriculum and pedagogy.

Background

There is a growing consensus that all students in general and African American students in particular are being taught a Eurocentric history in the United States (Epstein, 2008; Grande, 2004; King, 2011; Swartz, 2009). As King and Goodwin (2006) have observed:

> The continuing omission and misrepresentation of the experiences, histories, and realities of African American students and other people of color from the curriculum—including recent immigrants of color—has resulted in the massive alienation and disengagement of these same students from school and schooling.
>
> *(p. 1)*

Black doctoral students, many of whom are education professionals, also experience alienating omission and misrepresentation, often in the form of extensive exposure to cultural deficit theorizing; and they are rarely exposed to the growing body of research that demonstrates positive impacts of Black students' racial identification on their engagement, academic learning, and general school success (Carter, 2008; Harper, 2007; King, Akua, & Russell, 2014; Wakefield & Hudley, 2007). Nor does doctoral student training typically include consideration of the conceptualization of school success for African Americans as both academic and cultural excellence (NABSE, 1984).

According to Asante (1991), "The fact that an African-American or an Hispanic person—in order to master the white cultural information—has had to experience the death of his or her own culture does not register with most teachers" (p. 29). Further, Asante has made a connection between the content of the curriculum and what teachers can do about student "dislocation" and alienation: "By 'centering' their students of color, teachers can reduce feelings of dislocation engendered by our society's predominantly 'white self-esteem curricula'" (p. 28). Several implications for research on teacher learning follow from Asante's observation. First, this observation points to cultural knowledge that teachers need in order to center Black students' learning in their African cultural heritage. Second, many teachers do not realize and even reject the possibilities of Afrocentric education. This rejection has been fueled by ideological assimilationist propaganda that disparages African American group belonging and identification with Africa masquerading as scholarly discourse (Ginwright, 2000; Merry & New, 2008; Ravitch, 2010). Afrocentric education has been called separatist, segregationist, divisive, romantic, irrational, dogmatic, ethnocentric, and even a "taboo" topic for research (Shockley, 2009). Doctoral students are even advised that Afrocentric education is not a credible topic worthy of study.

Meanwhile, researchers using narrative inquiry and practitioner self-study (Clandinin & Connelly, 2000; Samara & Freese, 2006) are producing a rich body of empirical knowledge about teacher learning more generally, but have not taken up the problem of teachers' knowledge (or lack of knowledge) and practice within the Afrocentric theoretical perspective that Asante has articulated (Asante, 2007, 1980/1988). Nor have such forms of inquiry investigated how collaborating with parents might support curriculum and pedagogy along these lines. This is so in spite of the fact that in the decades since Asante's call for theoretical and pedagogical re-direction, converging empirical evidence across a number of disciplines shows positive impacts of *parental* racial socialization on Black students' learning. Research by Wang and Huguley (2012), for example, shows that parents' use of racial socialization (e.g., "talking to their children or engaging in activities that promote feelings of racial knowledge, pride, and connection") offsets potentially negative impacts of racism on students' academic development (*African Globe*, 2013). However, research on parents' roles in their children's education is typically limited to family literacy activities and parents as "teachers in the home" supervising homework without attention to the importance of parents' worldview (Hill, 2010; Lawson, 2003; Williams & Baber, 2007).

There is a dearth of research on teacher and parent collaboration focused on students' cultural well-being and belonging, that is to say, on cultural excellence, let alone how such engagement can serve as a context for teacher learning (Edwards, 2008). In her study of culturally relevant pedagogy, Ladson-Billings (1994) sought the help of parents to identify excellent teachers. A parent illustrated the contribution parents can make by articulating a comprehensive understanding of cultural excellence for African American children. This parent advised Ladson-Billings that an excellent teacher can teach my child "to hold his own in the classroom without forgetting his own in the community" (Ladson-Billings, 1994, p. 147). Unfortunately, culturally informed practices that can produce what this parent has advised have been outpaced by top-down market-oriented school privatization "reforms" and Eurocentric "core" curricula and accountability regimes. These approaches give primacy to student and teacher testing and leave no room for meaningful parent involvement.

Parental Involvement Approaches

With regard to African American communities, parental involvement approaches are woefully limited (Doucet, 2008; Gutman & McLoyd, 2000; Jackson & Remillard, 2005; Lawson, 2003). In U.S. public schools, parental involvement tends to carry an image of bake sales, Parent-Teacher Association (PTA) meetings, and chaperoning field trips (Robinson, 1997; Warren, Hong, Rubin, & Uy, 2009). Fundraising and other extracurricular activities do little to involve parents in the academic lives of their children. As Mattingly, Prislin, McKenzie, Rodriguez, and Kayzar (2002) observe, most parent involvement programs were developed with a top-down approach that did not include parent input. As a result, the predominant but narrow conception of parental involvement ignores the value that a child's family community can contribute to his or her education and socialization for academic and cultural excellence (Hill & Taylor, 2004; Jackson, Martin, & Stocklinski, 2004; Sanders, Allen-Jones, & Abel, 2002). Also, in addition to their deficit views of parents, educators' perceptions of race, culture, and language can inhibit parental engagement as well as recognition of its potential academic benefits (Barton, Drake, Perez, St. Louis, & George, 2004; Cooper, 2009).

A broader conception of learning or academic success that includes viewing parents as "intellectual resources" for their children (Jackson & Remillard,
2005) and the value of community assets recognizes that teachers, administrators, and students are not the only ones who need to be engaged with learning
in school spaces (King, 2008). When parents learn to "activate other forms
of capital, such as [the] ability to question the school system" (Barton et al.,
2004, p. 7), in addition to more traditional ways of participating, parents can
be engaged in new spaces, including curriculum, standards, and governance. In
"funds of knowledge" research, for example, teachers collaborate with families
to produce curricula using family knowledge and skills that are "… essential
for household or individual functioning and well-being" (Olmedo, 1997, p.
14). This research illustrates a shift toward the belief that communities can offer
something of value to children's learning (Marshall & Toohey, 2010; Moll,
Amanti, Neff, & Gonzalez, 1992). This shift broadens the definition of parent
involvement, viewing parents' knowledge, worldview perspectives, and ways
of being as having value.

Culturally Authentic Assessment for Academic and Cultural Excellence

When teachers place the community at the center of their work, they can more
effectively meet the academic and cultural needs of students (Blank, Johnson,
& Shah, 2003; Murrell, 1997, 2001). However, there is very little research on
teacher learning along these lines. Parents have knowledge about their children
as members of a community-family, and they have a right to expect that their
children's academic success will not be achieved at the cost of forgetting about
their community (e.g., cultural alienation). This knowledge and these expectations can be incorporated by teachers in the form of culturally authentic assessment criteria collaboratively produced with parents. This collaboration in the
identification of learning and socialization expectations for academic and cultural excellence is then a broader basis (than high stakes test scores) for assessing
student work (King, 2008; Robinson, 1997). Parents bring understanding of
their children's needs as members of their community. This focus on group
belonging contrasts with the dominant society's individualistic conception of
education. Teachers' professional education does not typically sensitize them to
this difference in worldview perspective, while their content knowledge is likewise limited by the omissions and misrepresentations that often exist in school
knowledge (Hill, 2010; King, 1992).

Black Studies scholarship has recognized that if parents have the opportunity to critically examine what is being taught in schools and to share their
perspectives and understanding of their lived experience, they will more likely
be able to advocate for knowledge and practices that accord with their values,
expectations, and epistemology (King, 1992, 2005, 2008; King & Mitchell,

1995; Reay & Mirza, 1997). Woods (1998) has identified specific examples of Black working-class thought and theorizing in the blues (as epistemology), for example, that illustrate this critical capacity. While several teacher preparation models have community partnerships that include parental involvement (Hyland & Meacham, 2004; Murrell, 2001), parents and teachers are not involved in co-constructing mutually agreed upon expectations regarding educational purposes from within the African worldview perspective discussed in the next section.

African Worldview: Recovering Heritage Knowledge and Culture

The National Black Education Agenda (NBEA) has stated that the uniqueness of Black people's historical experience "has left us without a heritage language and a sense of home and renders our children and families culturally and emotionally debilitated, threatening the future of our communities" (NBEA, 2012). There has been little research in the use of African American home language or African heritage languages as resources for students' well-being and belonging (Kynard, 2013; Paris, 2009). At the same time, and as stated above, there is evidence that educational experiences that promote a strong racial-ethnic identity among African American youth encourage academic success and cultural excellence (Chavous et al., 2003; Boutté, Kelly-Jackson, & Johnson, 2010; Bowman & Howard, 1985; Graham & Anderson, 2008; Lee, 2007; Oyserman, Harrison, & Bybee, 2001; Spencer, Noll, Stoltzfris, & Harpalani, 2001; Whaley & Noël, 2012). In the curriculum, pedagogy, collaborative practices, and data collection methods used in this case study, the Seven Cardinal Virtues of *Ma'at* and the *Nguzo Saba* (Seven Principles of Kwanzaa)—which embody the African worldview in classical African and Diaspora contexts, respectively—represent that (missing) "sense of home." Songhoy cosmology, language, and cultural concepts also embody an African worldview and are used in this study. Thus, the teacher educator's practice incorporated heritage knowledge and pedagogical practices that used African philosophical principles and virtues, African (Songhoy) language study, African naming, and Afrocentric scholarship designed to support the cultural well-being and belonging of both the doctoral students teaching in the Songhoy Club and the middle school students they taught. (See the Preface for descriptions of both "heritage knowledge" and "cultural knowledge.)

Kwanzaa Principles: "Education for Beautiful Ways of Being and Acting"

Karenga (1996) formulated the *Nguzo Saba* (Kwanzaa Principles) upon which people of African ancestry can "build and sustain an Afrocentric family, community and culture" (p. 543). The Seven Principles of the *Nguzo Saba* are *Umoja* (unity), *Kujichagulia* (self-determination), *Ujima* (collective work and responsibility), *Ujamaa* (cooperative economics), *Nia* (purpose), *Kuumba* (creativity), and *Imani* (faith). These principles provide a framework for the cultural unity that communitarian African societies share in common. Karenga posits that adherence to these ideals will serve several basic functions, including the "recovery and reconstruction of lost historical memory and cultural legacy in the development of an Afrocentric paradigm of life and achievement" (pp. 543–544). The Songhoy Club used a Rochester Teacher Center poster entitled "Education for Beautiful Ways of Being and Acting" to guide instruction and expectations for student learning and behavior (RTC, 2009). This poster adapts the Kwanzaa Principles to "articulate the elements of character needed to live within and by these Principles." These principles were modeled in the Study Group; they guided teaching and expectations for student behavior in the Songhoy Club and our reflections on teaching practice.

Ma'at: *An Epistemology for Afrocentric Research and Praxis*

Shockley (2009) and King and Mitchell (1995) note that collaboratively seeking community input in research is consistent with Afrocentric values and ways of knowing. King and Mitchell identified the values of reciprocity and mutuality in the Afrocentric research methodology used in their participatory study of Black mothers' education and socialization practices. Swain (2011) demonstrates how the Virtues of Ma'at (Reciprocity, Balance, Harmony, etc.) can inform data collection methods. For example, guided by the Virtues of Reciprocity and Balance, researchers view data collection as a mutual exchange of information that benefits the "subjects" of research as much as the researchers, rather than a one-way withdrawal of data. Another value that shapes culturally informed praxis in the African tradition is that students learn in order to serve the community and learning is for community-building. Thus, knowledge in the research-as-pedagogy contexts in this inquiry was produced for and about the Black community.

Pedagogy and Standards for Heritage Knowledge

King and Goodwin's (2006) *Criterion Standards for Contextualized Teaching and Learning about People of African Descent* support curriculum development as well as teaching values-based, standards-aligned lessons that link learning to heritage knowledge (King, 2006). Pedagogy that is guided by these *Criterion Standards,* which are informed by Afrocentric scholarship, centers African American children in their education by locating people of African ancestry on the "map of human geography." John Henrik Clarke, one of the "Founding Fathers" of Africana Studies, put it this way:

> History is not everything, but it is a starting point. History is a clock that people use to tell their political and cultural time of day. It is a compass they use to find themselves on the map of human geography. It tells them where they are, but more importantly, what they must be.
>
> *(Acree, n.d.)*

These 19 standards, which can inform the cultural knowledge teachers need, clarify how crucial it is for us to know that "African humanity and civilization are anterior in the recorded history of world" (Standard 1, p. 2) and that "African diasporan histories begin in Africa with human history, not with the period of enslavement" (Standard 2, p. 2). These standards reflect not only a more comprehensive account of the past, but also the value system of people of African ancestry that schools and teacher preparation programs in the U.S. typically fail to acknowledge, but which remains part of African American culture as heritage knowledge. The Afrocentric concepts that inform this value system (see Table 2.3 in chapter 2)—framed here as standards—represent cultural knowledge of students' community and heritage that teachers can know about and use.

Methodology

Our overarching methodology is co/auto ethnography, which is a form of collaborative practitioner inquiry into cultural phenomena—a narrative approach to raising the critical consciousness of self and others (Patton, 2002). Coia and Taylor (2006) describe co/auto ethnography as a participatory and contextualized process of sharing narratives, collaboratively conducting cultural analyses, and exchanging new levels of self-awareness. This overarching method involves the outward and inward looking of the researcher(s) and participants who are both subjects of the research, and whose views of cultural phenomena are embedded in the narratives they produce (Chang, Ngunjiri, & Hernandez, 2013; Dyson, 2007; Fournillier, 2009).

As seen in Table 8.1, there are five practice-based methods or data sources—participant observations, self-reflection, written responses to interview questions, group conversations, and review of documents and artifacts used to collect data in four data-collection sites (Study Group, Research Team Meetings, Songhoy Club, and Parent Workshops). By blending these more traditional qualitative methods with co/auto ethnography, using the narratives of all participants—including those of the researchers—we expand our data-gathering options in the interests of revealing "what happened" in this collaborative investigation of preparing doctoral students using Afrocentric curriculum and pedagogy.

The first method or data source, *participant observation,* refers to the teacher educator and doctoral students/practitioner researchers making, recording, and sharing observations in all four of the data-collection sites. These data were recorded in field notes and e-mails in order to collect "here-and-now"

TABLE 8.1 Methods/Data Sources and Data-Collection Sites

Data Collection Sites	Methods/Data Sources			
	Study Group	Research Team Meetings	Songhoy Club	Parent Workshops
Participant Observation (teacher educator, doctoral students)	x	x	x	x
Self-Reflection (teacher educator, doctoral students)	x	x	x	x
Written Responses to Questions (doctoral students, teacher educator)		x		
Group Conversations (doctoral students, teacher educator, parents)			x	
Review of Documents and Artifacts (teacher educator, doctoral students, parents)	x	x	x	x

experiences in which observers attempt to understand cultural phenomena as those being observed do, but in this case with a reflexive, inter-subjective focus on gathering data that narratively elicits and connects the voices of research-ers and participants (Dyson, 2007; Kemmis & McTaggart, 2000; Lincoln & Guba, 1985). The second method or data source, *self-reflection,* involves taking a thoughtful, deliberate, and questioning look at what is going on in the contexts of a research project in order to produce knowledge that includes findings and what they mean (Swartz, 2004). The teacher educator and doctoral students recorded and shared self-reflections and observations in field notes, memos, and e-mails. The third method or data source consists of *written responses to inter-view questions* produced by the doctoral students/practitioner researchers after attending Research Team Meetings. They responded in writing to questions posed to them by the teacher educator and shared those in e-mails and drafts of this chapter. The fourth method or data source, *group conversations,* refers to oral exchanges and discussions between and among doctoral students/practitioner researchers, the teacher educator, and parents (King & Mitchell, 1995). These data were collected through transcripts of video- and audio-recordings of con-versations during the Parent Workshops. The fifth and final method, *review of documents and artifacts,* was a way for the teacher educator, doctoral students, and parents to examine various teaching resources, including student texts, vid-eos, lesson plans, and other print materials and websites related to African his-tory and culture and lived experience. Data from the participants in the Study Group, Research Team Meetings, Songhoy Club, and Parent Workshops were recorded and shared through e-mails, notes, descriptions of assignments, les-son plans, and transcripts of oral discussions. The gathering of all five data sets involved collaboration and the formal and informal exchange of ideas among the study's participants.

Analysis of the five data sets proceeded recursively by going back-and-forth among them to prepare visual representations of the data, discuss and analyze the data, and to produce and share drafts in Research Team Meetings that identified themes and explored emerging findings. The presentation of findings and the interpretation of what they mean were co-constructed in stages, as portions of the chapter were collaboratively written and revised.

Participants

The participants in this case study include the teacher educator, two Study Group participants (doctoral students/practitioner researchers) and two Songhoy Club parents. The two doctoral students/practitioner researchers, Adrienne C. Goss and Sherell A. McArthur, collaboratively participated in this study organized and led by Joyce E. King, the teacher educator. Ms. McArthur was a third-year doctoral student and elementary school teacher. Ms. Goss, a high school math teacher, was also a third-year doctoral student at the time this study was conducted. Neither had yet identified a doctoral research topic.

The two mothers who participated in the Parent Workshops were actively involved Songhoy Club parents. Both had two children in the program and, on many occasions during the first year, observed and participated in lessons when they came to pick up their children. Ms. Ruby Jackson (a pseudonym) is a parent of four, two of whom, a girl and a boy, participated in the Songhoy Club afterschool program in the charter school where it was located. Ms. Jackson is originally from a community near the school. She chose the charter school because she believed that other Atlanta public schools, where her children had previously attended had failed her son. Changing her children's school was convenient given where they lived, and she believed the reputation of the school made it worth a try.

Ms. Veralynn Williams (also a pseudonym) is a mother of three children, all of whom attended the charter school in which the study was conducted. During the study, only her eldest child was still attending the school and the Songhoy Club. Ms. Williams is originally from Montgomery, Alabama, and she relocated to Georgia over 15 years ago to attend college. She enrolled her children in the charter school because she was pleased that the school leadership, including the principal, was all Black, which she thought would be good for her son.

Research-as-Pedagogy Contexts

There were three research-as-pedagogy contexts: A Study Group, the Songhoy Club, and Parent Workshops. As stated above, research-as-pedagogy is an iterative inquiry practice in which both teaching and data gathering take place. The three research-as-pedagogy teaching contexts generatively link to each other, with each being a space for teaching and practitioner inquiry. Consistent with an Afrocentric culturally informed praxis, the knowledge produced in these contexts is intended to serve the Black community.

Study Group meetings took place at the University and a K-8 public charter school on Tiger Flowers Drive in Dixie Hills, a Black neighborhood in Southwest Atlanta. The Songhoy Club and the Parent Workshops were held at the school site.

The Study Group

The curriculum used in the Study Group was also used in the Songhoy Club. The Afrocentric theoretical concepts discussed in chapter 2 shaped the Study Group's work: Collective Consciousness, Collective Responsibility, Centrality/Location, Self-Determination, Subjects with Agency, Reclamation of Cultural Heritage, and Anteriority of Classical African Civilizations (see Table 2.3 in chapter 2 for descriptions of these concepts). Collaborative preparation for Songhoy Club teachers/practitioner researchers in the Study Group included ongoing reflection on pedagogy and lesson planning using recovered historical/cultural content, which refers to content that is typically missing or distorted in school knowledge. The framework we used to select lesson content and design various learning activities—often with a community service/capacity-building focus—was called "From the Nile to the Niger to the Neighborhood." This moniker represents the same journey or trajectory that doctoral students were encouraged to consciously experience and exemplify in the lessons they designed using recovered content. Our discussions focused on how to construct lessons that could engage middle school students in learning about their community in relation to their heritage, culture, and identity in this way. Study Group topics, such as those listed below, were explored based on doctoral students' interests, teaching expertise, and Songhoy Club lesson assignments:

1. Sacred Science and Philosophy in Ancient Kemet;
2. African People's East to West Migration;
3. Songhoy Civilization, including the ancient universities of Timbuktu, Gao and Djenné; Songhoy Emperors Sunni Ali Ber (1464–1492) and Askya Mohammed (1493–1538); Abdul Rahman Ibn Sori (1762–1829), *Prince Among Slaves* (PBS, 2006);
4. African/African American literacy continuities, from Songhoy folktales to African American folktales, the African American toast tradition to Hip hop (Jackson, 1974; Maiga, 2010);
5. Origins of the Civil Rights Movement in Atlanta: The Washer Woman's Strike (Myrick-Harris, 2008); Eyewitness accounts of the 1906 Atlanta Race Riot (White, 1995);

6. The history of Dixie Hills and "Sweet Auburn" Avenue in Atlanta (interviews with community elders and community historians); The Hayti Project (which is recovering the history of the Hayti community) in Durham, North Carolina (interviews with community historians and residents) (Allen, 2006); and

7. Black women's historical mistreatment, portrayal in the media (e.g., films, rap videos, and Hip hop music), and depiction in school knowledge (e.g., fiction student text on enslavement) (Goodwin, 2008).

Two pedagogical strategies were modeled as part of the Study Group: question-driven pedagogy and problem-based lesson planning.

Question-Driven Pedagogy

Question-driven pedagogy is an emancipatory pedagogy that engages teachers and students in the co-construction of knowledge in response to problem-posing questions (Goodwin, 2004). Question-driven pedagogy was used in both the Study Group and the Songhoy Club. The following Study Group questions were re-visited throughout the year:

> In *Balancing Written History with Oral Tradition: The Legacy of the Songhoy People*, Dr. Hassimi Maiga (2010) traces the origins of West Africans in migration patterns from East Africa (Nubia and Kemet) westward. In *The Journey of the Songhai People*, Dr. Edward Robinson (Robinson & Robinson, 1992) posits that African Americans are heirs of the classical West African civilization built by the Songhoy (Songhai) people. How would you go about teaching middle school students in order to foster their positive identification with their African cultural heritage? And how would you engage students with this content in order to foster their cultural well-being and sense of belonging as people of African ancestry?

The Study Group curriculum content, which was also taught in the Songhoy Club, began with the origins of humanity in Africa and proceeded from East Africa (Kemet) to West African civilizations (specifically the Songhoy Empire) to the journey of the Songhoy people into the Americas. This recovered historical and cultural content included African language (Songhoy-senni), philosophy, and cosmology. The students had the opportunity to meet Dr. Hassimi Maiga, education researcher and Paramount Chief of Songhoy, and in addition to his Songhoy language textbook (Maiga, 1996/2003), we also used his family story as primary source documentation (e.g., his family genealogy as far back as emperors Sunni Ali Ber and Askya Mohammed). This content contextualized teaching about African people's culture and heritage in Africa, the Diaspora, and the southwest Atlanta neighborhood where students went to school (King & Goodwin, 2006).

Problem-Based Lessons

Developing and collaboratively reflecting on Songhoy Club lessons that focused on recovered historical and cultural content and identity reclamation (for the doctoral students and middle school students alike) was the primary teaching "problem" that guided the Study Group process. Thus, considering how to teach content to re-orient students toward identifying positively with their African heritage (including the neighborhood) and toward "community-mindedness" (King, 2005; Tedla, 1995) was the primary problem-based focus for the Study Group. Online Songhoy-senni (language) and culture lessons served this purpose. An animated Songhoy-senni lesson illustrates positive meanings of "blackness" in this language using proverbs and concepts such as *wayne bibi*—black sun, *hari bibi*—black water, and *labu bibi*—black earth (Maiga, King, & RaShon, 1999a). For example, *wayne bibi* refers to the black sun when it reaches its most brilliant stage in the noonday sky; *hari bibi* or black water refers to the deepest place in the middle of the Niger river where the purest water can be found.

An online math lesson (counting) was introduced in the Study Group using a Songhoy-senni lesson that included a video of a traditional Songhoy wedding event (Maiga, King, & RaShon, 1999b). The video showcases the bride's gifts and her generosity sharing the gifts with her sisters-in-laws. When every tenth gift is held aloft and counted out loud, the guests cheer because the bride will give a tenth of her gifts to her husband's sisters. This "counting lesson" teaches African family values of reciprocity, generosity, and mutuality.

Another lesson that illuminates the recovered historical and cultural content in our curriculum framework, "From the Nile to the Niger to the Neighborhood," made explicit connections between Songhoy folktales and the African American oral tradition, and from folktales to long oral poems and "toasts" like the "Signifying Monkey" (Jackson, 1974) to the poetry of rap and hip-hop lyrics. These lessons provided access to deep knowledge and cultural continuity within the indigenous worldview of African people—from the continent to the Diaspora—and expanded our pedagogical focus on African American students' language rights within a larger understanding of their linguistic cultural heritage that is typically missing from the school curriculum (Asante, 2010; Kynard, 2013; Smitherman, 1999).

The Study Group curriculum also included "re-membered" history drawn from document-based instructional materials the Rochester Teacher Center produced about Austin Steward, the first Black businessman in Rochester, New York (Goodwin & Swartz, 2009). This student text was used in the Study Group to demonstrate an important Afrocentric theoretical concept called "Centrality/Location." We enacted this concept by using recovered historical and cultural content to locate/identify values Black people have lived by. This "re-membered" content about Austin Steward was used to model and inspire other place-based lessons focused on: Atlanta's historic Black economic hub, "Sweet Auburn" Avenue, historic "Hayti" in Durham, North Carolina, which is another example of Black business success, and Tiger Flowers—a local early 20th century Black hero who used his business acumen and personal wealth for Black community building in Atlanta and in the Dixie Hills community where the charter school was located. None of this curricular content is taught in schools in the community. Recovering this knowledge for doctoral students and middle school students was especially important given the extreme opposite economic conditions they now experience in their school community. In addition to using historical documents and artifacts (websites, maps, photos, etc.) to prepare lessons, doctoral students also interviewed community elders and community-based academic researchers about the history of local communities and history makers, such as Tiger Flowers and others.

The Songhoy Club

The Songhoy Club was the second research-as-pedagogy context for presenting lessons about the topics listed in the section above. Doctoral students/practitioner researchers taught these lessons about African and Diasporan history, heritage knowledge, and African language, which provided interdisciplinary academic instruction for African American middle school students in our after-school program. The district in which the Songhoy Club's host charter school was located expected charter schools in the district to serve as laboratories for meaningful learning in order to model improved education for "regular" schools. To that end, Songhoy Club students were introduced to the idea that their learning in the club was purposeful. For example, they would help club teachers develop learning materials that other teachers and students at their school could use. This expectation of purposeful, place-based learning-by-doing (Gibbs, 1988; Maiga, 1995) in service to the school and community was also conveyed by Kwanzaa principles such as *Ujima* (to build and maintain our community together) and in the Student Creed that was recited at the beginning of each session:

> The resurrection of my people and the redemption of humanity depend on whether or not I accept the call to a higher consciousness today, tomorrow, and evermore.
>
> *(Akua, 2012, p. 95)*

Instructional materials provided content about our African worldview and its principles, virtues, and values (e.g., the Songhoy cosmology, the Seven Cardinal Virtues of *Ma'at*, the *Nguzo Saba* or Seven Principles of Kwanzaa). We did this by (a) using African-centered scholarship to create values-based, standards-aligned lessons that linked learning to heritage knowledge; (b) using *Criterion Standards* (King & Goodwin, (2006) as part of recovering our heritage; (c) using

Kwanzaa Principles as Beautiful Ways of Being and Acting that allowed students to experience a community-building classroom environment rather than a "managed" classroom environment; and (d) collectively producing knowledge for and about the community so that students could have the experience of serving their school and community. As stated in the above section about the Study Group, lessons on ancient Kemet (East Africa) were followed by lessons on Songhoy civilization (West Africa). Students received Songhoy names and they learned Songhoy folktales and proverbs as well as how to count and say basic greetings in Songhoy-senni.

A lesson on *The Songhai Princess* (E. Robinson, 1990) illustrates developmentally appropriate content about our African worldview used in the Songhoy Club. In this 25-minute animated video, King Sunni Ali Ber and Queen Dara host their daughter's naming ceremony in Timbuktu, "one of the great cities of the Songhoy Empire." Scenes show "beautiful buildings, wide avenues and beautiful, dignified [African] people dressed in colorful flowing robes." The Good Queen of the Waters gives the princess her name, Nzinga, and two magic rubies to protect her, yet the Wicked Witch of the Mountain kidnaps the princess. Years later, the Good Queen of the Waters helps Nzinga's childhood friend, Imhotep—who is a Timbuktu University medical student—to rescue her. At Nzinga's insistence, they bring the older couple, who found and raised the princess as their own daughter, back to the palace with them. These people were of good character and had put the magic rubies, which saved them all, away for safekeeping.

The King and Queen reward Imhotep with Nzinga's hand in marriage and half the kingdom and everyone "lived happily ever after." Although this film uses several Western fairy tale tropes, it is infused with African cosmological constructs and it valorizes African family relationships, African people's historic intellectual accomplishments, and the virtues of community-mindedness, loyalty, and courage. After viewing this video, the students were asked to write reflections in response to the following question: How might other students benefit if teachers showed this video? Constructing this assignment with a thought-provoking question exemplifies a problem-posing lesson used in the Songhoy Club. Many other lessons based on the seven broad topics listed in the above Study Group sub-section were introduced and taught in the Songhoy Club.

Parent Workshops

Parents were invited to review and discuss Songhoy Club lessons, and their views were sought about an expanded role for parents in collaborating with teachers to support children's academic and cultural excellence. We discussed the kinds of educational experiences that parents believe children need for success in today's society, their views about the role parents should play in their children's education, whether the Songhoy Club was beneficial, and how to teach certain lessons given the subject matter and students' ages. The doctoral students/practitioner researchers demonstrated two Songhoy Club lessons for parents: "*The Songhai Princess*" (Workshop 1) and "Media Portrayals of Black Women" (Workshop 2). In the final session (Workshop 3), we read and discussed a "re-membered" text about Isabella Dorsey from *Remembering Our Ancestors* (Swartz, 2011). In Rochester, New York, in the early 1900s, Isabella Dorsey and her husband, Thomas Dorsey, cared for children who had no relatives to take them in. Others in the community, including a reverend (Dr. James E. Rose) and a doctor (Dr. Charles T. Lunsford), helped the Dorseys care for the children. The Dorseys continued to take in children until the city of Rochester stopped allowing families to take in more than one or two children. This change forced the Dorseys to close their home in 1928. Participants identified and discussed the African worldview elements in this "re-membered" student text, such as unity, self-determination, care for the community, and reciprocity.

Findings

This case study explored two questions: What happens when a teacher educator models the use of Afrocentric curriculum and pedagogy to support doctoral students teaching middle school students? And, what happens when parents are engaged with practitioner researchers in reviewing and discussing Afrocentric curriculum and pedagogy that their middle school children experienced?

Afrocentric Agency

In response to our first research question, *Afrocentric Agency* is the finding that emerged from analysis of data collected in the Study Group, Research Team Meetings, Songhoy Club, and Parent Workshops. Using the narratives generated from participant observation, self-reflection, written responses to questions, group conversations, and the review of documents and artifacts, we found that doctoral students developed new knowledge and the will and capacity to critically analyze recovered historical and cultural content and related lesson plans in the Study Group and Research Team Meetings. As practitioner researchers, doctoral students also developed the confidence to use and examine Afrocentric curriculum and pedagogy with middle school students in the Songhoy Club and in conversations with parents. We call these findings (i.e., new knowledge, will, capacity, confidence) *Afrocentric Agency* because doctoral students demonstrated the facility to center and locate themselves and the students in learning about their heritage by using the Afrocentric pedagogical strategies of question-driven pedagogy and problem-based lessons that were modeled by the teacher educator in the Study Group and discussed in Research Team Meetings. In her reflections, Dr. King wrote:

I wanted to emphasize that our pedagogy should present recovered historical content in ways that students would find personally meaningful in order to co-create knowledge for cultural connectedness and to experience a sense of belonging.... I encouraged and modeled ways the doctoral students/Songhoy Club teachers could prepare problem-based lessons and activities that provided opportunities for the middle school students to identify with the character qualities of African family ancestors as far back as the pharaohs of ancient Kemet—also drawing on their own personal family heritage that we were attempting to connect to the past through our curriculum framework titled "From the Nile to the Niger to the Neighborhood." This expectation is consistent with Afro-centric concepts of Centrality/Location and Collective Consciousness. My doctoral students and the middle school students they are teaching need to see themselves as a location from which the past and present can be understood. This is a way to maintain the continuity of the African spirit and excellence traditions within our collective African family.

In their self-reflections and written responses to questions, doctoral students explored their interest in African history and culture and their efforts to center students in heritage knowledge while meeting subject area state standards. The words of Adrienne C. Goss represent this development:

During my first year as a doctoral student, I became very interested in African-centered education. I started reading about how schools and educators approach it [elsewhere] in the country. I reached out to schools in the area with the hope that some might let me see them in action. Working with the Songhoy Club gave me an experience that I could not get elsewhere—I was able to see first-hand how the students responded to our pedagogy over the course of several months. In turn, I learned more about how to teach Black students in a way that centers them in their learning.... I found that it was quite easy to connect our work to the Georgia Performance Standards (GPS).... [E]ven when the state requires certain standards for learning, we can still center children in an experience that teaches them about their culture and history without ignoring the state's requirements. In spite of the ease that I had with this in developing the Songhoy Club lessons, I still struggle with this in my daily practice as a high school math teacher because so much of what my students learn is abstract. I do continue to strive to find ways to help them connect what they are learning to the real world and potentially to their everyday lives. I imagine how much more applicable learning would be if schools were structured in a way that allowed for the interdisciplinary approach that we use in the Songhoy Club.... More than anything, teaching in the Songhoy Club improved my interactions with my students. [Now] I focus on the "knower" in each student. I never allow myself to believe that any child is not worth the extra effort that it may take to get him or her to work at full potential.

Even though the Songhoy Club was an afterschool program, our work existed in the context of the charter school in which we were located. We had our own curriculum and pedagogy, and there were times when we applied our Afrocentric practices as a response to school practices that came to our attention. Dr. King describes one of these situations:

> We discovered that 6th graders had read a novel about a 12-year-old enslaved girl growing up on a Georgia planation. While the book is about the struggle for literacy among enslaved people, it begins with the historical practice of "slave breeding." In the Study Group, we wondered whether teaching this historical injustice was age-appropriate. We wondered what parents would say about this. A community elder shared stories with us about the racist abuse of Black women and girls that he heard about while growing up. He reported that such abuse was one of the reasons Black people had left the "country" and moved to Atlanta to settle in Dixie Hills. My interest was to engage both doctoral students and Songhoy Club students in critical studyin' [King, 2006] that contextualizes current community problems in everyday life and in our collective memories. In fact, the Songhoy Club curriculum is titled "*Naarumey*: A Healing Journey Back Home," with *naarumey* meaning "journey" in Songhoy-senni.

Afrocentric Agency was also embodied in the doctoral students' identification with and application of the Seven Cardinal Virtues of *Ma'at* and the Seven Principles of the *Nguzo Saba* (Kwanzaa Principles). Examples of doctoral students' work suggest that they were able to use Black cultural ideals (e.g., unity, self-determination, purpose) and values (e.g., caring/kindness, right action/ respect, community mindedness), to invite students to think critically about the past and its relationship to the present. Related to the case of the novel read by sixth graders about a 12-year-old enslaved girl growing up on a Georgia planation, Dr. King asked her two doctoral students to co-develop and teach a lesson that connected the historical abuse of Black women and girls to current examples of violence such as the widely publicized news report that celebrity hip-hop artist Chris Brown attacked his celebrity girlfriend, Rihanna. As the practices of White supremacy/racism are at the root of this violence, how might Songhoy Club teachers help middle school students understand this? Dr. King sensed her students' tentativeness about this assignment and asked, "Are you skeptical about doing this?" In a written response to Dr. King's question, Sherell A. McArthur stated:

> [A]s I started thinking about the historical implications of how enslaved Africans were treated, especially in relation to African American women being used as breeders, I realized that the "breeder mentality" has not escaped our society. The historical roots of the oppression of Black women lie within the foundation of United States … thus, she is always

defending her name and her honor. The victimization of Black women is inextricably tied to Chris Brown's attack on Rihanna. The way women are portrayed and treated is connected to our torrid history here as Africans in America.

Ms. McArthur and Ms. Goss worked together to develop a lesson, and co-reflecting upon their practice in a Research Team Meeting, they described what they wanted to accomplish. Dr. King asked them to provide a written response to the following question: "Can you identify any Black cultural ideals that informed your lesson?" Ms. Goss wrote:

> I would have to say a combination of *Umoja* (Unity), *Nia* (Purpose), and *Kujichagulia* (Self-Determination). I wasn't necessarily conscious of these at the time; I just knew that I wanted to communicate to the students the importance of honoring Black women, and somehow get them to see that the media portrayals of Black women have likely warped their views on the way that they should treat Black women and girls in their lives. Unity embraces more than just the Black race; it also refers to unity in the family. *Nia* is about restoration and *Kujichagulia* is about naming ourselves. In this lesson I wanted the students to think about the distorted ways in which others have attempted to "name" Black women (e.g., breeders, promiscuous, expendable) and help them to understand that although it is not necessarily their fault that they may view women/girls in this way, it is up to them to change how they "name" (view and respond to) women/girls from this point on. It is up to them—up to all of us—to restore the unity in the Black family and community and put us back in a position to walk in our purposes.

In response to Dr. King's question, Ms. McArthur wrote:

> My pedagogical stance in creating this lesson was *Kujichagulia*: "to define ourselves, name ourselves, create for ourselves and speak for ourselves." While I wanted us to discuss and tease out many of the intricacies of our history here in America, I could not end the lesson on this note. I concluded our lesson with a question: What images should we see of Black women? I brought magazines for the students to participate in a hands-on activity in which they found images of Black women that provided a counter-narrative to the images that they see in the media. They not only found, [and] cut out and pasted these images to paper, but they also expressed to the club how their particular chosen images challenge the images in the media.

We often discussed students and community needs in our Research Team Meetings. Teachers in the school sometimes dropped in to the Songhoy Club to share their observations about individual students or they brought us "hard

cases." Ms. Goss observed how one of these "hard cases" responded to a Songhoy language lesson:

> One of the other new students ... was kicked out of two other clubs
> before being escorted to ours. Amazingly, we had absolutely no problems
> with him. He was fully engaged right away, learning the Songhoy vocab-
> ulary as Alfagaa M. (Teacher in Songhoy-senni) explained the terms, and
> he repeated every phrase after her clearly, audibly. He made flash cards
> and desired to write them correctly, asking for clarification from students
> around him. I loved watching what an affirming environment can do for
> a student who had spent the last few weeks being perceived as difficult
> and perhaps [as] a troublemaker.

Walking in Our Own Purpose

Our second research question explored what happens when parents are engaged
with practitioner researchers in reviewing and discussing Afrocentric curriculum and pedagogy that their middle school children experienced? By collecting
data using the methods of *participant observation, self-reflection, group conversations,*
and *the review of documents and artifacts,* we found that parents expressed Black
cultural ideals such as unity in the family and community, collective responsibility, and community purpose. Their commentary on these cultural ideals was
a counterpoint to the current challenges and deficit narratives that predominately describe our communities. They had specific ideas about what families
and educators could do to change the conditions that threaten their children
and their community, and in so doing, pointed out that the community needed
its own collective purpose to pursue; and in conversations with doctoral students and the teacher educator, parents also identified the value in recuperating
ideas and practices from the past to apply them to the present. We adapted a
phrase that Ms. Goss used in one of her written responses (above), and called
this second finding *Walking in Our Own Purpose.* Thus, expressing Black cultural ideals, offering ideas about how to change threatening conditions, affirm-
ing the value system Black people have lived by, using our spiritual traditions,
identifying the need to develop a collective community purpose, and looking
to the past for ideas to apply to the present exemplify and describe *Walking in
Our Own Purpose.*

We showed *The Songhai Princess* video (E. Robinson, 1990) and talked
with the parents about how it was used with Songhoy Club students. We then
introduced the *Criterion Standards* (King & Goodwin, 2006) that informed
our Songhoy Club curriculum, particularly pointing out those standards that
describe the extensive African history that preceded enslavement in the Americas. The following exchange occurred between Dr. King, Ms. Jackson, and
Ms. Williams:

Ms. Jackson: What did the children think about the film?

Dr. King: I think they were impressed, because if we just look at television and movies, you don't often see a story like this.... We now have the Disney Princess, but that's the only one.

Ms. Williams: The only one we got is kissing a frog. [Everyone laughs].

Ms. Jackson: Nzinga's commitment to her foster parents reflects the African value of dedication to one's family and to one's people—the Black community.... That part of the video reminded me of Naomi and Ruth in the *Bible*. That is, the Songhoy Princess showed the same kind of dedication to her foster parents that Naomi showed for her mother-in-law Ruth.

Parents expressed how African people's cultural ideals need to be at the center of shaping a collective response to current community realities. After experiencing the doctoral students' lesson on the portrayals of Black women and girls—including negative lyrics in hip-hop, media misrepresentations, and the historical disrespect and abuse of Black women—Ms. Williams described how she prepared her children to resist what she called "propaganda" by providing them a very different narrative as her "home-teaching" strategy:

It's the [music] industry, so you have to teach them in the home first. If they are not getting properly taught in the home they will have those influences.... We need to learn our culture and keep the culture alive [and] learn our culture before slavery.... A lot of times [people think] our history over here begins with slavery. If people think they [only] came from that, then they won't have anyone or anything to aspire to. I mean, if all my ancestors did was be slaves, then they weren't that great anyway.

Ms. Jackson immediately referred to our previous discussion about the Songhoy Empire.

[Y]ou have to see the Songhai queens. You missed the movie. [Ms. Williams had arrived late.] We were kings and queens in Africa. That is where we come from. They [are] the ones that came and got us. We were fine. We had our different tribes [Nations] and so on, but you got to see the Songhoy Queen [*The Songhai Princess*].

Ms. Williams: I'm just saying that is where our history begins over here for a lot of people and that is where they teach it from the time we hit the shores over here, and [they say], "This is all your people have contributed." Not knowing that our people started astronomy, had vast empires, traveled all over the world—China, Japan, India, Mexico, over here—before Europeans came. So, they are not taught that. And then

when they colonized your image of God—that really messes you up. ...
A slave mentality is still with us.

The parents also cited society's double standard regarding how Black women
and men are viewed. They suggested children become aware of this lingering
after-effect of slavery and that teachers provide content about the ways Black
people were treated as less than human, for example, but always in the context
of knowing that our history does not begin there. In order to set a context and
tone for studying the African American experience of enslavement, Ms. Williams also thought it was worth considering how Europeans have treated each
other, referring to Hitler's attempt to breed a superior race.

Recovering the Past to "Re-Member" Ourselves

In response to both research questions taken together, *Recovering the Past to "Re-
member" Ourselves* is the third finding that emerged in the conversations that
occurred in the Parent Workshops. We found that recovering African history
and culture ("From the Nile to the Niger to the Neighborhood") illuminates
not only the seemingly abstract, yet centuries-old cultural ideals and values of
people of African ancestry, but that it has a healing outcome of reconnecting
our cultural selves. From analysis of data generated by all five methods/data
sources, we found that the study's participants narratively identified connections between themselves and their family, community, and culture through
the experience of engaging with "re-membered" historical knowledge. When
African history is recovered and is then available as heritage knowledge, the
cultural ideals and values embedded in that knowledge are restored as well. In
other words, the palpable presence of these cultural ideals and values becomes a
guide toward healing and wholeness—toward a conscious reconnection of our
cultural selves that has been severed in many ways, not the least of which is the
omission and distortion of our heritage. We found that this "re-membering" of
ourselves is linked to the academic and cultural excellence we seek for our children. For example, in the materials experienced by doctoral and middle school
students and parents, the lives of historical figures on the African continent
and in the United States (e.g., Emperor Sunni Ali Ber, Austin Steward, Isabella
Dorsey)—embody Black cultural ideals such as self-determination, unity in
the family and the community, collective consciousness, and care for the community. In conversations with parents, we learned that they saw the connection
between what they emphasized in their "home teaching" and the values and
actions of these historical figures; and they saw how these Black cultural ideals
could guide their children toward cultural excellence, well-being, and belonging in the context of recovering their cultural identity.

The question of the teachers' role in fostering cultural excellence loomed
large in our conversations. Ms. Jackson said, "When you [teachers] see they

[students] are about to fall, you lift them up." Ms. Williams said, "Well, they [teachers] have got to care first, from the beginning. They have to work with their [students'] self-esteem as well, because kids are just little people." She complained, however, that teachers often say, "We are not here to be a counselor to your kids.... I get that a lot," she said. "Well I'm not a counselor [either], but sometimes you can counsel without being trained. Teachers need to let the kids know 'I'm here for you regardless'...." These parental comments indicate the concerns parents have about the absence of Black cultural ideals (e.g., collective responsibility, reciprocity, caring, mutuality) in the pedagogical practices of the teachers and in the culture of the school. This was echoed in an encounter Dr. King had with a teacher at the charter school:

> I first learned about Tiger Flowers when a teacher who grew up in the neighborhood surreptitiously handed me a booklet that included a story about Tiger Flowers that the district had produced some time ago. Looking apprehensively over her shoulder, she whispered, "You all might want to know about this." While her sharing the material was valuable, I realized that teaching to recover such knowledge about this community was apparently taboo in the culture of the school. In fact, we encountered a lot of resistance from some teachers and administrators. Although this booklet was actually very helpful, I suspect the recovery of neighborhood history wasn't something she felt she could do in her own practice, that is, to connect heritage knowledge to teaching and learning. The absence of such a connection separates us from ourselves and jeopardizes our reach for academic and cultural excellence.

This absence of cultural consciousness, which was exhibited by some, but not all teachers and parents in the school, placed cultural well-being and belonging further out of reach. When we invited parents to share their ideas about how parents can support teaching for academic and cultural excellence, they indicated that Isabella Dorsey's story would be especially helpful for children in Rochester. Reading the story of Mrs. Dorsey afforded both the doctoral students/ practitioner researchers and parents the opportunity to recognize dedication as an important value that their elders as well as ancestors had passed on to them. Parents identified several Black cultural ideals in the story, leading to a lengthy discussion about how children in the Dorsey home were raised. This "re-membered" biography also led the parents to recount positive virtues regarding what life used to be like in the Black community when they were growing up. Black neighborhoods used to have "Big Mamas," women like Isabella Dorsey, who took care of others in the community, including those who were not blood relatives. Such dedication to people who are not necessarily blood relatives is also part of the African value system and a dimension of cultural excellence. Likewise, in an earlier workshop, both mothers talked about ways they attempted to be a positive influence with children other than their own.

The parents lamented the loss of "community" as seen in the way most families no longer eat together and the change in standards for how children should dress in public. Taking note of a photograph in the Dorsey biography that shows the Dorseys having lunch with more than a dozen children in their care, Ms. Williams remarked: "Back then, people used to eat together. People don't eat together these days. They are always in front of the TV." Other pictures evoked comments regarding the children's appearance. Ms. Jackson said, "They were crisp and they were neat. They probably did not have a lot, but you can tell that what they had was clean and neat...." Parents remembered that there were different expectations for taking care of your clothing during that time. Children were not allowed to play in their "good clothes."

We all laughed when Ms. Williams quipped that the only princess we have is kissing a frog—referring to Disney's Black princess in a recent animated children's film. This and other egregious media portrayals were interrogated in Songhoy Club lessons. The doctoral students and parents could see how these media portrayals contrast with the legacy of Ms. Dorsey and the sacrifice and generosity of the "Big Mamas" whose lives of commitment and service deserve to be studied and honored. Ms. Dorsey's story in *Remembering Our Ancestors* (Swartz, 2011) makes it possible to discuss these cultural ideals in counterpoint to current community challenges, deficit narratives, and flawed conceptualizations in master scripts about enslavement. The Parent Workshops demonstrated how "re-membered" history democratizes knowledge that reflects African descent people's cultural ideals and community realities. Along with the biography of Ms. Dorsey, other biographies in *Remembering Our Ancestors* also exemplify the *Nguzo Saba* and the Virtues of *Ma'at* by teaching children to remember the cultural ideals demonstrated by their ancestors.

These biographies also illustrate community ideals, that is to say, Black cultural ideals ordinary people demonstrate in their lives. For example, Mrs. Dorsey's life illustrates the ideals of *Umoja* (unity), *Kujichagulia* (self-determination), and the *Ma'atian* virtue of reciprocity. The responses of the parents in the workshops also attest to the ideals of *Umoja* (cultural unity caring for one another, acting in solidarity), *Kujichagulia* (self-determination—naming and defining ourselves), as well as *Nia* (purpose—recognizing the historical and cultural experience, knowledge, and beauty of our ancestors who gift our legacy to the next generation), and *Imani* (faith in our cultural inheritance and spiritual resilience to free ourselves). The group conversation also delved into Biblical narratives as well as African traditional spirituality as resources for personal and community problem-solving. Both Ms. Williams and Ms. Jackson referred to spiritual ways of knowing and being and the power of faith as an important virtue to maintain and pass along. With quiet conviction Ms. Williams said, "Your ancestors are always ready to help. They are already a part of you."

It was important to demonstrate to the parents that children in the Songhoy Club learned about their heritage as starting on the African continent with human history, not in the Americas with slavery. In our conversation about *The Songhai Princess* video, the parents affirmed that the African values/ Black cultural ideals depicted in the film continue to inform and shape the lives of African Americans—even though Black communities are under assault. These parents also expressed clear expectations that a teacher has to be honest about the oppression of Black people in America. They also emphasized that the home environment needs assistance so that parents have knowledge about their heritage, which can help all of our children to become more successful. Thus, the workshop participants exchanged ideas with the doctoral students/ practitioner researchers and the teacher educator about how to teach children regarding where we as an African people came from, where we are now as a people, and where we are headed. Parents saw the importance of getting this information at school, as long as parents and communities defined the purposes of education and what parental involvement looked like—all in the interest of fostering the cultural well-being and belonging of their children.

In a written response, Ms. Goss describes the interactions between the Research Team and parents as lively and open; and reflecting humor, candor, and reciprocity:

> The parents in our workshop(s) spoke with us openly and freely about controversial topics, including racism and misogyny, and personal infor- mation about their children and home lives. We did not only ask them to answer our questions; we shared a little about ourselves and our own experiences. In doing so, we showed some level of reciprocity in the workshops ... Importantly, my experience in the Songhoy Club, particu- larly during the Parent Workshops, developed me as a researcher. I saw firsthand that engaging with research participants in conversations is a valuable approach to generating data.

The data that was gathered and the co-constructed analysis that the teacher educator and doctoral students produced in the three research-as-pedagogy contexts (Songhoy Club, Study Group, and Parent Workshops) resulted in three major findings: *Afrocentric Agency, Walking in Our Own Purpose, and Recovering the Past to "Re-member" Ourselves.* During this iterative "inquiry on inquiry" within inquiry, the teacher educator learned that using Afrocentric curriculum and pedagogy with her doctoral students facilitated their learning about and using Black cultural ideals; and that these experiences resulted in her students gaining the knowledge, confidence, and capacity to in turn teach these ide- als grounded in practical everyday life lessons to their middle school students. Over the course of the study, doctoral students not only gained new knowledge and pedagogical approaches, but they also learned how to frame their teaching and interactions with parents using *Nguzo Saba* Principles and *Ma'atian* Virtues. Parents identified the importance of retrieving elements of the past, the ways in which teachers need to support students, and the responsibility of parents

to engage in "home-teaching" as a counter to the negative media representations and historical misrepresentations of Black people. Parents also thought
that awareness of African people's cultural ideals (e.g., caring, dedication to
one's family and one's people, a collective community purpose) is necessary to
shaping a response to current community realities and centuries of oppression.

Conclusion

The Black cultural ideals found in the *Nguzo Saba* Principles and *Ma'atian*
Virtues underpin the Afrocentric curriculum and pedagogy used in this case
study. These ideals, such as collective responsibility, collective consciousness,
self-determination, reciprocity, and community mindedness, provide a unique
vantage point, as the doctoral students indicated, for critical cultural analysis
and for gaining new levels of self-awareness regarding teaching Black students.
Moreover, the Study Group, Songhoy Club, and Parent Workshops represent a viable model of school-based Afrocentric professional development that
includes parent engagement with what is taught in co-consideration of how
students are guided toward cultural well-being and belonging.

This study's focus was not on providing evidence of middle school students'
learning. However, the study's three main findings—*Afrocentric Agency, Walking
in Our Own Purpose,* and *Recovering the Past to "Re-member" Ourselves*—suggest
that using Afrocentric curriculum and pedagogy with doctoral students who
are teaching middle school students and with parents can place community
ideals and values at the center of teaching and learning. As doctoral students
developed *Afrocentric Agency*—which is seen in their new knowledge, will,
capacity, and confidence to use Afrocentric curriculum and pedagogy—they
developed lessons designed to center and locate themselves and middle school
students in learning about their heritage. What might account for this? The
Afrocentric culturally informed praxis modeled by the teacher educator who
exposed doctoral students' to question-driven pedagogy and problem-based
lessons based on recovered historical materials, and the conversations with parents both around the curriculum their children were experiencing, as well as
their acute awareness of community needs, shifted our location as researchers
from outsiders to insiders, as we co-constructed a research context in which
parents and teachers learned from each other. Together, as we discussed culturally informed praxis, we envisioned and experienced cultural well-being and
belonging as mutually agreed upon outcomes. Thus, this collaborative inquiry
was an opportunity for teachers and parents to realize our natural alliance in
replacing Eurocentric practices that continue to be an assault on the identity of
our children.

As parents expressed Black cultural ideals such as unity in the family and
community, collective responsibility, and community purpose, they offered
ideas that could challenge the current deficit narratives that predominately

describe parents of African ancestry as well as our schools and communities (Edwards, 2010). What might account for this? Engaging parents with the same Afrocentric curriculum that their children were experiencing created a context in which parents could do something with the Black cultural ideals that they themselves embodied, knew about from the past, or had identified in instructional materials. What they did was to identify the need for communities—including school communities—to have a collective purpose to pursue—to do what we call *Walking in Our Own Purpose*. Having a collective purpose empowers parents to participate in the teaching and learning process and the governance of their children's schools. This study suggests that not only is this different approach warranted, but that it is possible.

Viewing and discussing instructional materials that recovered African history and culture, were opportunities for the study's participants to either become familiar with and/or experience the centuries-old cultural ideals and virtues of people of African ancestry. Knowledge and use of these African ideals and virtues has the healing potential to reconnect or put back together our cultural selves—what we refer to as *Recovering the Past to "Re-member" Ourselves*. So, what might account for this? The recovery of African history restores our heritage knowledge and reveals the continuing relevance of the cultural ideals and virtues embedded in that knowledge. Parents knew that these ideals and virtues—examples of which they identified in Songhoy Club curriculum artifacts like *The Songhai Princess* video—still exist. Shining a light on these cultural ideals and virtues can guide teachers, parents, and students toward a conscious "re-membering" of our cultural selves, which is essential to our children's academic and cultural excellence.

Citing Asa Hilliard and other revolutionary theoreticians—Amilcar Cabral, Paulo Freire, and Aimé Césaire—Nunn (2011) explains that culture is a requirement for community viability: "… culture holds a community together … [and] supplies the most efficient tool to combat oppression" (p. 147). Nunn references Hilliard's prodigious understanding that "one of the key determinants of oppression is control of language and of names" (p. 146). According to Wynter, "there is always something else going on besides the dominant cultural logic" (Scott, 2000, p. 164). Study participants identified what else was really "going on" for them as they focused on the power of naming ourselves as a counterpoint to narratives of slavery and disparaging discourses about Black women, parents, and communities that continue to alienate African American children from their heritage and identity. The power of language is also demonstrated in this inquiry—in the form of naming ourselves—to resist "practices of subjugation" (McKittrick, 2006, p. 13) and in African language study as a resource for critical intervention to resist assaults on cultural blackness (King, 2008). Parents reclaiming memories of the "Big Mamas" and their community-minded virtues in contrast to the "socioeconomic mapping of blackness" onto impoverished neighborhoods like Dixie Hills as the epitome of "demonic grounds" (McKittrick, 2006, p. 13) is another form of resistance to the "dominant logic." Cultural recovery from alienating historical omissions and distortions requires our participation—our naming ourselves, which was evident in raised critical consciousness and "new levels of self-awareness" as doctoral students and parents affirmed the value of Afrocentric curriculum and pedagogy.

The Black Studies curriculum revolution of the 1960s has been all but stymied so far as K-12 education is concerned by the current high stakes testing regime, the predominance of "scripted" teaching in urban schools, and policy efforts to establish national "core" curricula. A call for engaging parents in partnership with teachers about what and how their children are learning—in light of the concerns and the needs in the community today—is our response to this current policy/political climate. By demonstrating how to increase the confidence and capacity of teachers to use Afrocentric curriculum and pedagogy, include parents' ideas and experiences as a source of learning, and connect community purposes to what happens in schools, academic and cultural excellence for Black students can become the rule, not the exception. While this study is small in size, it is large in its conceptualization of how to connect knowledge about the past to changing conditions in our present Diasporan communities.

References

Acree, E. (n.d.) J. H. Clarke: Historian, scholar, teacher. Cornell University Library. Retrieved from: http://africana.library.cornell.edu/africana/clarke/index.html

African Globe. (2013). "Black teens with racial pride do better in school." *African Globe*, January 1. Retrieved from: http://www.africanglobe.net/headlines/black-teens-racial-pride-school/

Akua, C. (2012). *Education for transformation: The keys to releasing the genius of African American students.* Conyers, GA: Imani Enterprises.

Allen, K. D. (2006). *Looking back to move forward: Reconciling the past, liberating the future.* Bloomington, IN: AuthorHouse.

Asante, M. K. (1980/1988). *Afrocentricity.* Trenton, NJ: Africa World Press.

Asante, M. K. (1991). Afrocentric curriculum. *Educational Leadership, 49*(4), 28–31.

Asante, M. K. (2007). *An Afrocentric manifesto.* Malden, MA: Polity Press.

Asante, M. K. (2010). *Speaking my mother's tongue: An introduction to African-American language.* Forth Worth, TX: Temba House Press.

Barton, A. C., Drake, C., Perez, J. G., St. Louis, K., & George, M. (2004). Ecologies of parental engagement in urban education. *Educational Researcher, 33*(4), 3–12.

Blank, M. J., Johnson, S. D., & Shah, B. P. (2003, Spring). Community as text: the community as a resource for learning in community schools. *New Directions for Youth Development, 97*, 107–120.

Boutté, G., Kelly-Jackson, C., & Johnson, G. L. (2010). Culturally relevant teaching in science classrooms: Addressing academic achievement, cultural competence, and critical consciousness. *International Journal of Multicultural Education, 12*(2), 1–20.

Bowman, P. J., & Howard, C. (1985). Race-related socialization, motivation, and academic achievement: A study of Black youths in three-generation families. *Journal of the American Academy of Child Psychiatry, 24,* 134–141.

Carter, D. J. (2008). Achievement as resistance: The development of a critical race achievement ideology among Black achievers. *Harvard Educational Review, 78*(3), 466–497.

Chang, H., Ngunjiri, F. W., & Hernandez, K. C. (2013). *Collaborative autoethnography.* Walnut Creek, CA: Left Coast Press.

Chavous, T. M., Bernat, D. H., Schmeelk-Cone, K., Caldwell, C. H., Kohn-Wood, L., & Zimmerman, M. A. (2003). Racial identity and academic attainment among African American adolescents. *Child Development, 74*(3), 1076–1090.

Clandinin, D. J., & Connelly, F. M. (2000). *Narrative inquiry: experience and story in qualitative research.* San Francisco, CA: Jossey-Bass.

Cochran-Smith, M., Barnatt, J., Friedman, A., & Pine, G. (2009). Inquiry on inquiry: Practitioner research and students' learning. *Action in Teacher Education, 31*(2), 17–32.

Coia, L. & Taylor, M. (2006). From the inside out and the outside in: co/autoethnography as a means of professional renewal. In C. Kosnik, C. Beck, A. R. Freese, & A. P. Samaras (Eds.), *Making a difference in teacher education through self-study* (pp. 19–33). Amsterdam, Netherlands: Springer.

Cooper, C. W. (2009). Parent involvement, African American mothers, and the politics of educational care. *Equity & Excellence in Education, 42*(4), 379-394.

Doucet, F. (2008). How African American parents understand their and teachers' roles in children's schooling and what this means for preparing preservice teachers. *Journal of Early Childhood Teacher Education, 29*(2), 108–139.

Dyson, M. (2007). My story in a profession of stories: Auto ethnography—an empowering methodology for educators. *Australian Journal of Teacher Education, 32*(1), 35–48.

Edwards, P. A. (2008). The education of African-American students: Voicing the debates, controversies, and solutions. In D. W. Rowe, R. Jimenez, D. Compton, D. Dickinson, Y. Kim, K. Leander, & V. Risko (Eds.), *57th Yearbook of the National Reading Conference* (pp. 1–31). Oak Creek, WI: National Reading Conference.

Edwards, P. A. (2010). Village or villain: The role of African American families. In P. Edwards, G. T. McMillon, & J. D. Turner (Eds.), *A change is gonna come: Transforming literacy education for African American students* (pp. 93–131). New York, NY: Teachers College Press.

Epstein, T. (2008). *Interpreting national history: Race, identity and pedagogy in the classroom.* New York, NY: Routledge.

Fournillier, J. (2009). Trying to return home: A Trinidadian's experience of becoming a "native" ethnographer. *Qualitative Inquiry, 15*(4), 740–765.

Gibbs, G. (1988). *Learning by doing: A guide to teaching and learning methods.* London, England: FEU Publishers.

Ginwright, S. (2000). Identity for sale: The limits of racial reform in urban schools. *The Urban Review, 32*(1), 87–104.

Goodwin, R. (2008). Control after dark: Slave owners and their control of slaves' intimate relationships, or "Who's your daddy?" *Journal of History and Culture, 1*(1), 12–24.

Goodwin, S. (2004). Emancipatory pedagogy. In S. Goodwin & E. E. Swartz (Eds.), *Teaching children of color: Seven constructs of effective teaching in urban schools* (pp. 37–48). Rochester, NY: RTA Press.

Goodwin, S., & Swartz, E. E. (2009). *Document-based learning: Curriculum and assessment.* Rochester, NY: RTA Press.

Graham, A., & Anderson, K. A. (2008). "I have to be three steps ahead": Academically gifted African American male students in an urban high school on the tension between an ethnic and academic identity. *Urban Review, 40,* 472–499.

Grande, S. (2004). *Red pedagogy: Native American social and political thought.* Lanham, MD: Rowman & Littlefield.

Gutman, L. M., & McLoyd, V. C. (2000). Parents' management of their children's education within the home, at school, and in the community: An examination of African-American families living in poverty. *The Urban Review, 32*(1), 1–24.

Harper, B. E. (2007). The relationship between Black racial identity and academic achievement in urban settings. *Theory Into Practice, 46*(3), 230–238.

Hill, N. E. (2010). Culturally-based worldviews, family processes, and family-school interactions. In S. L. Christenson & A. L. Reschley (Eds.), *Handbook of school-family partnerships* (pp. 101–128). New York, NY: Routledge.

Hill, N. E., & Taylor, L. C. (2004). Parental school involvement and children's academic achievement: Pragmatics and issues. *Current Directions in Psychological Science, 13*(4), 161–164.

Hyland, N. E. & Meacham, S. (2004). Community knowledge-centered teacher education: A paradigm for socially just educational transformation. In J. L. Kincheloe, A. Bursztyn, & S. R. Steinberg (Eds.), *Teaching teachers: Building a quality school of urban education* (pp. 113–134). New York, NY: Peter Lang.

Jackson, B. (1974). *Get your ass in the water and swim like me: African-American oral poetry from the oral tradition.* Cambridge, MA: Harvard University Press.

Jackson, S., Martin, N., & Stocklinski, J. (2004). Families as partners. In E. T. Joyner, M. Ben-Avie, & J. P. Comer (Eds.), *Transforming school leadership and management to support student learning and development* (pp. 105–126). Thousand Oaks, CA: Corwin.

Jackson, K., & Remillard, J. T. (2005). Rethinking parent involvement: African American mothers construct their roles in the mathematics education of their children. *The School Community Journal, 15*(1), 51–73.

Karenga, M. (1996). The Nguzo Saba (the Seven Principles). In M. K. Asante & A. S. Abarry (Eds.), *African intellectual heritage: A book of sources* (pp. 543–554). Philadelphia, PA: Temple University.

Kemmis, S., & McTaggart, R. (2000). Participatory action research. In N. K. Denzin & Y. S. Lincoln (Eds.), *Handbook of qualitative research* (pp. 567–605). Thousand Oaks, CA: Sage.

King, J. E. (1992). Diaspora literacy and consciousness in the struggle against miseducation in the Black community. *Journal of Negro Education, 61*(3), 317–340.

King, J. E. (2005). A transformative vision of Black education for human freedom. In J. E. King (Ed.), *Black education: A transformative research and action agenda for the new century* (pp. 3–17). Mahwah, NJ: Erlbaum for the American Educational Research Association.

King, J. E. (2006). If justice is our objective: Diaspora literacy, heritage knowledge and the praxis of critical studyin' for human freedom. In A. Ball (Ed.), *With more deliberate speed: Achieving equity and excellence in education—realizing the full potential of Brown v. Board of Education* (pp. 337–360). National Society for the Study of Education, 105th Yearbook, Part 2. New York, NY: Ballenger.

King, J. E. (2008). Critical & qualitative research in teacher education: A Blues Epistemology for cultural well-being and a reason for knowing. In M. Cochran-Smith, S. Feiman-Nemser, D. J. McIntyre, & K. E. Demers (Eds.), *Handbook of research on teacher education: Enduring questions in changing contexts* (3rd ed., pp. 1094–1136). New York, NY: Routledge.

King, J. E. (2011). "Who dat say (we) too depraved to be saved?" Re-membering Haiti/ Katrina (and beyond): Critical studyin' for human freedom. *Harvard Educational Review, 81*(2), 343–371.

King, J. E., Akua, C., & Russell, L. (2014). Liberating urban education for human freedom. In H. R. Milner & K. Lomotey (Eds.), *Handbook for research on urban education* (pp. 52–107). New York, NY: Routledge.

King, J. E., & Goodwin, S. (2006). *Criterion standards for contextualized teaching and learning about people of African Descent.* Rochester, NY: Author.

King, J. E., & Mitchell, C. A. (1995). *Black mothers to sons: Juxtaposing African American literature with social practice.* New York, NY: Peter Lang.

Kynard, C. (2013). "I want to be African": Tracing Black radical traditions with "students' rights to their own language." In C. Kynard, *Vernacular insurrections: Race, Black protest, and the new century in composition-literacies studies* (pp. 73–105). Albany, NY: SUNY Press.

Lawson, M. A. (2003). School-family relations in context: Parent and teacher perceptions of parent involvement. *Urban Education, 38*(1), 77–133.

Lee, C. (2007). *Culture, literacy and learning: Taking bloom in the midst of the whirlwind.* New York, NY: Teachers College Press.

Lincoln, Y. S. & Guba, E. G. (1985). *Naturalistic inquiry.* Beverly Hills, CA: Sage.

Maiga, H. O. (1995). Bridging classroom, curriculum, and community: The Gao School Museum. *Theory Into Practice, 34*(3), 209–215.

Maiga, H. O. (1996/2003). *Conversational Sonay language.* Atlanta, GA: Murehm Books.

Maiga, H. O. (2010). *Balancing written history with oral tradition: The legacy of the Songhoy people.* New York, NY: Taylor & Francis.

Maiga, H. O., King, J. E., & RaShon (1999a). *Black is.* In The people who could fly: Commission on Research in Black Education demonstration projects—lessons. Retrieved from http://www.coribe.org/SONGHOY/Pages/frameset.html

Maiga, H. O., King, J. E., & RaShon (1999b). *Counting lesson.* In The people who could fly: Commission on Research in Black Education demonstration projects—lessons. Retrieved from: http://www.coribe.org/SONGHOY/Pages/frameset.html.

Marshall, E., & Toohey, K. (2010). Representing family: Community funds of knowledge, bilingualism, and multimodality. *Harvard Educational Review, 80*(2), 221–241.

Mattingly, D. J., Prislin, R., McKenzie, T. L., Rodriguez, J. L., & Kayzar, B. (2002). Evaluating evaluations: The case of parent involvement programs. *Review of Educational Research, 72*(4), 549–576.

McKittrick, K. (2006). *Demonic grounds: Black women and the cartographies of struggle.* Minneapolis: University of Minnesota Press.

Merry, M. S., & New, W. (2008). Constructing an authentic self: The challenges and promise of African-centered pedagogy. *American Journal of Education, 115*(1), 35–64.

Moll, L. C., Amanti, C., Neff, D., & Gonzalez, N. (1992). Funds of knowledge for teaching: Using a qualitative approach to connect homes and classrooms. *Theory Into Practice, 31*(2), 132–141.

Murrell, P. C. (1997). Digging again the family wells: A Freirian literacy framework as emancipatory pedagogy for African American children. In P. Freire, T. McKinnon, D. Macedo, & J.W. Fraser (Eds.), *Mentoring the mentor: A critical dialogue with Paulo Freire* (pp. 19–58). New York, NY: Peter Lang.

Murrell, P. C. (2001). *The community teacher: A new framework for effective urban teaching.* New York, NY: Teachers College.

Myrick-Harris, C. (2008). The origins of the Civil Rights Movement in Atlanta, 1880–1910. American Historical Association. Retrieved from: http://www.historians.org/perspectives/issues/2006/0611/0611ann5.cfm

NABSE (National Alliance of Black School Educators). (1984). *Saving the African American child, task force report.* Washington, DC: Author.

NBEA (National Black Education Agenda) (2012). Declaration of academic and cultural excellence for all African American children, families and communities. National Black Education Agenda. Retrieved from http://www.ipetitions.com/petition/declaration-of-academic-and-cultural-excellence

Nunn, K. B. (2011). The Black nationalist cure to disproportional minority contact. In N. Dowd (Ed.), *Justice for kids: Keeping kids out of the juvenile justice system* (pp. 135–156). New York, NY: New York University Press.

Olmedo, I. M. (1997). Family oral histories for multicultural curriculum perspectives. *Urban Education, 32*(1), 45–62.

Oyserman, D., Harrison, K., & Bybee, D. (2001). Can racial identity be promotive of academic efficacy? *International Journal of Behavioral Development, 25*(4), 379–385.

Paris, D. (2009). "They're in my culture, they speak the same way": African American language in multiethnic high schools. *Harvard Educational Review, 79*(3), 428–448.

Patton, M. Q. (2002). *Qualitative research and evaluation methods* (3rd ed.). Thousand Oaks, CA: Sage.

PBS (2006). "Prince Among Slaves." Retrieved from http://www.pbs.org/programs/prince-among-slaves/

Ravitch, D. (2010). *The death and life of the great American school system.* New York, NY: Basic Books.

Reay, D., & Mirza, H. S. (1997). Uncovering genealogies of the margin: Black supplementary schooling. *British Journal of Sociology of Education, 18*(4), 477–499.

Robinson. C., & Robinson, E. (1992). *The journey of the Songhai people.* Philadelphia, PA: Songhai.

Robinson, E. (1990). *The Songhai princess* [video]. Philadelphia, PA. New Dawn Productions.

Robinson, J. J. (1997). Parents as allies for alternative assessment. In A. L. Goodwin (Ed.). *Assessment for equity and inclusion: Embracing all our children* (pp. 297–303). New York, NY: Routledge.

RTC (Rochester Teacher Center) (2009). *Education for beautiful ways of being and acting.* Rochester, NY: Author.

Samara, A. P., & Freese, A. R. (2006). *Self-study of teaching practices: Primer.* New York, NY: Peter Lang.

Sanders, M. G., Allen-Jones, G. L., & Abel, Y. (2002). Involving families and communities in the education of children and youth placed at risk. In S. Stringfield & D. Land (Eds.), *Educating at-risk students: Yearbook of the National Society for the Study of Education, 101* (pp. 171–188). Chicago, IL: National Society for the Study of Education.

Scott, D. (2000, September). The re-enactment of humanism: An interview with Sylvia Wynter. *Small Axe: A Caribbean Journal of Criticism, 8,* 119–207.

Shockley, K. G. (2009). A researcher "called" to "taboo" places?: A burgeoning research method in African-centered education, *International Journal of Qualitative Studies in Education, 22*(2), 163–176.

Smitherman, G. (1999, February). CCC's role in the struggle for language rights. *College Composition and Communication, 50*(3), 349–376.

Spencer, M. B., Noll, E., Stoltzfris, J., & Harpalani, V. (2001). Identity and school adjustment: Revisiting the "acting White" assumption. *Educational Psychologist, 36*, 21–30.

Swain, A. (2011). 21st century freedom fighters: African descent teachers' use of culturally relevant pedagogy as a liberation tool (Unpublished doctoral dissertation). Georgia State University, Atlanta.

Swartz, E. E. (2004). Casing the self: A study of pedagogy and critical thinking. *Teacher Development, An International Journal of Teachers' Professional Development, 8*(1), 45–65.

Swartz, E. E. (2009). Diversity: Gatekeeping knowledge and maintaining inequalities. *Review of Educational Research, 79*(2), 1044–1083.

Swartz, E. E. (2011). *Remembering our ancestors*. Rochester, NY: Rochester City School District.

Tedla, E. (1995). *Sankofa: African thought and education*. New York, NY: Peter Lang.

Wakefield, W. D., & Hudley, C. (2007). Ethnic and racial identity and adolescent well-being. *Theory Into Practice, 46*(2), 147–154.

Wang, M., & Huguley, J. P. (2012). Parental racial socialization as a moderator of the effects of racial discrimination on education success among African American adolescents. *Child Development, 83*(5), 1716–1731.

Warren, M. R., Hong, S., Rubin, C. L., & Uy, P. S. (2009). Beyond the bake sale: A community-based relational approach to parent engagement in schools. *Teachers College Record, 111*(9), 2209–2254.

Whaley, A. L., & Noël, L. (2012). Sociocultural theories, academic achievement, and African American adolescents in a multicultural context: A review of the cultural incompatibility perspective. *Journal of Negro Education, 81*(1), 25–38.

Williams, E. R., & Baber, C. R. (2007). Building trust through culturally reciprocal home-school-community collaboration from the perspective of African-American parents. *Multicultural Perspectives, 9*(2), 3–9.

White, W. (1995). *A man called White: The autobiography of Walter White*. Athens, GA: University of Georgia Press.

Woods, C. (1998). *Development arrested: The blues and plantation power in the Mississippi Delta*. London, England: Verso.

9

CODA

What "Re-Membered" Texts "Re-Member"

When democratized knowledge is used in the classroom, what are the implications for change in the educational system?

Recovering History

In this volume we have presented an Afrocentric culturally informed praxis for recovering history through a process of "re-membering." This process produces democratized knowledge that more fully represents the past—knowledge that can replace the standard social studies content still used in schools across our nation. Even after decades of critique and assistance from well-known scholars in multicultural and culturally responsive education, corporate publishers of social studies materials have not changed the grand narratives that frame curricula and instructional materials, and these narratives have been further enshrined in state standards and high stakes tests. It is these grand narratives—and the master scripts that teach them—that obstruct critical dialogues with the past and therefore the present; and in the absence of such dialogues, a hierarchy of human worth is perpetuated in educational policies and practices that maintains euro-epistemic dominance.

As a counter response to the limitations and distortions of grand narratives and master scripts, we have used Afrocentric theory and concepts and the principles of culturally informed curricular practice to frame and write "re-membered" student texts that demonstrate how democratized knowledge is able to reconnect the multiple and shared knowledge bases and experiences that shaped the past. We have also developed a "re-membered" standards model using both state and culturally informed standards. In these ways, we offer "re-membering" as a realizable alternative to gatekeeping and the hegemonic standards and silenced accounts produced by those with the power and resources to widely disseminate knowledge. Rather than being held in the grip of state standards and related curricula and instructional materials, we invite teachers at all levels to take an emancipatory stance—to select democratized content and standards that bring the benefits of historical recovery to students.

Learning from Practitioner Inquiry

Practitioner inquiry is the third element of our praxis of historical recovery. In addition to "re-membering" both student texts and standards, we asked in-service and pre-service teachers and teacher educators to examine the use of "re-membered" content in classrooms and community. Below are summaries of these four practitioner case studies.

Campbell Case Study and "Re-Membering"

In chapter 5, third-grade teacher Linda Campbell explained how her own school experience and the school experience she in turn provided for students had separated her and her students from knowledge of their African heritage. After reading the "re-membered" student text "Austin Steward: Self-Determination and Human Freedom" (Goodwin & Swartz, 2009) and Steward's (2004) autobiography *Twenty-Two Years a Slave and Forty Years a Freeman,* she wrote, "It was now personal and I could share a renewed desire to learn more about my history as a Black person who is part of a family that was once enslaved and lived during the same era as Austin Steward." This renewed desire propelled Ms. Campbell's efforts to alter her relationships with students and parents. When she invited parents to participate in developing student assessments related to the "re-membered" text about Steward, and when parents engaged with their children in a unit related to that text, she found that she was no longer isolated and disconnected from parents, students, and her own heritage. In her study's findings and conclusion, she put it this way:

> It became very clear to me that the system that I had become thoroughly assimilated and raised in was no longer comfortable. It was not only a misfit for my students, but for me as well.... As a result of this project I now have more communication with parents. I make ways for us to be in contact with each other, either in person or through phone conferencing. I know I need family support, and as a result, I have become more approachable. It is a "we" thing now, not an "I" thing.

Now seeing herself as part of a family classroom, Ms. Campbell stopped using rules and point systems and sending students to the office. Instead she responded to students—even the most challenging students—as she would her own children, by building relationships and being loving and genuine with them. This included the use of "re-membered" content guided by both state and culturally informed standards. No longer was the content of the curriculum a misfit for her and her students. This shift in her way of seeing herself, parents, and students represented a shift in her cultural consciousness that was informed by learning about the African cultural platform upon which Austin Steward stood. His self-determination, community mindedness, collective responsibility, collaborative and reciprocal interactions with others—and what these ways of being, values, and practices produced in his life—showed her the benefits of interdependence and relationship building. For parents to actually be included in the instructional process was so strikingly positive that Ms. Campbell and parents wondered together why it wasn't the norm in school. As she moved from being a controlling classroom manager to a collaborative classroom leader, she observed that student outcomes and parent engagement improved.

As the first completed case study, Linda Campbell's findings were an early indication that "re-membered" texts might be contexts for "re-membering" more than historical knowledge. In her study, using "re-membered" content was instrumental in "re-membering" relationships that were disconnected, for example between her and her cultural identity and between students' cultural identities and the curriculum. As the three other case studies were completed, we began to see a pattern. Using "re-membered" texts prompted or pointed the way not only to changing classroom-related outcomes, but also to "re-membering" disconnections with systemic implications.

Lemons-Smith Case Study and "Re-Membering"

In chapter 6, math educator Shonda Lemons-Smith examined urban, elementary pre-service teachers' construction of mathematics lessons using the "re-membered" text *Freedom and Democracy: A Story Remembered* (Swartz, 2013). Equity and social justice were themes in her course readings, discussions, assignments, and field experiences. Yet, in her study, most pre-service math-methods teachers selected "safe" mathematical operations for their lesson plans and did not write lessons that encouraged elementary students to use math concepts to explore the historical or political content in *Freedom and Democracy*. Likewise, in small group discussions most pre-service teachers restated historical facts rather than raise thoughtful points and issues about the content. As part of the design of her study, Dr. Lemons-Smith did not intervene in students' small-group discussions and activities. She wanted to learn how students—without her input—approached instructional planning based on a "re-membered" text. The study's findings suggest that pre-service teachers do need guidance to engage in interdisciplinary learning and to integrate cultural knowledge in lesson planning. Lemons-Smith noted that her students' responses were aligned with the literature about how most pre-service teachers are reluctant to engage with cultural diversity and that this tendency is exacerbated by teacher preparation programs that typically rely on one "culture course":

> Preparing teachers who can engage in integrated, critical, and culturally and historically grounded content and pedagogy requires extending beyond the designated culture course to make connections through interdisciplinarity across content disciplines such as mathematics. If preservice teachers are to develop the skills to critically engage with curriculum for all students, teacher preparation programs must rethink how they prepare teachers.

The change sought by Dr. Lemons-Smith is a response to the segregation of knowledge about the heritage of "others" in a designated "culture course"—an institutional practice that has disconnected this "other" knowledge from most course content in teacher preparation.

López Case Study and "Re-Membering"

In chapter 7, pre-service teacher Ericka López found that using a "re-membered" text, *Freedom and Democracy: A Story Remembered* (Swartz, 2013), altered the teacher-centered approach to constructing lessons that she had learned in her master's program. She began her study by using culturally informed principles to examine both corporate social studies textbooks and a "re-membered" social studies text. It wasn't long before she identified gaps in her own historical knowledge and realized how extensively African and Indigenous Peoples were omitted and misrepresented in social studies textbooks. She also identified how emancipatory pedagogy—in particular question-driven pedagogy that draws out students' ideas and voices—was compatible with "re-membered" texts that rely on multiple voices to provide comprehensive accounts. Guided by both state and culturally informed standards, Ms. López found that student collaboration and group-based dialogue were a good fit for a lesson based on "re-membered" text and emancipatory pedagogy compared to the traditional teacher-centered approach where the knowledge worth knowing is presented through the dominant voice of teacher and text:

> Instead of professing the information and being the sole holder of knowledge, the role is one of a teacher as a guide. The lesson plan under study encourages a teacher to create an environment through questioning in which students construct their own knowledge through collaborative and communal interactions.

Ms. López also noted that traditional approaches to teaching ESOL students view their cultural backgrounds as an impediment to learning, not as a resource, with ESOL students often being placed in low ability tracks that negatively impact their higher education and employment opportunities. She suggests that lesson planning can be part of changing this marginalization of ESOL students if it includes their cultural and linguistic backgrounds along with challenging content and pedagogy that encourage student cooperation.

King, Goss, and McArthur Case Study and "Re-Membering"

In chapter 8, teacher educator Joyce E. King and two of her doctoral students, Adrienne C. Goss and Sherell A. McArthur, collaboratively conducted a study that investigated what happened when doctoral students and parents engaged with Afrocentric curriculum and pedagogy in an afterschool program called the Songhoy Club. As Dr. King explained:

> I encouraged and modeled ways the doctoral students/Songhoy Club teachers could prepare problem-based lessons and activities that provided opportunities for the middle school students to identify with the character qualities of African family ancestors as far back as the pharaohs of ancient Kemet—also drawing on their own personal family heritage that we were attempting to connect to the past through our curriculum framework titled "From the Nile to the Niger to the Neighborhood."

In a series of workshops, the research team invited the parents of students in the Songhoy Club to review and discuss the curriculum that their children experienced. As part of this curriculum the "re-membered" student text *Remembering Our Ancestors* (Swartz, 2011) gave the doctoral students/practitioner researchers and parents additional access to Black cultural ideals (e.g., unity, self-determination, collective responsibility, community purpose) as evident in the lives of African family ancestors.

This case study produced three findings that the researchers referred to as *Afrocentric Identity, Walking in Our Own Purpose, and Recovering the Past to "Re-member" Ourselves*. During the study, doctoral students gained new knowledge and developed the will, capacity, and confidence to use Afrocentric curriculum and pedagogy (*Afrocentric Agency*); parents identified the need to establish a collective and purposeful response to current community realities and the deficit narratives that persist about people of African ancestry, their schools, and communities (*Walking in Our Own Purpose*); and the study's participants agreed that a conscious "re-membering" of heritage knowledge—and the Black cultural ideals embedded in it—leads to cultural well-being and belonging and, in turn, to academic and cultural excellence (*Recovering the Past to "Re-member" Ourselves*).

When "Remembered" Texts are the Context

In *Freedom and Democracy: A Story Remembered* (Swartz, 2013), Afrocentric concepts direct us to look for that which was conceptually African,

Haudenosaunee, and European in 17th-century North America when these three groups met, that is, to identify the cultural platforms that carried the knowledge, ways of being, traditions, beliefs, values, and practices of each group (Asante, 1980/1988). Bringing these cultural platforms together—and applying the same set of culturally informed principles to writing about each cultural group—is central to the process we used to democratize knowledge. Thus, when "re-membered" texts are the context for writing lessons, making curricular and pedagogical choices, designing student assignments, and as the basis for interacting with parents, these experiences and practices are likely to be informed by Afrocentric concepts and culturally informed principles. By taking another look at Linda Campbell's case study (chapter 5), we can see how a "re-membered" text, with its Afrocentric concepts and culturally informed principles, not only impacted her classroom practices, but also "re-membered" several disconnections she identified in her curriculum and pedagogy—an outcome with implications for systemic change.

The Influence of Afrocentric Concepts and Culturally Informed Principles

In Linda Campbell's case study (chapter 5), the "re-membered" text about Austin Steward is framed by several Afrocentric concepts. Steward stands at the center of his own recovered story—the result of framing it with the Reclamation of Cultural Heritage (the conscious recovery of African history, culture, and identity) and Centrality/Location (placing Africa and African people and experiences at the center of phenomena as a standing place from which the past and present can be viewed and understood). The Afrocentric concepts of Subjects with Agency, Self-Determination, and Collective Responsibility framed accounts of his self-liberation, reciprocal and interconnected relationships with Black and White people, and the decisions he made to advocate for justice in the collective interests of his people. The principles of representation, accurate scholarship, indigenous voice, and the idea of a collective humanity guided the writing of the student text about Steward and those with whom he interacted.

Keep in mind that Austin Steward in a "re-membered" account is very different than Austin Steward in a standard account that would fit him into a dominant version of early 19th-century colonial settlement. In a standard account, his enslavement and business accomplishments would be mentioned, but the above Afrocentric concepts and culturally informed principles would not inform the account. Readers would not learn about his collaborative efforts to act in and on the world in service to freedom and the collective needs of his people. It is Afrocentric concepts that bring forward that which is African about Steward—the idea that freedom is a human entitlement and that reciprocity is essential to achievement and excellence. And it is the power of these concepts in the "re-membered" body of knowledge that moved Ms. Campbell's pedagogy toward fostering connections with students and parents—whom, along with herself, she now viewed as family:

> Most importantly, what I have called a "home-style" of teaching, plan-ning, and assessment that includes parents and families, has changed my ideas and practices about their role in teaching and learning.... We became partners. I no longer see parents and families as "out there," dis-connected from me and what we do in the classroom.... In a sense, we—students, parents, and teacher—have been "re-membered" or put back together just like the Austin Steward text we used.

As Ms. Campbell learned about Austin Steward, she described how knowl-edge of the past can shape the present: "I learned that Austin Steward is a model of empowerment. If he could accomplish all that he did with all that was against him, *it is because of him* that we can accomplish even more" [italics added]. It is Afrocentric concepts that present Steward as a model of empowerment—a man representative of his cultural community rather than an exception to (the rule of) his people. In a euro-script, he is an exceptional who is fit into the margins; in a "re-membered" text, culturally informed principles put him at the cen-ter of a democratized story that concurrently reflects his empowerment and is empowering for teachers, students, and parents.

As Ms. Campbell enacted Afrocentric concepts by centering students and their heritage in the curriculum, collaborating with parents, and making deci-sions that considered the collective needs of the classroom community, students' achievement, motivation, and cooperation increased, along with the engage-ment of parents in her instructional program and in other school activities. Specifically, she enacted Collective Consciousness by building genuine familial relationships with her students and their parents, which required the will and capacity to be collaborative and reciprocal (Subjects with Agency and Collec-tive Responsibility). As she became conscious of her heritage knowledge as a community member, and increased her cultural knowledge as a professional, she positioned African knowledge as a location for viewing and understanding the past (Centrality/Location), which lead to the Reclamation of Cultural Her-itage. Enacting these Afrocentric concepts reduced the disconnections between herself and students, herself and parents, and the curriculum and students' iden-tities—disconnections that she described as characteristic of her curriculum and pedagogy prior to this teacher research project. In other words, when Ms. Campbell used "re-membered" content, the Afrocentric concepts that framed that content also framed her interactions with students and parents. As she changed her practices, many of the disconnections that had unwittingly been driving her classroom practices were removed. No longer were her practices reproducing systemic outcomes such as student disengagement, low achieve-ment, limited parent involvement, and a devaluation of what parents in urban schools can contribute to the education of their children (Barton, Drake, Perez,

St. Louis, & George, 2004; Doucet, 2008; Edwards, 2010; Hill, 2010; Hill & Taylor, 2004).

Implications of Using "Re-Membered" Texts

In this volume's four case studies, practitioner researchers identified several implications of using "re-membered" texts for classrooms. However, it wasn't until we looked at all four completed case studies that we saw how their findings consistently suggested that using "re-membered" texts also "re-membered" or pointed the way toward a second type of "re-membering"—one with systemic implications. For generations, the preponderance of euro-spun content and standards has obstructed exposure to the heritage knowledge of liminal groups and to the cultural knowledge of all oppressed groups (Asante, 2007; Grande, 2004; Wynter, 2006). Thus, these knowledge bases have been disconnected from curricular and pedagogical choices, social studies content, ways of interacting with students' families, and institutional practices (King, 2006; Wynter, 1992). The findings of our four case studies exemplify how a number of these disconnected relationships and practices—which have become rooted in the educational system—were "re-membered":

- A teacher's cultural consciousness was "re-membered" with her choices of content and pedagogy and how she interacted with parents (chapter 5);
- Pre-service teachers' lack of engagement with the cultural knowledge of liminal groups pointed the way toward "re-membering" diverse cultural knowledge throughout teacher preparation programs (chapter 6);
- ESOL students' cultural and linguistic backgrounds were "re-membered" with lesson planning (chapter 7); and
- Heritage knowledge was "re-membered" with cultural well-being and belonging, that is, with academic and cultural excellence (chapter 8).

If increasing numbers of teachers raise their cultural consciousness and develop reciprocal relationships with students and parents; if increasing numbers of teacher preparation programs prepare teachers with a broad cultural knowledge base; if increasing numbers of teachers center students by connecting what is being taught in classrooms to their identities; and if increasing numbers of teachers and parents draw upon heritage and cultural knowledge to create learning experiences that foster academic and cultural excellence, a very different educational system comes into focus—one that places students at the center of the curriculum and the content of the curriculum at the center of a system that intends to equitably educate all groups of students (Asante, 1991/1992; Goodwin, 2004, 2013; Swartz, 1996).

Concluding Thoughts

The case studies in this volume show how recovering history and using "re-membered" student texts that reflect that recovery, reconnect more than the torn and dismembered pieces of the past that grand narratives foster and master scripts teach. As part of our Afrocentric culturally informed praxis, practitioner inquiry about the use of "re-membered" texts has brought the knowledge bases of diverse cultural platforms to bear on the relationships teachers build with students, families, and the institutions in which they work. Using practitioner inquiry adds to the democratizing potential of an Afrocentric culturally informed praxis by removing the inequitable power relations that determine who controls ideas about effective teaching and learning. Just as we can study and reconstruct the past from multiple vantage points, knowledge bases, and experiences, practitioner inquiry positions teachers as professionals who can study and reconstruct their present classroom practices rather than submit to practices that either fail to meet the academic and socio-cultural needs of students or worse, reproduce the very systemic outcomes that most teachers denounce.

What we have learned so far suggests that democratizing historical knowledge has a profound impact on social studies content; on grounding students, parents, and teachers with more accurate accounts of their heritage and history; on making fundamental changes in pedagogy; on building relationships among teachers, students, and families; and on shaping culturally informed and purposeful responses to the state of schools and the communities in which we live. While the scale of findings in our four case studies is small, the pattern in these findings suggests a potential line of research related to exploring the impact of using "re-membered" texts on both classroom practices and changing the hegemonic educational system we have inherited. It is our hope that varying iterations of practitioner inquiry related to "re-membering" will emerge from those who read this volume.

References

Asante, M. K. (1980/1988). *Afrocentricity*. Trenton, NJ: Africa World Press.
Asante, M. K. (1991/1992). Afrocentric curriculum. *Educational Leadership, 49*(4), 28–31.
Asante, M. K. (2007). *An Afrocentric manifesto*. Malden, MA: Polity Press.
Barton, A. C., Drake, C., Perez, J. G., St. Louis, K., & George, M. (2004). Ecologies of parental engagement in urban education. *Educational Researcher, 33*(4), 3–12.
Doucet, F. (2008). How African American parents understand their and teachers' roles in children's schooling and what this means for preparing preservice teachers. *Journal of Early Childhood Teacher Education, 29*(2), 108–139.
Dyson, M. (2007). My story in a profession of stories: Auto ethnography—an empowering methodology for educators. *Australian Journal of Teacher Education, 32*(1), 35–48.

Edwards, P. A. (2010). Village or villain: The role of African American families. In P. Edwards, G. T. McMillon, & J. D. Turner (Eds.), *A change is gonna come: Transforming literacy education for African American students* (pp. 93–131). New York, NY: Teachers College Press.

Goodwin, S. (2004). Emancipatory pedagogy. In S. Goodwin & E. E. Swartz (Eds.), *Teaching children of color: Seven constructs of effective teaching in urban schools* (pp. 37–48). Rochester, NY: RTA Press.

Goodwin, S. (2013, June). Conceptualizing culturally-connected, consciousness-raising teacher/parent-led schools, Paper presented at a professional development session of the Rochester Teacher Association, Rochester, NY.

Goodwin, S., & Swartz, E. E. (2009). *Document-based learning: Curriculum and assessment.* Rochester, NY: RTA Press.

Grande, S. (2004). *Red pedagogy: Native American social and political thought.* Lanham, MD: Rowman & Littlefield.

Hill, N. E. (2010). Culturally-based worldviews, family processes, and family-school interactions. In S. L. Christenson & A. L. Reschley (Eds.), *Handbook of school-family partnerships* (pp. 101–128). New York, NY: Routledge.

Hill, N. E., & Taylor, L. C. (2004). Parental school involvement and children's academic achievement: Pragmatics and issues. *Current Directions in Psychological Science, 13*(4), 161–164.

King, J. E. (2006). "If justice is our objective": Diaspora literacy, heritage knowledge and the praxis of critical studyin' for human freedom. *Yearbook of the National Society for the Study of Education, 105*(2), 337–360.

Steward, A. (2004). *Twenty-two years a slave, and forty years a freeman.* Rochester, NY: William Alling. (Original work published 1857)

Swartz, E. E. (1996). Emancipatory pedagogy: A postcritical response to "standard" school knowledge. *Journal of Curriculum Studies, 28*(4), 397–418.

Swartz, E. E. (2011). *Remembering our ancestors.* Rochester, NY: Rochester City School District.

Swartz, E. E. (2013). *Freedom and democracy: A story remembered.* Rochester, NY: Omnicentric Press.

Wynter, S. (1992). *Do not call us "Negroes": How multicultural textbooks perpetuate racism.* San Francisco, CA: Aspire Books.

Wynter, S. (2006). On how we mistook the map for the territory, and re-imprisoned ourselves in our unbearable wrongness of being, of Désêtre: Black studies toward the human project. In L. R. Gordon & J. A. Gordon (Eds.), *Not only the master's tools: African American studies in theory and practice* (pp. 107–169). Boulder, CO: Paradigm.

APPENDIX A

Four Identity-Group Narratives

This appendix includes narratives of the four identity-groups that shaped the development of freedom and democracy in North America. Each of these narratives is framed by Afrocentric metatheory and concepts and written with the principles of culturally informed curricular practice. It should be noted that the scholars whose work we have drawn upon may or may not have consciously used the specific Afrocentric concepts and culturally informed principles described in this volume. In either case, their scholarship provides knowledge that allows us to construct historical accounts that *do* consciously use these concepts and principles to frame and write identity-group narratives.

Several Afrocentric theoretical concepts (see definitions in Table 2.3 in chapter 2) frame each of the four narratives. Keep in mind that Afrocentric theory can be used to frame accounts of any identity-group, as, at its human-centric core, is the idea of locating each culture or group at the center of phenomena, not on the periphery. With each group's cultural platform as a location (Asante, 1980/1988), it is possible to replace eurocratic knowledge with democratized knowledge. Thus, when the Afrocentric concept of Collective Responsibility is used to frame knowledge about Haudenosaunee governance, it refers to the reciprocal and interconnected relationships among the Haudenosaunee that produced and maintain emancipatory practices such as participatory democracy and women in leadership positions. Likewise, when Centrality/Location is used to frame knowledge about the White colonial founding fathers, their cultural platform (e.g., cultural ideals, beliefs, values, ways of knowing and being) becomes the location from which to view their concerns about the leveling spirit of democracy.

You will notice that, due to the cultural base of Afrocentric theoretical concepts, a number of them are more identifiable in collectively oriented cultures than in individually oriented cultures. For example, Self-Determination is an Afrocentric concept in which individuals make decisions and control their lives, but they do this within the context of considering the common interests and sovereignty of the group. Thus, while Afrocentric concepts such as Centrality/ Location, Subjects with Agency, and Reclamation of Cultural Heritage can be used to frame accounts of all cultures and groups, concepts such as Collective Consciousness, Collective Responsibility, and Self-Determination are only used to frame accounts of groups with cultural tenets that foster ontologically based beliefs and values that are collective. The names of Afrocentric theoretical concepts that framed the content in identity-group narratives are placed in brackets at the end of paragraphs in each narrative.

Following each identity-group narrative is a sub-section that shows the connection between Afrocentric concepts and the principles of culturally informed curricular practice. We explain how specific culturally informed principles were used to actualize specific Afrocentric concepts when writing each narrative.

Haudenosaunee Narrative

An account of the Haudenosaunee related to freedom and democracy begins with knowledge about an Indigenous worldview. While not monolithic or static, Indigenous Peoples share commonalities of worldview such as the connectedness of all life, accountability to the collective whole—including ancestors and descendants, and the shared responsibility for maintaining balance and harmony of the total environment (Cajete, 1994; Cook, 1993; Dumont, 2002; Forbes, 2001; Tayac, 2004). Dating to the 12th century, the Haudenosaunee, or People of the Longhouse, became a League or Confederacy composed of five Nations (Mohawk, Oneida, Onondaga, Cayuga, Seneca) and later a sixth Nation (Tuscarora) throughout what is known today as New York State (Johansen, 1995). The history of this Confederacy begins with Tekanawita, the Peacemaker, who forged a union of five Nations by calling upon the laws of the universe and its Creator at a time when these Nations had set aside any commitment to peace and coexistence (Lyons, 1992; Tehanetorens, 1970/1999). His success in overcoming civil strife and war resulted in the unity of these Nations into the League of Five Nations. The Peacemaker also taught the principles of peace, justice, harmony, and freedom from coercion. These principles applied equally to men and women and were central to the Confederacy's governing tradition—a participatory democracy with practices of government by consent, the right to speak, freedom of religion, separation of powers, and confederation (Grinde, 1992; Lyons, 1992). The social and political structures developed by Tekanawita were recorded on Wampum Belts, one for each of the 117 sections in the Confederacy's Great Law of Peace (*Kaianerekowa*) (Ganienkeh Territory Council Fire, 2011; Tehanetorens, 1970/1999). Some sections explain how the Haudenosaunee Confederacy came about; others describe how the Nations are joined together, the structure of governance, symbols of the League, how leaders are chosen, and practices for dealing with other sovereignties. For example, in Wampum #57, Tekanawita describes the symbol of unity and what it means for the present and future generations:

> Five arrows shall be bound together very strong and shall represent one Nation each. As the five arrows are strongly bound, this shall symbolize the complete union of the Nations. Thus are the Five Nations completely united and enfolded together, united into one head, one body, and one mind. They therefore shall labor, legislate, and council together for the interests of future generations.
>
> *(Tehanetorens, 1970/1999, p. 28)*

[Collective Consciousness, Collective Responsibility, Centrality/Location, Self-Determination, Subjects with Agency, Reclamation of Cultural Heritage]

Haudenosaunee social structures are matrilineal, which means that women are central in maintaining the continuity of leadership, the sacredness of life, and the well-being of families (Shenandoah, 1988). This is evident in many sections in the Great Law of Peace that refer to their responsibilities. For example, Wampum #44 states:

> The lineal descent of the people of the Five Nations shall run in the female line. Women shall be considered the progenitors of the Nation. They shall own the land, and the soil. Men and women shall follow the status of their mothers.
>
> *(Tehanetorens, 1999, p. 22)*

Wampum #45 states, "The women heirs of the chieftainship titles of the League shall be called Oianer or Otiianer (Noble) for all time to come" (p. 22). These women heirs are thought of as *good path makers* (Ganienkeh Territory Council Fire, 2011). If a Chief errs in ways such as not attending the League or Grand Council, not following the rules of the Great Law of Peace, or in other ways failing to keep in mind the welfare of the people, a Clan Mother can begin a process to remove the Chief. If, after three complaints and warnings, the Chief is still disobedient, the Council of War Chiefs will take away the Chief's title, as stated in Wampum Belt #19, "by order of the women in whom the title is vested" (Tehanetorens, 1999, p. 10). Thus, while male leaders' titles are held by women, their power comes from serving the will of the people (Grinde & Johansen, 1991) [Collective Responsibility, Centrality/Location, Subjects with Agency].

Five hundred years after the forming of the Haudenosaunee Confederacy, Europeans arrived and began to settle on Haudenosaunee land. By the mid- to late 17th century, the Confederacy was strategically positioned between the English and French who fought over land and the fur trade. As long as they remained neutral, the Haudenosaunee (called Iroquois by the French) held the balance of power and were able to treat with both colonial powers. During this and the following century, the Haudenosaunee bore significant influence on colonial economies through trade, as well as colonial politics through land holdings (Boyd, 1943; Jennings, 1776; Johansen, 1982). Colonists also understood the authority that the Haudenosaunee held with other Indigenous Nations. In the early 1700s, James Logan, the most informed colonial administrator in charge of "Indian affairs" in the Pennsylvania colony stated, "If we lose the Iroquois, we are gone" (Van Doren & Boyd, 1938, p. xx). However, notwithstanding the regular making of treaties to purportedly assure that land would not be taken unless purchased, continued colonial expansion—both official and unofficial—made states of freedom and sovereignty increasingly difficult to maintain. The Haudenosaunee responded by strengthening alliances with other Indigenous Nations (as far west as the Appalachians), negotiating with British and French colonists, and later with the American colonists, and so remained central in diplomatic relations in the decades prior to the American Revolution (Fenton, 1998) [Centrality/Location, Self-Determination, Subjects with Agency, Reclamation of Cultural Heritage].

Since the 17th century, cultural contact between the Haudenosaunee and English colonists included interactions on formal and informal visits and as peers at conferences, ceremonies, and treaty councils. Indicative of the power held by the Haudenosaunee, the English became familiar with and carefully followed Haudenosaunee protocols in meetings and treaty councils, including brightening the Covenant Chain of friendship, using a form of the Condolence Ceremony, exchanging Wampum Belts to record agreements, giving gifts, making speeches related to concerns and interests, and providing time for reflection—often a day or two—before responding in negotiations (Grinde, 1992; Van Doren & Boyd, 1938). In the same way that colonists became skilled in negotiating with the Haudenosaunee, they became predisposed to considering Haudenosaunee political concepts and related symbols such as unity (a chain of interlocking links) and confederated strength (a bundle of arrows), which were placed on colonial coinage, broadsides, and the Great Seal of the United States (Grinde, 1992; Grinde & Johansen, 1991; Johansen, 1982). Haudenosaunee leaders and spokesmen such as Canassateego, Tiyanoga (Hendrick), and Kaintwakon (Cornplanter) presented concepts of unity and confederation when meeting with colonial leaders such as Benjamin Franklin, John Adams, and James Madison, suggesting by example that the preservation of the 13 colonies depended upon unifying as one federation (Van Doren & Boyd, 1938; Grinde, 1992; Venables, 1992). In fact, the 1854 Albany Plan of Union was modeled in part on what Benjamin Franklin learned about unity from the Haudenosaunee, which he viewed as an Indigenous American precedent for this political concept (Boyd, 1943). Tiyanoga was present in Albany as colonists and Haudenosaunee assembled to discuss Franklin's Albany Plan. He spoke on behalf of the 200 Haudenosaunee who attended, describing the ways in which unity was a central part of Haudenosaunee governance structures (Johansen, 1991) [Centrality/Location, Subjects with Agency, Reclamation of Cultural Heritage].

The Great Law of Peace still exists and preserves community by respecting the inherent freedom and will of the people. The Onkwehonwe (the Haudenosaunee People)—and all people—are understood as having a common right and shared responsibility to maintain their cultures without interference. This common right to maintain culture is expressed in the Canandaigua Treaty of 1794. While this treaty has been violated several times by the U.S government and corporations in western New York (e.g., dam construction and the flooding of Haudenosaunee land, industrial pollution of Haudenosaunee land and water, dumping drums of toxic solvents on Haudenosaunee land), it has provided legal recourse for some of these violations, thereby protecting to some extent the sovereignty of Haudenosaunee Nations today (Jemison, 1995). Governance that values sovereignty fosters a concern for the whole—a way of being that continues to be seen in Haudenosaunee advocacy for collective responsibility related to environmental restoration and ecological, economic, and human sustainability (Lickers, 1995; Mohawk, 2002; Shenandoah, 1988; Summit of Elders, 1995; Swamp, 1997) [Collective Consciousness, Collective Responsibility].

Writing the Haudenosaunee Narrative

The Afrocentric concepts that frame the contours of the above narrative bring into view a cultural platform (Asante, 1980/1988) that carries the knowledge, beliefs, values, and ways of being, knowing, and doing of the Haudenosaunee. With this cultural platform as a location, the principles of culturally informed curricular practice "wrote" this narrative. For example, the principles of accurate scholarship and indigenous voice actualized the Reclamation of Cultural Heritage by dating the origin of the Haudenosaunee Confederacy more accurately than dates given in eurocratic accounts, and by providing some history of the Confederation and the cultural tenets recorded in the Great Law of Peace. The principle of a collective humanity—the idea that all humanity is one and there is no hierarchy of human worth—enacted the Afrocentric concepts of Collective Consciousness, Collective Responsibility, and Centrality/Location by writing about Haudenosaunee practices such as the connectedness of all life, the inherency of freedom, and the common right to maintain culture without interference. These three principles, along with inclusion and critical thinking, realized the concepts of Self-Determination and Subjects with Agency when writing about the centrality of the Haudenosaunee in diplomatic relations with colonists in the Northeast during a century and a half of varied types of interaction. This content provides opportunities for critical thinking that are typically obstructed by truncated euro-bound accounts of 17th- and 18th-century cross-cultural relations. The principle of indigenous voice enacted the concepts of Collective Responsibility and Subjects with Agency when writing content about Haudenosaunee matrilineal social structures in which women and men collaborate in practices of governance. And the principle of representation actualized the concepts of Centrality/Location, Subjects with Agency, Self-Determination, and Reclamation of Cultural Heritage when writing content that positioned Haudenosaunee leaders within their communal cultural practices as they modeled and presented political concepts such as unity, sovereignty, and confederation to colonial leaders.

Africans in the Diaspora Narrative

An account of African men and women in the Diaspora related to freedom and democracy represents their experiences of freedom at home, and their efforts to consistently pursue human freedom in the Diaspora long before the founding of this country up to the present day (Bennett, 1975; Quarles, 1961; Robinson, 2000). The wellspring of this ongoing pursuit is the understanding that freedom is an inherent and shared right and responsibility to bring goodness, justice, and rightness into the world—an understanding shaped by African cultural orientations of harmony, collectivity, and interdependence, and cultural tenets such as the oneness of being and the sanctity of all life (Azuonye, 1996; Dixon, 1971; Karenga, 2006; Sindima, 1995). This ancient (Kemetic) and enduring way of thinking about and viewing life framed the socio-political and spiritual practices of African Nations. For example, in the West African Songhoy *Gandawey* (Empire) of the 1400s and 1500s, justice and rightness were leading principles of governance, with public accountability for leaders who were evaluated based on their caring for people using a system of just/fair treatment (J. E. King, personal communication, June 2, 2011). Decisions were a shared responsibility made by agreement among the living, as well as attending to the knowledge of ancestors. The Head of State consulted with a Wisdom Council of Elders called the San Hu (House of Scholars), the Queen Mother, the Head of State's Sisters, and a cabinet of experts (Maiga, 2010). People could approach leaders with ideas and concerns, there was freedom to practice more than one religion (e.g., African traditional religions, Islam), and a peacekeeping strategy that involved showing respect for the cultures and traditions of local populations. There were no prisons that took away individuals' freedom. Instead, wrongdoers gave back to their community by providing some service [Collective Consciousness, Collective Responsibility, Centrality/Location, Subjects with Agency, Reclamation of Cultural Heritage, the Anteriority of African Civilization].

As explained by Maulana Karenga (2006), Harriet Tubman exemplifies an African worldview (such as the Songhoy worldview illustrated above) by sidestepping individualism (interest in only achieving her own freedom) to pursue a "collective practice of self-determination in community" (facilitating freedom for others) (p. 247). He explains how Tubman's communal orientation comes from a longstanding African tradition of knowing that human freedom is a shared responsibility. This can also be seen in the hidden communities throughout the Americas organized by thousands of men and women—some of royal ancestry—who chose freedom not only from enslavement, but freedom to maintain culture on their own terms as a common right and responsibility (Hilliard, 1995; Piersen, 1993). In Jamaica and the United States, the people who liberated themselves from enslavement and established these hidden communities are called Maroons (Hart, 1985/2002). In Puerto Rico and Panama these men and women are called *Cimarrones;* in Colombia and Cuba, *Palenques;* and in Brazil, *Quilombolas* (Hilliard, 1995). *Palmares,* begun in the late 16th century, was the name of a *Quilombo* community of over 15,000 people that governed itself for almost 100 years (Gomez, 2004; Tomaz, Espíndula, & Pedrini, n.d.). Evidence of *Palmares* being a culturally diverse community exists, indicating that Angolans and their direct descendants lived in this fortified community along with other people of African descent—both free and self-liberated, poor immigrants of diverse cultural origins, and Indigenous People (Anderson, 1996) [Collective Consciousness, Collective Responsibility, Centrality/Location, Self-Determination, Subjects with Agency, Reclamation of Cultural Heritage].

Another example that allows us to see the cultural orientations, traditions, values, and practices related to freedom that African people brought with them to the Americas is the life's work of mathematician and astronomer Benjamin Banneker, including how he resisted and wrote against the system of slavery on behalf of his people (Swartz, 2013). The ethos of freedom can also be seen in the spirituals and other music traditions created by people of African descent—traditions traced back to the African aesthetics of Mali, Ghana, and Songhoy (Thiam, 2011). According to Cone (1992), these traditions come from a holistic worldview, and the spirituals in particular—which do not distinguish between the secular and the sacred—suggest that it was not the freedom-denying Christian religion, but African traditions of freedom that were the source of this music [Collective Consciousness, Collective Responsibility, Centrality/ Location, Self-Determination, Subjects with Agency, Reclamation of Cultural Heritage].

The knowledge and skills that African people brought to the Americas and that European/White enslavers exploited is documented (Carney, 2001; Hall, 2005; Holloway, 1990; Littlefield, 1981; Piersen, 1993; Walker, 2001). What is less well known are African ideas about freedom. Once in the Americas, primary sources such as colonial military and plantation records, court suits, petitions for freedom, letters, and other documents articulate Africans' freedom-seeking thoughts and actions, with frequent reference to never having given up their natural right to freedom (Aptheker, 1951/1969; Bennett, 1975; Hart, 1985/2002; Kaplan, 1973). These accounts uncover how African men and women throughout the Americas engaged in continuous revolts and collective resistance to enslavement throughout the *Maafa* (European enslavement of African people)—from the time of their forced arrival, and often in connection with Indigenous Americans (Bennett, 1975; Franklin, 1992; Price, 1979; Quarles, 1969; Thompson, 1987; Williams, 2010) [Collective Responsibility, Centrality/Location, Self-Determination, Subjects with Agency, Reclamation of Cultural Heritage].

Free and enslaved Africans were well represented in the struggle for freedom from England—among Stamp Act rioters, in street demonstrations, and in confrontations with British soldiers quartered in Boston (Bennett, 1968; Zobel, 1970). They served as soldiers and sailors in the major battles of the Revolutionary War, beginning at Lexington and Concord up until the British surrender at Yorktown (Kaplan, 1973). Whether fighting with the colonists or the British, Black people who were enslaved saw participating in the war as a pathway to freedom. Before and after the war, free men like Paul Cuffee, Prince Hall, Richard Allen, James Forten, and Absalom Jones hoped that political separation from England and ideas of democracy would lessen the restrictions under which they lived. For example, Cuffee and six other men of African ancestry petitioned the legislature in Massachusetts in 1780 to either give Africans the right to vote or to stop taxing them. Their petition sought the same right of representation that White colonists sought from England. Not only was their petition denied, they were jailed for refusing to pay taxes. In another case, Prince Hall, a community leader and founder of the first African Masonic Lodge in Boston, worked with others in his community to organize petitions in 1787 and 1788 for the end of slavery and for equal education, which were also denied. These examples indicate that while the war opened a few doors to freedom for soldiers and sailors, African rights would remain severely restricted even as the new United States was being established. Enslavement and other systemic restrictions denied African people the right to maintain their ancestral cultures as well as establish and maintain an unimpeded cultural presence suited to life in the Americas. These denials happened at the same time as colonists were seeking to end English rule and establish an independent cultural presence for themselves [Centrality/Location, Self-Determination, Subjects with Agency, Reclamation of Cultural Heritage].

Due to the power of patriarchy, the court battles for freedom of Jenny Slew and Mum Bett in the Massachusetts colony and later state are rarely if at all mentioned in standard instructional materials (Giddings, 1984; Kaplan, 1973). Slew was a free woman until 1762 when she was kidnapped and enslaved at the age of 43. She sued for her freedom that year in a Massachusetts court. While her right to sue was contested by her "owner," that colony did allow enslaved people to bring cases to court. She argued that her right to freedom ensued from her free-born mother—a law in some colonies that a child's status followed that of the mother. She won her case in 1766 when a Superior Court in

Salem overturned the decision of a lower court (Bruns, 1983). In 1781, Mum Bett petitioned a Massachusetts court for her freedom based on the new state Constitution, which stated in its Bill of Rights that "All men are born free and equal, and have certain natural, essential, and unalienable rights" (Kaplan, 1973). Upon gaining her freedom from a jury in Great Barrington, Massachusetts, Mum Bett changed her name to Elizabeth Freeman. Her case set a precedent for a series of cases (Quok Walker cases) that led to ending enslavement in that state. It is not surprising that one of Freeman's great grandchildren was the scholar, author, and human rights advocate W. E. B. Du Bois. In addition to these precedent-setting cases of resistance, African women—often only known by their first names—participated in other forms of resistance and revolt. Some poisoned their "owners," others used fire (Giddings, 1984). In 1681, Maria and two men tried to burn down the home of their "owner" in Massachusetts. One man was banished, one hung, and Maria was burned alive at the stake. The same fate was experienced in 1708 by a woman in Newton, Long Island, who was part of a revolt in which seven White people were killed. Women were similarly part of and punished for revolts in New York City and numerous Southern colonies throughout the 1700s. Many of these revolts were jointly planned and executed by African women and men, and in some cases supported by Indigenous and White Americans (Aptheker, 1993; Bennett, 1975). While less documentation is currently available related to African women, it is clear that they joined with African men in ongoing resistance to enslavement and in the pursuit of human freedom [Centrality/Location, Self-Determination, Subjects with Agency, Reclamation of Cultural Heritage].

As the system of slavery continued for more than another half century, African men and women such as David Walker (1965), Frederick Douglass (1881/1983), Harriet Tubman, Sojourner Truth (1850), Henry Highland Garnett (1972a & b), Richard Allen, Samuel Cornish, and John B. Russwurm (Bennett, 1968) provided written and spoken critiques of oppression that were congruent with their actions. They established institutions such as newspapers, churches, schools, and mutual aid societies and lived lives that actualized self-determination and communal concepts such as collective responsibility, reciprocity, justice, and right action (Anderson, 1988; Hutton, 1993; Lincoln & Mamiya, 1990; Mabee, 1979; West, 1972; Winch, 2002). These communal concepts were further evidenced in the coalescing of abolition forces and the Underground Railroad and the ongoing conceptualization and enactment of legal, social, educational, and political interventions against unjust laws and inequalities (Franklin, 1992; Quarles, 1969; Still, 2007). These critiques and actions taken for human freedom were central to both maintaining African culture and pushing the practice of democracy toward concurrence with its stated principles. These critiques and actions consistently occurred following emancipation and Reconstruction, and in events related to Jim Crow, segregation, and civil rights (Carruthers, 1999; Du Bois, 1935/1972, 1945, Foner,

2005; Grant, 1998; Wells, 1892). This steady African search for democratic congruence for all people continues today, for example, in efforts to expose and counteract disenfranchisement caused by profit-making schemes to privatize urban schools and expand the prison-industrial complex (Duncan, 2007; King, 2005) [Collective Consciousness, Collective Responsibility, Centrality/ Location, Self-Determination, Subjects with Agency, Reclamation of Cultural Heritage].

Writing the Africans in the Diaspora Narrative

The Afrocentric concepts that frame the contours of the above narrative bring into view a cultural platform (Asante, 1980/1988) that carries the knowledge, beliefs, values, and ways of knowing, being, and doing of Africans in the Diaspora. With this cultural platform as a location, the principles of culturally informed curricular practice "wrote" this narrative. For example, the principles of inclusion, accurate scholarship, and a collective humanity enacted the Afrocentric concepts of Collective Consciousness, Collective Responsibility, Centrality/Location, Subjects with Agency, Reclamation of Cultural Heritage, and the Anteriority of African Civilization when writing about the ancient and enduring elements of an African worldview and its collective, reciprocal, and interdependent characteristics. Examples of this worldview from the Songhoy of West Africa and the early records and practices of free and enslaved Africans support the claim that African people brought with them the knowledge that freedom is an inherent and shared right. These same three principles along with representation actualized the concepts of Self-Determination and Subjects with Agency by connecting this Continental African knowledge about freedom to the substantive pursuit of human freedom in the Diaspora since the early 16th century in North America. This pursuit is detailed with content about the hidden liberation communities throughout the Americas that demonstrated the common right to maintain culture, written evidence about African claims to never having given up their inherent right to freedom, and knowledge about varied forms of collective resistance and revolts. By using the principles of representation and critical thinking, the actions of individual men and women who worked for human freedom remain connected to their culture's values and pursuits, rather than presenting these individuals as decontextualized exceptions to their race/culture. Using this knowledge during instruction opens up the text for critical thinking opportunities about the cultural context of responses to enslavement and oppression that are typically omitted in social studies standards and curricula. And the principles of indigenous voice and a collective humanity realized the concepts of Collective Consciousness, Collective Responsibility, Centrality/Location, Self-Determination, Subjects with Agency, and Reclamation of Cultural Heritage when writing about the centuries-long, collaborative efforts of Africans in the Diaspora (e.g., establishing institutions, enacting varied interventions against unjust laws and inequalities) to bring democracy closer to its stated ideals for all people.

European/White Colonists Narrative

An account of freedom and democracy related to European/White colonists begins with knowledge about Europeans prior to arrival in North America. Whether they were indentured servants, poor farmers, artisans, mechanics, merchants, or landed aristocrats, Europeans were subject to monarchies and oligarchies. Obedience to authority, hard toil, debtors' imprisonment, and excessive taxes were exacted from the masses in exchange for one step from starvation subsistence (Cohen, 1952; Johnson, 1909). While the wealthy fared better than peasants, artisans, and merchants, everyone's lives were shaped by tyrannical social, political, and economic systems. The concepts and practices of freedom and democracy did not exist in Europe at this time.

Not long after arrival in North America, (mostly northern) Europeans of different nationalities formed loose bonds through the commonalities of survival, the negotiation with, but increasingly frequent assaults on Indigenous Peoples, and the emerging fixated binary of Europeans as White and superior, Africans as Black and inferior, and Europeans and their descendants as civilized and all "others" as not (Deloria, 2004; Mills, 1997; Morrison, 1992; Wynter, 1992). This Black/White binary conceptualized whiteness as all that was rational and good—what it meant to be human—with Blackness as its opposite (King, 2006; Wynter, 1992, 2000). Actualizing this racial belief structure, which depended upon the subjugation and exploitation of African and Indigenous Peoples and the appropriation of their lands, was at the core of advancing the colonial project, building wealth, and preserving European cultures and power in North America. With this racial duality hinged to the social, political, and economic practices of colonial life, White colonists carved out some liberties for themselves and engaged in self-government despite their colonial status. In fact, prior to 1776, colonists were practicing elements of democracy among themselves beyond anything that existed in Europe at the time (Di Nunzio, 1987). However, since White colonists created an occupational and class structure similar to that which existed in England, these experiences in self-government were only in the hands of the upper class, mostly English men who owned large amounts of land (Martin, 1973) [Centrality/Location, Subjects with Agency, Reclamation of Cultural Heritage].

Before the Revolution, colonial leaders interacted with Indigenous Peoples in numerous contexts for 150 years, observing and learning, among other things, about their practices of freedom and democratic political organization (Grinde & Johansen, 1991; Johansen, 1991; Mohawk, 1992). They also studied various European forms of government, but in 1787, many members of the Constitutional Convention noted the absence of democratic principles and practices in contemporary European nation states (Grinde, 1992). Franklin, in particular, stated in the records of that convention that "none of their Constitutions [are] suitable to our circumstances" (Farrand, 1911, p. 451). What the convention produced was a radically different constitutional document than any that existed in Europe—one that reflected some aspects of the Haudeno-saunee Great Law of Peace. The *Federalist Papers* provide a further window into the thinking of the country's new leadership, many who were large landown-ers (Hamilton, Madison, & Jay, 1787-1788/1961; Millican, 1990). While these upper-class leaders saw value in the practices of unity and government by con-sent, excerpts from the *Federalist* and other colonial pamphlets, newspapers, and letters indicate that the Founding Fathers viewed the leveling spirit of democ-racy as potentially disruptive of their control over the disenfranchised masses. They preferred a federally controlled system of representation that limited property rights and solidified their economic and political interests (Adams, 1875; Bailyn, 1965; Beard, 1914; Grinde, 1992). White leaders—be they Feder-alists or Antifederalists—spoke and wrote about the natural rights of freedom. Yet, this rhetoric existed at a time when they directly or indirectly participated in and greatly profited from (a) the system of slavery and severe restrictions on free Black people; (b) government supported land theft from Indigenous Nations; (c) the legal and social subjugation of women; and (d) the suppression of poor and "common" White people through disenfranchisement, marginal-ized political influence for those with voting rights, and economic exploitation of workers and tenant farmers (Deloria, 2004; Drinnon, 1980/1997; Franklin, 1992; Gage, 1980; Jennings, 1776; Martin, 1973; Quarles, 1961). What beliefs, assumptions, and practices can account for such massive contradictions? The White belief structure of race (Wynter, 1992, 2000), including the perceptions of racial difference as a deficit, the assigned status of African and Indigenous Peoples as less than human, the assumed inferiority of women embedded in law and custom, the social and political privileging of individuals who rose above their peers in power and wealth, and the assumption that only Europeans had the right to maintain their culture, exemplify this group's ontological and epistemological orientations of individualism, difference, domination, survival of the fittest (only the strongest individuals and cultures survive), and authority (Dixon, 1976; Nobles, 1991). Such a worldview, into which successive groups of European immigrants were assimilated as they became "White," engendered practices of cultural supremacy and exploitation, not practices in line with the natural rights discourse in the new republic's founding documents. After all, it took generations of struggle to pass numerous constitutional amendments that placed legal restraints on the race, class, and gender oppression supported by the original U.S. Constitution [Centrality/Location, Subjects with Agency, Reclamation of Cultural Heritage].

There was a small sub-group of White colonists who did not support the oppressive practices of colonial and later U.S. leaders and governments. They were not a coherent group and different concerns motivated them. Some were members of religious groups, others were workers and farmers, and a few were members of the upper class. However, the ideas and actions of these men and women demonstrate their varied commitments to freedom and justice, and clarify that, while White colonists were the dominant group, there were members among them who thought otherwise. While most White colonists, North and South, supported the system of slavery, there were some who published anti-slavery tracts, pamphlets, and books on the immorality and inhumanity of enslavement (Aptheker, 1993; Bailyn, 1965; Quarles, 1961). For example, Samuel Hopkins (1776–1787/1854) was a minister who, in 1776, called for the immediate release of all enslaved Africans in the 13 colonies. He made a direct connection between the freeing of Africans, who had never forfeited their liberty, and the freeing of the 13 colonies from England—stating that asking for liberty while denying it to others was the greatest of moral and practical contradictions. Hopkins went further to state that the enslavement of Africans was one reason for the oppressive situation in which the American colonists found themselves in relation to England. However, while Hopkins's exhortations against slavery were unyielding, his view of African peoples as uncivilized resulted in his equally strong recommendation that resettlement in Africa for the purpose of Christianizing African people should follow emancipation [Centrality/Location, Subjects with Agency, Reclamation of Cultural Heritage].

The Quakers are typically thought of as a religious group opposed to slavery, but many members of the Society of Friends were slave owners in the 17th and 18th centuries. Some Quakers such as George Keith, John Woolman, Anthony Benezet, Benjamin Rush, and Lucretia Mott spoke and wrote against enslavement in the 17th, 18th, and 19th centuries, and, along with other Quakers, became abolitionists and participated in the Underground Railroad (Brookes, 1937; Drake, 1950; Hallowell, 1884; Keith, 1889; Runes, 1947). Many of these Quakers worked with the first abolitionists—African men and women—and were inspired by their logical arguments and actions for freedom. But, Quaker abolitionists were more the exception than the rule. They typically experienced hostility in their Quaker Meetings—especially from the hierarchy of established ministers, were often disowned and expelled, and had to form their own Friends groups (Aptheker, 1993; Hallowell, 1884). However, most Friends groups that opposed slavery—first within their own ranks and then in the general society—were gradualists, adherents of colonization schemes, and slow to admit Black people as members (Drake, 1950). The Society of Friends fully disconnected from the system of slavery only shortly before the Civil War (Aptheker, 1956) [Centrality/Location, Subjects with Agency, Reclamation of Cultural Heritage].

In the early years of most colonies—prior to legalizing slavery for life in the mid-1600s—there were close relations between Black and White indentured servants, with documented alliances formed to escape indenture (Aptheker, 1993; Bennett, 1975). There were White colonists who agreed that the natural right of freedom applied to Black people, and some men and women such as James Hall Mumford and Delia Webster assisted liberation efforts and/or participated in African revolts against enslavement (Aptheker, 1993). A lynch mob forced a White Georgia printer, Elijah H. Burritt, to flee to the North for distributing *David Walker's Appeal* (Walker, 1829); and a White Boston seaman, Edward Smith who distributed the same book was fined and jailed for a year (Aptheker, 1993). In this book, David Walker revealed the hypocrisy and inhumanity of enslaving his people and called for resistance. There were also men like Charles Thomson who called for fair treaties with Indigenous Peoples and truthfully wrote down and reported colonial treaty negotiations (Hendricks, 1979). And there were named and unnamed White working people who—driven by the hope of freedom and equality—engaged in the struggle to end British rule. Shortly after the Revolutionary War, this drive for equality remained evident in civil protests begun by mostly White small farmers in western Massachusetts. Government officials were seizing and selling the land and livestock of these farmers for a fraction of their value. Given the cascading economic crisis following the war, small farmers—many of whom had just fought in the war—were unable to pay their taxes and other debts and they were being sentenced to debtor's prison (Szatmary, 1980; Zinn, 1980/2003). After several fruitless years of petitioning and offering solutions to the monetary crisis, the farmers moved from reform to revolt. Named after one of their leaders, Daniel Shay, the Shaysites armed themselves in 1786, surrounded the courthouses in their communities, and stopped the courts from repossessing their property and sentencing farmers to debtor's prison. The professional class of merchants, land speculators, lawyers, large landowners, and public officials—who benefited from these seizures of property—vilified and stood against the Shaysites (Szatmary, 1980). Before the rebellion ended in 1787, there were similar actions in New Jersey, Pennsylvania, South Carolina, Virginia, and Maryland. These rebellions—and the legislative and military responses of those in power to crush them—are credited with solidifying support for a Federalist Constitution that would give the national government increased powers to put down future domestic uprisings, both free and enslaved [Centrality/ Location, Subjects with Agency, Reclamation of Cultural Heritage].

The ideas of 18th-century wealthy White women are seen in the writing of intellectuals such as Judith Sargent Murray, Abigail Adams, and Mercy Otis Warren. While they protested British tyranny and taxation without representation and warned against English government as a model, their protests against the subordination of women were limited (Adams, 1875, 1878/1972; Cohen, 1983; Kerber, 1980; Sargent Murray, 1994; Zagarri, 1995). Accounts of White women workers who engaged in street protests and textile production to boycott British goods, participated in the war as spies and messengers,

and disguised themselves as soldiers shows how they responded to their gender and class oppression and to ideas of freedom (Norton, 1980). However,
clear class distinctions existed among White women. The upper class received
legal and economic benefits unavailable to poor and indentured White women,
and White women in general fared better than women of color (Hoff Wilson,
1976). Thus, White women were similarly affected by the race and class hierarchies of human worth that defined the interactions of their male counterparts
with others related to practices of freedom. These hierarchies of human worth
can still be seen in the social, political, and economic inequalities that exist
today, with, for example, White women and therefore White families receiving
more benefit from affirmative action than other disenfranchised groups, such as
women of African ancestry and their families (Massey & Denton, 1993; Robinson, 2000; Walters, 1982) [Subjects with Agency, Reclamation of Cultural
Heritage].

Writing the European/White Colonists Narrative

The Afrocentric concepts that frame the contours of the above narrative bring
into view a cultural platform (Asante, 1980/1988) that carries the knowledge,
beliefs, values, and ways of being, knowing, and doing of European/White
colonists. With this cultural platform as a location, the principles of culturally informed curricular practice "wrote" this narrative. The principles of
inclusion, accurate scholarship, representation, indigenous voice, and critical
thinking enacted the Afrocentric concepts of Centrality/Location, Subjects
with Agency, and Reclamation of Cultural Heritage that frame the European/
White colonist narrative. These principles enacted these concepts by writing
about the political and economic conditions of Europeans prior to arrival in
the Americas and about the ways in which they conceptualized and used race
after their arrival. Thus, there is content in the narrative about Europeans'
experience of monarchy and tyranny—not freedom or democracy, and about
the emerging Black/White binary they fostered once in North America. This
content locates the cultural ideals, values, and ways of knowing and being of
Europeans and their White descendants at the center of phenomena, which
creates opportunities for critical thinking about the seeming inevitability of
racial division and White domination, which are still the messages provided
in standard curriculum. The principle of representation "wrote" content about
European/White ways of being (ontological orientations such as individualism,
difference, and survival of the fittest), knowing (epistemological orientation of
authority), and doing (subjugation and exploitation), as seen in evidence of their
interactions with Indigenous and African Peoples. The principles of accurate
scholarship and indigenous voice made it possible to write about the contradictions between White rhetoric and actions, and the preference of colonial
leaders for a federally controlled system of representation that excluded people

of color, women, and poor White people, positioning White, wealthy colonial men as the primary beneficiaries of democracy. And the principles of inclusion, indigenous voice, and accurate scholarship actualized the concepts of Centrality/Location, Subjects with Agency, and Reclamation of Cultural Heritage when writing about a sub-group of White colonists who acted against inequalities and unjust hierarchies experienced by African and Indigenous Peoples and poor White people. In so doing, this sub-group of White colonists participated in the reach for a more inclusive and just democracy before and after the Revolutionary War.

European Enlightenment Philosophers Narrative

Elementary, middle, and high school textbooks still identify only European sources (e.g., ancient Greece, the Magna Carta, European Enlightenment philosophers) as influences on the origin of U.S. democracy (Banks et al., 2005; Boyd et al, 2011; Cayton, Israels Perry, Reed, & Winkler, 2007; Garcia, Ogle, Risinger, & Stevos, 2005). For example, England's John Locke is consistently featured for his influence on the thinking of Thomas Jefferson. There is no doubt that the theories of European Enlightenment philosophers affected what happened in colonial America, but affect also occurred in the opposite direction (Arneil, 1996). European explorers and travelers to the Americas from the late 16th into the 18th century observed and wrote about Indigenous Americans. Those who traveled in the Northeast wrote about the Haudenosaunee, Huron, and other Indigenous Nations, and many published accounts of their experiences when they returned home (Grinde, 1992; Mohawk, 1992). These accounts included details about egalitarian practices, governance structures that were democratic, and what travelers observed as the natural state of freedom from want, coercion, and oppression [Centrality/Location].

This natural state of freedom was of interest to English and French philosophers such as Thomas Hobbes, John Locke, Jean Jacques Rousseau, and Charles De Montesquieu. They read these travelogues, but only used those portions that supported the various natural law theories they proposed for the management and improvement of European societies—which they referred to as civil (Hobbes, 1977; Locke, 1988; Montesquieu, 1952; Rousseau, 1952). They mostly ignored evidence provided by European explorers and travelers about Indigenous institutions, governance systems, and land cultivation. While meeting all the requirements of civil society—even as defined by Europeans—these Indigenous practices did not fit with dichotomous Enlightenment theories. For example, Enlightenment philosophers claimed that Indigenous Americans lived in a state of nature—a precursor of civil society and an Edenic source from which theories of natural law could be fashioned. In this way, they "explained" how, over time, common land necessarily becomes private (a European interest) through cultivation as people "progress" (Arneil, 1996). As colonial aggression increased and Indigenous Americans defended their home-lands, Europeans shifted their cultural perception of Indigenous Americans from noble and innocent (potential converts to the "civilizing" influence of Christianity) to ignoble and diabolical (irredeemable "others" whose presence obstructed colonial interests). In both dichotomous, seemingly contradictory perceptions—an Edenic state of nature as opposite civil society, and noble/innocent Indigenous Americans as opposite those who were ignoble/diaboli-cal—Enlightenment philosophers solipsistically viewed Indigenous Peoples at a stage of human development below that of Europeans whose "more advanced" cultures were more worthy of continuance than Indigenous and later African cultures. While the colonizing tactics of European countries varied, Enlight-enment philosophers commonly claimed European cultural supremacy—a spurious claim that was used to justify conquest, land appropriation, cultural destruction, and enslavement [Centrality/Location, Subjects with Agency, Reclamation of Cultural Heritage].

Enlightenment philosophers lived and worked in countries ruled by monar-chal and oligarchic governments. In addition to providing political theories in support of colonial expansion and empire building abroad, they sought to reform their governments at home. Influenced by the reported—but typically unacknowledged—freedoms and egalitarian practices in Indigenous American societies, they proposed an enlightened absolutism. For example, John Locke admonished 17th-century English monarchs to rule more justly, but his alter-native to monarchy and the divine right to rule was not a public empowered to participate in government; it was a government led by property-owning aristo-crats (Di Nunzio, 1987). By way of contrast, Nations of Indigenous Americans modeled freedom and justice, and the Haudenosaunee in particular exhibited a participatory democracy. For over 150 years colonists observed and experi-enced these Indigenous practices, many which they took on and altered to serve their purposes. It was 19th-century historians who ignored these Indigenous influences in order to position the political theories of Enlightenment figures as central to the origin of U.S. democracy. In this interpretation, European theo-ries trumped American empiricism, which continues to be the case in standard school knowledge. Colonialism is still justified and Indigenous influences on ideas and practices of freedom, justice, and democracy are still omitted from curriculum and instructional materials [Subjects with Agency, Reclamation of Cultural Heritage].

So what do we owe European Enlightenment philosophers, and why are they selected as one of the four identity-groups who bore influence on the ideas and practices of freedom and democracy in colonial America? As upper-class men of mostly English and French nationality, these philosophers had a profound influ-ence on their ontologically similar but distant counterparts in North America. These philosophers can be credited with laying the exclusionary and therefore contradictory groundwork that guided democracy's euro-driven development in the West from the late 18th century to the present (Keita, 2000). The period's pseudo-scientific biological theories of race were used by European and White American philosophers, authors, and statesmen (e.g., Gobineau, Hegel, Hume, Kant, Jefferson) to justify European domination and White racial supremacy as seen in its modern age practices of colonialism, imperialism, capitalism, and now discredited "sciences" such as phrenology, craniology, degeneracy theory, and eugenics (Biddiss, 1966; Gilman, 1983; Gould, 1981; Keita, 2000; Mills, 1997; Sanders, 1969). The exclusion of people of color, women, poor people, and the differently abled in the purportedly inclusive concepts of freedom and democracy can better be understood by accurately representing knowledge about Enlightenment philosophers. This identity-group's European cultural orientations—further informed by its upper-class status, western-euro-national identity, and gender—resulted in political theories, practices, and scientific productions in which "others" were viewed as deviations from the norm of whiteness, maleness, upper-classness, and ableness, and, in the case of Hegel's (1900, p. 99) view of African people as "no historical part of the world" (Asante, 2003; Kliewer & Fitzgerald, 2001; Wynter, 1992, 2005) [Subjects with Agency, Reclamation of Cultural Heritage].

Perhaps the most catastrophic and enduring outcome of Enlightenment philosophers' political theories is the support they provided for the rapine of entire continents. Political theorist John Locke—who gained in personal wealth through his involvement in the administrative affairs of the Carolina colony—defended England's right to "vacant" land in the Americas (Tully, 1993). In his *Two Treatises of Government,* Locke's labor theory of property defined property as land that is enclosed and cultivated—a theory that was consistently used to circumvent the right of thousands of years of occupancy claimed by Native Americans (Arneil, 1996; Locke, 1988). If land wasn't being "used," it could be taken according to the constructed theories of Enlightenment philosophers. Linking the individual right to own private property in a civil society to its cultivation through labor became the pretext for English colonial practices of massive land appropriation that preserved European communities and cultures. Bolstered by the Protestant work ethic, Enlightenment justifications for taking Indigenous land and turning it into private property and wealth in the Americas became part of a contradictory framework for a new nation claiming to be a democracy based on freedom. As one example among much shameless irrationality, the knowledge, skills, and labor of enslaved Africans (also viewed as private property and a source of wealth) were used to decorate federal buildings that symbolized freedom and democracy (Robinson, 2000). Freedom and the right to maintain their cultures were denied to Indigenous and African Peoples. White colonial leaders, perceiving themselves as the primary beneficiaries of democracy, systemically embedded hierarchal Enlightenment ideas in the context of democracy, denied freedom and democracy to "others," and maintained a privileged class through structured inequalities. Social science has continued to recycle these hegemonic ideas with genetic explanations of and deficit-oriented approaches to altering racial and socio-economic "gaps" in education and other fields (Herrnstein & Murray, 1994; Jensen, 1972; Payne, 2001; Riessman, 1962). Another remnant of the Enlightenment and its claim to cultural supremacy is ongoing opposition to expanding school knowledge beyond the canons of European civilization (Bloom, 1987; Hirsch, 1987; Schlesinger, 1992; Wood, 2003) [Centrality/Location, Subjects with Agency, Reclamation of Cultural Heritage].

Writing the European Enlightenment Philosophers Narrative

The Afrocentric concepts that frame the contours of the above narrative bring into view a cultural platform (Asante, 1980/1988)—shaped by class and nationality—that carries the knowledge, beliefs, values, and ways of being, knowing, and doing of European Enlightenment philosophers. With this platform as a location, a number of principles of culturally informed curricular practice "wrote" this narrative. For example, the principles of accurate scholarship and representation enacted the Afrocentric concepts of Subjects with Agency, and the Reclamation of Cultural Heritage when writing about how Enlightenment philosophers were influenced by the practices of Indigenous Peoples in North America. English and French philosophers developed political theories in support of colonization abroad, and they sought to create an enlightened absolutism at home by asking for just rule from their monarchs, not representative democracy for the masses. The principle of representation contextualizes the portrayals of these philosophers through their ways of being, knowing, and doing. Their ontological orientations of individualism, competition, difference, and domination over nature; and their epistemological orientations of (il)logic and (pseudo)science are evident in their writing about "others." Thus, accurate scholarship and representation reclaim parts of European cultural heritage that have been either omitted or misrepresented in standard accounts. The principles of inclusion, indigenous voice, and critical thinking actualized the concepts of Centrality/Location, Subjects with Agency, and the Reclamation of Cultural Heritage when writing about the substantive influences of these philosophers, in particular the credence they gave to theories of property and race used to support European cultural supremacy, conquest, and empire building. By using the principle of indigenous voice, these philosophers spoke for themselves and their worldview through their writing; and their work invites critical thinking about how a supremacist ideology is created and a hierarchy of human worth is maintained. The only way to "see" the principle of a collective humanity in the writing of this narrative is in its absence—as an opposite assertion of the ideas of Enlightenment philosophers. Their writings and the ways in which they have been used normalize oppression and stand opposed to the oneness of humanity.

References

Adams, C. F. (1875). *Familiar letters of John Adams and his wife Abigail Adams, during the Revolution with a memoir of Mrs. Adams.* Boston, MA: Houghton Mifflin.

Adams, C. F. (Ed.). (1878/1972). *Correspondence between John Adams and Mercy Warren.* New York, NY: Arno Press.

Anderson, J. (1988). *The education of blacks in the South, 1860–1935.* Chapel Hill: The University of North Carolina Press.

Anderson, R. N. (1996). The Quilombo of Palmares: A new overview of a Maroon state in seventeenth-century Brazil. *Journal of Latin American Studies, 28*(3), 545–566.

Aptheker, H. (1951/1969). *A documentary history of the Negro people in the United States: From colonial times through the Civil War* (Vol. I). New York, NY: The Citadel Press.

Aptheker, H. (1956). *Toward Negro freedom.* New York, NY: New Century.

Aptheker, H. (1993). *Anti-racism in U.S. history: The first two hundred years.* Westport, CT: Praeger.

Arneil, B. (1996). *John Locke and America: The defence of English colonialism.* New York, NY: Oxford University Press.

Asante, M. K. (1980/1988). *Afrocentricity.* Trenton, NJ: Africa World Press.

Asante, M. K. (2003). The Afrocentric idea. In A. Mazama (Ed.), *The Afrocentric paradigm* (pp. 37–53). Trenton, NJ: Africa World Press.

Azuonye, C. (1996). *Dogon.* New York, NY: Rosen Publishing Group.

Bailyn, B. (Ed.). (1965). *Pamphlets of the American Revolution, 1750–1776* (Vol. 1). Cambridge, MA: The Belknap Press.

Banks, J. A., Boehm, R. G., Colleary, K. P., Contreras, G., Goodwin, A. L., McFarland, M.A., & Parker, W. C. (2005). *Our nation.* New York, NY: Macmillan/ McGraw-Hill.

Beard, C. (1914). *An economic interpretation of the Constitution of the United States.* New York, NY: Macmillan.

Bennett, L., Jr. (1968). *Pioneers in protest.* Chicago, IL: Johnson Publishing Company.

Bennett, L., Jr. (1975). *The shaping of Black America.* Chicago, IL: Johnson Publishing Company.

Biddiss, M. D. (1966). Gobineau and the origins of European racism. *Race, 7*(3), 255–270.

Bloom, A. (1987). *The closing of the American mind: How education has failed democracy and impoverished the souls of today's students.* New York, NY: Simon & Schuster.

Boyd, C. D., Gay, G., Geiger, R., Kracht, J. B., Ooka Pang, V., Risinger, C. F., & Sanchez, S. M. (2011). *Communities.* Boston, MA: Pearson.

Boyd, J. P. (1943). Dr. Franklin: Friend of the Indians. In The Franklin Institute (Ed.), *Meet Dr. Franklin* (pp. 201–220). Lancaster, PA: Lancaster Press.

Brookes, G. S. (1937). *Friend Anthony Benezet.* Philadelphia: University of Pennsylvania Press.

Bruns, R. (Ed.). (1983). *Am I not a man and a brother: The antislavery crusade of Revolutionary America, 1688–1788.* New York, NY: Chelsea House.

Cajete, G. (1994). *Look to the mountain: An ecology of Indigenous education.* Durango, CO: Kivaki Press.

Carney, J. A. (2001). *Black rice: The African origins of rice cultivation in the Americas.* Cambridge, MA: Harvard University Press.

Carruthers, J. H. (1999). *Intellectual warfare.* Chicago, IL: Third World Press.

Cayton, A., Israels Perry, E., Reed, L., & Winkler, A. M. (2007). *America: Pathways to the present.* Boston. MA: Pearson Education/Prentice Hall.

Cohen, F. (1952). Americanizing the white man. *The American Scholar, 21*(2), 177–191.

Cohen, L. H. (1983). Mercy Otis Warren: The politics of language and the aesthetics of self. *American Quarterly, 35*(5), 481–498.

Cone, J. H. (1992). *The spirituals and the blues: An interpretation.* Maryknoll: NY: Orbis Book.

Cook, K. (1993). Seeking the balance, a Native women's dialogue. *Akwe:kon, X*(2), 16–29.

Deloria, V., Jr. (2004). Promises made, promises broken. In G. McMaster & C. E. Trafzer (Eds.), *Native universe: Voices of Indian America* (pp. 143–159). Washington, DC: National Museum of the American Indian, Smithsonian Institution/National Geographic Society.

Di Nunzio, M. R. (1987). *American democracy and the authoritarian tradition of the West.* Lanham, MD: University Press of America.

Dixon, V. J. (1971). African-oriented and Euro-American-oriented world views: Research methodologies and economics. *The Review of Black Political Economy, 7*(2), 119–156.

Dixon, V. J. (1976). World views and research methodology. In L. M. King, V. J. Dixon, & W. W. Nobles (Eds.), *African philosophy: Assumptions and paradigms for research on Black persons* (pp. 51–102). Los Angeles, CA: Fanon Research and Development Center.

Douglass, F. (1881/1983). *The life and times of Frederick Douglass.* Secaucus, NJ: Citadel Press.

Drake, T. E. (1950). *Quakers and slavery in America.* New Haven, CT: Yale University Press.

Drinnon, R. (1980/1997). *Facing west: The metaphysics of Indian-hating & empire-building.* Norman: University of Oklahoma Press.

Du Bois, W. E. B. (1935/1972). *Black reconstruction in America.* New York, NY: Atheneum.

Du Bois, W. E. B. (1945). *Color and democracy.* New York, NY: Harcourt Brace and Company.

Dumont, J. (2002). Indigenous intelligence. *Native Americas, XIV*(3 & 4), 15–16.

Duncan, G. A. (2007). From plantations to penitentiaries: Race making and new century schools. In M. Welsing (Ed.), *Without fear…claiming safe communities without sacrificing ourselves* (pp. 26–37). Los Angeles, CA: The Southern California Library for Social Studies Research.

Farrand, M. (Ed.). (1911). *The records of the Federal convention* (Vol. 1). New Haven, CT: Yale University Press.

Fenton, W. N. (1998). *The Great Law and the Longhouse: A political history of the Iroquois confederacy.* Norman: University of Oklahoma Press.

Foner, E. (2005). *Forever free: The story of emancipation and Reconstruction* (illustrations edited and with commentary by Joshua Brown). New York, NY: Alfred A. Knopf.

Forbes, J. D. (2001). Nature and culture: Problematic concepts for Native Americans. In J. A. Grim (Ed.), *Indigenous traditions and ecology: The interbeing of cosmology and community* (pp. 103–124). Cambridge, MA: Harvard University Press for the Center for the Study of World Religions, Harvard Divinity School.

Franklin, V. P. (1992). *Black self-determination: A cultural history of African American resistance.* Chicago, IL: Lawrence Hill Books.

Gage, M. J. (1980). *Women, church and state*. Watertown, MA: Persephone Press. (Original work published 1893)

Ganienkeh Territory Council Fire (2011). *Kayanerehkowa, the Great Law of Peace.* Retrieved from http://www.ganienkeh.net/thelaw.html

Garcia, J., Ogle, D. M., Risinger, C. F., & Stevos, J. (2005). *Creating America: A history of the United States*. Evanston, IL: McDougal Littell.

Garnet, H. H. (1972a). Address to the slaves of the United States of America (Rejected by the National Convention held in Buffalo, NY, 1843). In S. Stuckey (Ed.), *The ideological origins of Black nationalism* (pp. 168–170). Boston, MA: Beacon Press.

Garnet, H. H. (1972b). Speech to the Colored citizens of Boston, 1859. In S. Stuckey (Ed.), *The ideological origins of Black nationalism* (pp. 174–194). Boston, MA: Beacon Press. (Originally printed in *The Weekly Anglo African,* Volume 1, No. 9, September 19, 1859)

Giddings, P. (1984). *When and where I enter, the impact of Black women on race and sex in America*. New York, NY: Bantam Books.

Gilman S. C. (1983). Degeneracy and race in the nineteenth century: The impact on clinical medicine. *The Journal of Ethnic Studies, 10*(4), 27–50.

Gomez, M. (2004). *Reversing sail: A history of the African diaspora*. New York, NY: Cambridge University Press.

Gould, S. J. (1981). *The mismeasure of man*. New York, NY: Norton.

Grant, J. (1998). *Ella Baker: Freedom bound*. New York, NY: Wiley.

Grinde Jr., D. A. (1992). Iroquois political theory and the roots of American democracy. In O. Lyons & J. Mohawk (Eds.), *Exiled in the land of the free: Democracy, Indian nations, and the U.S. Constitution* (pp. 228–280). Santa Fe, NM: Clear Light Publishers.

Grinde Jr., D. A., & Johansen, B. E. (1991). *Exemplar of liberty: Native America and the evolution of democracy*. Los Angeles: American Indian Studies Center, University of California, Los Angeles.

Hall, G. M. (2005). *Slavery and African ethnicities in the Americas: Restoring the links*. Chapel Hill: University of North Carolina Press.

Hallowell, A. D. (1884). *James and Lucretia Mott: Life and letters* (A. D. Hallowell, Ed.). Boston, MA: Houghton Mifflin.

Hamilton, A., Madison, J., & Jay, J. (1787–1788/1961). *The Federalist papers* (C. Rossiter, Ed.). New York, NY: A Mentor Book, The New American Library.

Hart, R. (1985/2002). *Slaves who abolished slavery: Blacks in rebellion*. Kingston, Jamaica: University of the West Indies Press.

Hegel, G. W. F. (1900). *The philosophy of history* (rev. ed. from G. W. F. Hegel's original lecture manuscripts, 1830–1831). New York, NY: The Colonial Press. Hendricks, J. E. (1979). *Charles Thomson and the making of a new nation, 1929–1824*. Cranbury, NJ: Associated University Presses.

Herrnstein, R. J., & Murray, C. (1994). *The bell curve: Intelligence and class structure in American life*. New York, NY: Free Press.

Hilliard, A. G. III (1995). *The Maroon within us: Selected essays on African American community socialization*. Baltimore, MD: Black Classic Press.

Hirsch, E. D., Jr. (1987). *Cultural literacy: What every American needs to know*. Boston. MA: Houghton Mifflin.

Hobbes, T. (1977). *Leviathan, or the matter, forme, & power of a common-wealth ecclesiasticall and civil* (C. B. Macpherson, Ed.). New York, NY: Penguin Books. (Original work published 1651)

Hoff Wilson, J. (1976). The illusion of change: Women and the American Revolution.

In A. F. Young (Ed.), *The American Revolution: Explorations in the history of American radicalism* (pp. 383–445). De Kalb: Northern Illinois University Press.

Holloway, J. E. (Ed.) (1990). *Africanisms in American culture*. Bloomington: Indiana University Press.

Hopkins, S. (1776–1787/1854). *Timely articles on slavery*. Boston, MA: Congregational Board of Publication.

Hutton, F. (1993). *The early Black press in America, 1827 to 1860*. Westport, CT: Greenwood Press.

Jemison, G. P. (1995). Sovereignty and treaty rights — we remember. *Akwesasne Notes New Series, 1*(3 & 4), 10–15.

Jennings, F. (1776). The Indians' revolution. In A. F. Young (Ed.), *The American Revolution: Explorations in the history of American radicalism* (pp. 319–348). DeKalb: Northern Illinois University Press.

Johansen, B. E. (1982). *Forgotten founders: Benjamin Franklin, the Iroquois and the rationale for the American Revolution*. Ipswich, MA: Gambit.

Johansen, B. E. (1991 Summer). Native American roots for freedom of expression as a form of liberty. *Journal of Communication Inquiry, 15*(2), 48–69.

Johansen, B. E. (1995). Dating the Iroquois Confederacy. *Akwesasne Notes New Series, 1*(3 & 4), 62–63.

Johnson, A. H. (1909). *The disappearance of the small landowner: Ford lectures*. Retrieved from http://babel.hathitrust.org/cgi/pt?id=mdp.39015063841251

Kaplan, S. (1973). *The Black presence in the era of the American Revolution, 1770–1800*. Greenwich, CT: New York Graphic Society Ltd. in association with the Smithsonian Institution Press.

Karenga, M. (2006). Philosophy in the African tradition of resistance: Issues of human freedom and human flourishing. In L. R. Gordon & J. A. Gordon (Eds.), *Not only the master's tools: African American studies in theory and practice* (pp. 243–271). Boulder, CO: Paradigm.

Keita, M. (2000). *Race and the writing of history: Riddling the Sphinx*. New York, NY: Oxford University Press.

Keith, G. (1889). An exhortation and caution to Friends concerning buying or keeping of Negroes. *Pennsylvania Magazine of History and Biography, 13,* 265–270. (Original work published 1693)

Kerber, L. K. (1980). *Women of the Republic: Intellect and ideology in Revolutionary America*. Chapel Hill: The University of North Carolina Press.

King, J. E. (2005). A transformative vision of Black education for human freedom. In J. E. King (Ed.), *Black education: A transformative research and action agenda for the new century* (pp. 3–17). Mahwah, NJ: Erlbaum for the American Educational Research Association.

King, J. E. (2006). Perceiving reality in a new way: Rethinking the Black/White duality of our times. In A. Bogues (Ed.), *Caribbean reasonings. After Man toward the human. Critical essays on Sylvia Wynter* (pp. 25–56). Kingston, Jamaica: Ian Randle Publishers.

Kliewer, C., & Fitzgerald, L. May (2001). Disability, schooling, and the artifacts of colonialism. *Teachers College Record, 103*(3), 450–470.

Lickers, F. H. (1995). Haudenosaunee environmental action plan. *Akwesasne Notes New Series, 1*(3 & 4), 16–17.

Lincoln, C. E., & Mamiya, L. H. (1990). *The Black church in the African American experience*. Durham, NC: Duke University Press.

Littlefield, D. C. (1981). *Rice and slaves: Ethnicity and the slave trade in colonial South Caro-lina.* Baton Rouge: Louisiana State University Press.

Locke, J. (1988). *Two treatises of government* (P. Laslett, Ed.). New York, NY: Cambridge University Press. (Original work published 1690)

Lyons, O. (1992). The American Indian in the past. In O. Lyons & J. Mohawk (Eds.), *Exiled in the land of the free: Democracy, Indian Nations, and the U.S. Constitution* (pp. 14–42). Santa Fe, NM: Clear Light Publishers.

Mabee, C. (1979). *Black education in New York State: From colonial to modern times.* Syracuse, NY: Syracuse University Press.

Maiga, H. O. (2010). *Balancing written history with oral tradition: The legacy of the Songhoy people.* New York, NY: Routledge.

Martin, J. K. (1973). *Men in rebellion: Higher government leaders and the coming of the American Revolution.* New Brunswick, NJ: Rutgers University Press.

Massey, D. S., & Denton, N. A. (1993). *American apartheid: Segregation and the making of the underclass.* Cambridge, MA: Harvard University Press.

Millican, E. (1990). *One united people: The Federalist Papers and the national idea.* Lexington, KY: The University Press of Kentucky.

Mills, C. W. (1997). *The racial contract.* Ithaca, NY: Cornell University Press.

Mohawk, J. (1992). Indians and democracy: No one ever told us. In O. Lyons & J. Mohawk (Eds.), *Exiled in the land of the free: Democracy, Indian nations, and the U.S. Constitution* (pp. 44–71). Santa Fe, NM: Clear Light Publishers.

Mohawk, J. (2002). Nurturance is the responsibility of the nation and the people. *Native Americas, XIV*(3 & 4), 58–62.

Montesquieu, C. De (1952). *The spirit of laws* (T. Nugent, Trans., revised by J. V. Prichard). Chicago, IL: The University of Chicago and Encyclopedia Britannica. (Original work published 1748)

Morrison T. (1992). *Playing in the dark, whiteness and the literary imagination.* Cambridge, MA: Harvard University Press.

Nobles, W. W. (1991). African philosophy: Foundations for Black psychology. In R. Jones (Ed.), *Black psychology* (3rd ed., pp. 47–63). Berkeley, CA: Cobb and Henry.

Norton, M. B. (1980). *Liberty's daughters: The Revolutionary experience of American women, 1750–1800.* Boston, MA: Little, Brown.

Payne, R. K. (2001). *A framework for understanding poverty.* Highlands, TX: aha! Process.

Piersen, W. D. (1993). *Black legacy: America's hidden heritage.* Amherst, MA: University of Massachusetts Press.

Price, R. (Ed.) (1979). *Maroon societies: Rebel slave communities in the Americas* (2nd ed.). Baltimore, MD: The Johns Hopkins University Press.

Quarles, B. (1961). *Negro in the American Revolution.* Chapel Hill: University of North Carolina Press.

Quarles, B. (1969). *Black abolitionists.* New York, NY: Oxford University Press.

Riessman, F. (1962). *The culturally deprived child.* New York, NY: Harper & Brothers.

Robinson, R. (2000). *The debt: What America owes to Blacks.* New York, NY: Dutton.

Rousseau, J. J. (1952). *A discourse on the origin of inequality* (G. D. H. Cole, Trans.). Chicago, IL: The University of Chicago and Encyclopedia Britannica. (Original work published 1755)

Runes, D. D. (Ed.). (1947). *The selected writings of Benjamin Rush.* New York, NY: The Philosophical Library.

Sanders, E. R. (1969). The Hamitic hypothesis: Its origins and functions in time perspective. *Journal of African history, 10*(4), 521–532.

Sargent Murray, J. (1994). On the equality of the sexes. In P. Lauter (Ed.), *The Heath anthology of American literature* (2nd ed., pp. 1011–1016). Lexington, MA: D.C. Heath and Company. (Original work published in the *Massachusetts Magazine,* April and May, 1790)

Schlesinger, A. M., Jr. (1992). *The disuniting of America.* New York, NY: W.W. Norton.

Shenandoah, A. (1988). Everything has to be in balance. *Northeast Indian Quarterly, IV*(4) & *V*(1), 4–7.

Sindima, H. (1995). *Africa's agenda: The legacy of liberalism and colonialism in the crisis of African values.* Westport, CT: Greenwood.

Still, W. (2007). *The Underground Railroad: Authentic narratives and first-hand accounts* (I. F. Finseth, Ed.). Mineola, NY: Dover Publications. (Originally published 1872)

Summit of the Elders. (1995 fall). Summit of the Elders: Haudenosaunee environmental restoration strategy. *Akwesasne Notes New Series, 1*(3 & 4), 66–70.

Swamp, L. C. (1997). St. Regis Mohawk Tribe Environment Division. *Akwesasne Notes New Series, 2*(2), 16–17.

Swartz, E. E. (2013). Removing the master script: Benjamin Banneker "Re-membered." *Journal of Black Studies, 44*(1), 31–49.

Szatmary, D. P. (1980). *Shay's rebellion: The making of an agrarian insurrection.* Amherst, MA: The University of Massachusetts Press.

Tayac, G. (2004). Keeping the original instructions. In G. McMaster & C. E. Trafzer (Eds.), *Native universe: Voices of Indian America* (pp. 72–83). Washington, DC: National Museum of the American Indian, Smithsonian Institution/National Geographic Society.

Tehanetorens (Fadden, R.) (1970/1999). *Kaianerekowa Hotinonsionne: The Great Law of Peace of the Longhouse people.* Rooseveltown, NY: Akwesasne Notes/Mohawk Nation.

Tehanetorens (Fadden, R.) (1999). *Wampum belts of the Iroquois.* Summertown, TN: Book Publishing Company.

Thiam, P. K. (2011). *From Timbuktu to the Mississippi Delta.* San Diego, CA: Cognella.

Thompson, V. B. (1987). *The making of the African diaspora in the Americas 1441–1900.* New York, NY: Longman.

Tomaz, B. L., Espíndula, F. B., & Pedrini, I. (n.d.). *Roots of intolerance: Slavery in Brazil.* Retrieved from http://library.thinkquest.org/C008212F/resistence2.htm

Truth, S. (1850). *Narrative of Sojourner Truth, a northern slave emancipated from bodily servitude by the state of New York in 1828.* Boston, MA: J.B. Yerrington and Sons.

Tully, J.(1993). Placing the 'Two Treatises.' In N. Phillipson & Q. Skinner (Eds.), *Political discourse in early modern Britain* (pp. 253–280). New York, NY: Cambridge University Press.

Van Doren, C., & Boyd, J. P. (Eds.). (1938). *Indian treaties printed by Benjamin Franklin 1736–1762.* Philadelphia, PA: Historical Society of Pennsylvania.

Venables, R. W. (1992). The founding fathers, choosing to be Romans. In J. Barreiro (Ed.), *Indian roots of American democracy* (pp. 67–106). Ithaca, NY: Akwe:Kon Press.

Walker, D. (1965). *David Walker's appeal* (C. M. Wiltse, Ed.). New York, NY: Hill and Wang. (Original work published 1829)

Walker, S.,S. (Ed.). (2001). *African roots/American cultures: Africa in the creation of the Americas.* Lanham, MD: Rowman & Littlefield.

Walters, R. W. (1982). The politics of affirmative action. *The Western Journal of Black Studies, 6*(3), 175–181.

Wells, I. B. (1892). *Southern horrors: Lynch law in all its phases*. New York, NY: The New York Age Print.

West, E. H. (1972). *The Black American and education*. Columbus, OH: Charles E. Merrill Publishing Company.

Williams, E. (2010). The slaves and slavery. In L. Dubois & J. S. Scott (Eds.), *Origins of the Black Atlantic* (pp. 323–333). New York, NY: Routledge.

Winch, J. (2002). *A gentleman of color: The life of James Forten*. New York, NY: Oxford University Press.

Wood, P. (2003). *Diversity: The invention of a concept*. San Francisco, CA: Encounter Books.

Wynter, S. (1992). *Do not call us "Negroes": How multicultural textbooks perpetuate racism*. San Francisco, CA: Aspire Books.

Wynter, S. (2000). The re-enchantment of humanism: An interview with S. Wynter by D. Scott. *Small Axe 8*, 119–207.

Wynter, S. (2005). Race and our biocentric belief system: An interview with S. Wynter. In J. King (Ed.), *Black education: A transformative research and action agenda for the new century* (pp. 361–366). Mahwah, NJ: Erlbaum for the American Educational Research Association.

Zagarri, R. (1995). *A woman's dilemma: Mercy Otis Warren and the American Revolution*. Wheeling, IL: Harlan-Davidson.

Zinn, H. (1980/2003). *A people's history of the United States: 1492–present*. New York, NY: Harper Collins.

Zobel, H. B. (1970). *The Boston Massacre*. New York, NY: W.W. Norton & Company.

APPENDIX B

Lesson Summaries: Themes, Concepts, and Principles

Freedom and Democracy: A Story Remembered

Freedom and Democracy is a 45-page student text of six Lessons written for the fourth grade. A summary of each Lesson begins with describing the themes (see Table 3.1 in chapter 3) that guided us to include specific knowledge in that lesson. As explained in chapter 3, the power relations between groups in an inequitable society determine whether an identity-group's narrative reflects dominant themes, alterity themes, or marginalized themes. By using Afrocentric theory and culturally informed principles to frame and write narratives of the groups that participated in shaping a topic, the themes in these narratives avoid the euro-spun hegemonic versions of knowledge found in standard accounts—the versions that communicate the sole rightness and inevitability of the knowledge and actions of dominant groups. The Lesson summaries below also explain how Afrocentric concepts and the principles of culturally informed curricular practice were preserved in the framing and writing of each lesson to grade level. (For information regarding how to obtain copies of the student text *Freedom and Democracy,* contact omnicentricpress@gmail.com.)

Lesson 1

Lesson 1 is entitled "Knowing about Freedom and Democracy." The alterity themes in the narratives of the Haudenosaunee and Africans in the Diaspora, and a dominant theme in the narrative of European/White colonists—all identified in the historical record during the process of researching and writing identity-group narratives—direct us to include typically omitted knowledge about all three groups. Alterity themes refer to knowledge about how

Haudenosaunee and African people had centuries of experience with freedom, which they understood as an inherent right and shared responsibility. Other alterity themes describe leadership and decision making, the process of setting up Haudenosaunee democracy to bring about unity and protect freedom, and how African people brought ideas about freedom from their homelands to other parts of the world. A dominant group theme refers to knowledge about Europeans who experienced subjugation to tyranny within their social, political, and economic systems prior to arriving in North America. By "remembering" or bringing together the knowledge represented by both alterity and dominant themes in Lesson 1, we can describe who had knowledge of and experience with freedom and democracy when the Haudenosaunee, Africans, and Europeans came together in North America over 400 years ago. This combined knowledge lays a foundation for the events that followed and is thus the first Lesson in the text. Pictures and maps locate the homelands of the Haudenosaunee, Africans, and Europeans; and text describes each group's knowledge of and experience with freedom and democracy, including aspects of their governments.

In order to maintain Afrocentric theoretical concepts in framing the content in Lesson 1, we kept in mind the concepts of Centrality/Location, Subjects with Agency, and the Reclamation of Cultural Heritage so that this Lesson would show Haudenosaunee, African, and European people as locations for knowing about freedom and governance and for acting on the world prior to all three cultural groups coming together in North America. This represents a major departure from master-scripted texts that omit the centrality, agency, and heritage of Indigenous and African cultures related to this topic. We also used the Afrocentric concept of Collective Responsibility to frame content about African and Haudenosaunee understanding of freedom as a shared experience.

To write Lesson 1 to grade level, we used the culturally informed principles of inclusion, representation, and accurate scholarship to describe the substantive experiences of Haudenosaunee and African cultures with freedom, the development of Haudenosaunee democracy, and the absence of these experiences among Europeans. We enacted the principle of critical thinking by asking students a thought-provoking end-of-Lesson question: "Why do you think that sharing freedom causes people to act in ways that are caring and right?" Responding to this question involves students with a portion of Indigenous and African heritage knowledge that Lesson 1 has recovered.

Lesson 2

Lesson 2 is entitled "Haudenosaunee and Europeans Meet." The alterity themes in the narrative of the Haudenosaunee and the dominate themes in the narrative of European/White colonists—all identified in the historical record during the process of researching and writing identity-group narratives—direct us to include typically omitted or distorted knowledge about both groups. Thus, we include the Haudenosaunee understanding that democracy is a process requiring participation, equity, the right to speak, and consensus; and that agreement, unity, and peace among people preserve community and culture. Haudenosaunee alterity themes also describe practices of gender equity, leadership by the consent of the people, and the instruction of colonial leaders about the value of unity. Dominant themes describe what colonial leaders learned from Haudenosaunee leaders at the same time as they were engaged in taking Indigenous land and colonizing North America. By bringing together the knowledge represented by both alterity and dominant themes in Lesson 2, we can portray the beliefs, values, and actions of the Haudenosaunee and European/White colonists, how they interacted, and the interest that colonial leaders took in Haudenosaunee democracy.

In order to maintain Afrocentric theoretical concepts in framing the content in Lesson 2, we kept in mind the concepts of Centrality/Location and Subjects with Agency so that both Haudenosaunee and European/White colonists are shown as locations for knowing something about the past and acting on the world. The Collective Consciousness of the Haudenosaunee is preserved through text and images that exhibit their approach to bringing peace and equanimity into the world through the demonstration of interdependence as seen in the Two-Row Wampum Treaty and Ayonwatha Wampum Belts that are pictured and described; and Collective Responsibility and the Reclamation of Cultural Heritage are kept by framing text about how Haudenosaunee women and men worked together to keep their communities healthy and in harmony through democratic governance.

By paying attention to the culturally informed principles of inclusion, accurate scholarship, indigenous voice, and a collective humanity, we were able to write at grade level about Haudenosaunee social and political practices, their matrilineal social structure, and their interactions with European colonists. In so doing, text and images show the substantive participation of the Haudenosaunee in modeling how different cultures can live together in peace, how women and men have equal worth, and what European leaders learned from Haudenosaunee leaders. While master-scripted texts teach that colonization was an inevitable aspect of European interest in the Americas, this "re-membered" Lesson encourages critical thinking by describing colonial land theft, the wealth it brought to Europeans and White colonists, and Haudenosaunee efforts to protect their homelands. This is followed by stating that "Colonizing North America was not a right action." Taking an ethical stand on the colonial project makes a way for teachers and students to engage in a critical dialog with the past. Mindful use of the above five culturally informed principles when writing for students brought knowledge from the narratives of Haudenosaunee and European/White colonists into this lesson.

Lesson 3

Lesson 3 is entitled "African People in North America." The alterity themes in the narratives of Africans in the Diaspora and the dominant themes in the narratives of European/White colonists were identified in the historical record during the process of researching and writing identity-group narratives. These themes direct us to include typically omitted or distorted knowledge about Africans at home and in the Diaspora and about European/White colonists. Alterity themes were drawn from content about the centuries of freedom experienced by African people and about African elders/leaders who made decisions by agreement and were publicly accountable for being fair and just. African people brought these ideas about freedom and justice from their homelands. Once African people were enslaved in the Americas, resistance and revolt was immediate and ongoing. Resistance was also expressed in the speeches, petitions, and writing of African men and women in the Americas. Through pictures and text, Lesson 3 also includes the dominant theme that even though White colonists experienced African people's logical arguments and actions for freedom, they continued to engage in and benefit from the kidnapping, cruelty, and exploitation of African men, women, and children. By bringing together the knowledge represented by both alterity and dominant themes in this lesson, we were able to exemplify the longstanding African traditions of freedom through descriptions of the governance practices in the Songhoy Nation of West Africa. We also explained that during the *Maafa,* African people—who always asserted that they had never given up their natural right to be free—were forced to work for the benefit and wealth of Europeans and White colonists. Varied examples of African resistance and liberation efforts are described, including a biography of Benjamin Banneker that presents his advocacy for human freedom along with his other scientific and mathematical accomplishments.

In order to maintain Afrocentric theoretical concepts in framing the content in Lesson 3, we kept in mind three Afrocentric concepts—the Anteriority of African Civilization, Collective Consciousness, and Centrality/Location so that there would be content about the diverse disciplines of African knowledge that were developed over thousands of years, and about the social and political practices of governance that demonstrate the interdependent practices of African leaders and the freedoms experienced by citizens. We also preserved Centrality/Location, Self-Determination, Subjects with Agency, and Collective Responsibility so that African people in the Diaspora could be located at the center of knowing about freedom and its absence, and at the center of making decisions to collectively resist and revolt against the system of slavery. Centrality/Location and Subjects with Agency also frame knowledge about the actions of White colonists as they fought for freedom from England, even though they denied freedom to people of African descent and built massive wealth through a system of exploiting others. Recovering the above historical pieces preserves another Afrocentric concept, the Reclamation of Cultural Heritage.

By paying attention to the culturally informed principles of inclusion and a collective humanity, we were able to write at grade level about the substantive participation of African people in shaping ideas about freedom, pursuing human freedom, and expressing that the inherency and shared nature of freedom are normative. These ways of thinking and acting are all omitted in master-scripted social studies content. The principle of representation allowed us to contextualized Benjamin Banneker's freedom-seeking actions as African; and the principles of accurate scholarship and critical thinking made it possible to write about and picture the wealth and power of White colonists who benefit from kidnapping African people and stealing their knowledge and skills. The text raises an ethical question by stating that enslavement "was not a right action," which encourages students and teachers to engage in critical thought about the content detailed in this Lesson. Mindful use of the above five culturally informed principles when writing for students brought knowledge from the narratives of Africans in the Diaspora and European/White colonists into this Lesson.

Lesson 4

Lesson 4 is entitled "Learning from the Great Law of Peace." Alterity themes in the narrative of the Haudenosaunee and dominant themes in the narrative of European/White colonists—identified in the historical record during the process of researching and writing identity-group narratives—direct us to include typically omitted knowledge about the Haudenosaunee model of democracy and White/colonial leaders' exposure to it. Thus, we include some of the protocols and practices of Haudenosaunee democracy as recorded in the Great Law of Peace. Haudenosaunee alterity themes also reflect their understanding that agreement, unity, and peace preserved culture—all democratic concepts that were taught to colonial leaders. Dominant themes describe that these leaders learned about the practices of freedom and democracy from the Haudenosaunee and wrote a constitution including some of what they learned. Yet, they excluded African and Indigenous people, poor White men, and all women from the benefits of this constitution. By combining both alterity and dominant themes in Lesson 4, we explain and exemplify how Wampum Belts represent sections of the Great Law of Peace and describe how colonial leaders, such as Benjamin Franklin, learned about unity and other democratic practices from the Haudenosaunee. We also show how Haudenosaunee images and symbols were used in the design of the Great Seal of the United States.

In order to maintain Afrocentric theoretical concepts in framing the content in Lesson 4, we kept in mind the concepts of Collective Responsibility, Centrality/Location, Self-Determination, and Subjects with Agency in order to frame the Great Law of Peace as a living document and model of democracy. Locating Haudenosaunee people at the center of phenomena reveals their collective approach to decision making and the actions they took to teach colonial leaders about unity as a path to peace. Centrality/Location and Subjects with Agency are also preserved in text and images about European/White colonists who are a location for learning about those leaders who agreed with Haudenosaunee ideas about unification and who made decisions when writing the U.S. Constitution and developing the Great Seal of the United States. And the Reclamation of Cultural Heritage is kept as a way to recover knowledge about both groups as well as their interactions with each other.

By paying attention to the culturally informed principles of inclusion, representation, accurate scholarship, and indigenous voice, we were able to write at grade level about the Great Law of Peace; to make it clear that the Haudenosaunee influenced colonial thinking and action; and to allow leaders of *both* groups to speak for, name, and define their ideas in ways that locate them as normative subjects within their respective cultural contexts. The principle of critical thinking is seen in end-of-Lesson questions: "Why do you think that the right to speak freely is part of a democracy? How might having this right lead to peace within a community such as your classroom?" Being mindful of engaging students in critical thinking also resulted in text and images that encourage the evaluation of a rarely acknowledged source of the Great Seal of the United States. Using the above five culturally informed principles when writing for students brought knowledge from the narratives of Haudenosaunee and European/White colonists into this lesson.

Lesson 5

Lesson 5 is entitled "The Common Right of Culture." The alterity themes in the narratives of the Haudenosaunee and Africans in the Diaspora, a marginalized theme of a sub-group of White colonists in the narrative of European/White colonists, and the dominant themes in the narrative of European/White colonists were identified in the historical record during the process of researching and writing identity-group narratives. These themes direct us to include typically omitted knowledge about opposing assertions related to maintaining culture. The Haudenosaunee and Africans in the Diaspora claimed that culture is the common right of all peoples. For the Haudenosaunee, agreement, unity, and peace among people preserve community and culture as does serving and being accountable to people. African people claimed that having freedom for all, not just for some, preserves all cultures as does establishing institutions such as churches and schools. A marginalized theme about a subgroup of White colonists describes how they acted as allies and advocates of freedom and justice—some on behalf of their own disenfranchised or politically marginalized men and women and others on behalf of African and Indigenous Americans. Dominant group themes direct us to include knowledge about the claims of White colonists that only their culture deserved to be maintained, which depended on colonizing and subjugating Indigenous and African

Peoples in the Diaspora. By bringing together the knowledge represented by alterity, dominant, and marginalized themes in Lesson 5, we can reconnect or "re-member" what occurred related to cultural preservation and the pursuit of freedom and justice in the colonial period.

In order to maintain Afrocentric theoretical concepts in framing the content in Lesson 5, we kept in mind the concepts of Centrality/Location, Self-Determination, Collective Consciousness, Reclamation of Cultural Heritage, and Subjects with Agency so that Haudenosaunee and African Peoples are shown as locations for knowing about the maintenance of culture as a common right. The collective actions and decisions they made to share cultural knowledge and to speak and act for justice are evidence of an interdependent orientation and understanding of the oneness of humanity; and including knowledge framed by these concepts reclaims portions of cultural heritage related to these two groups. The concepts of Self-Determination, Subjects with Agency, and Reclamation of Cultural Heritage also made it possible to frame content about free Black people (e.g., Richard Allen, James Forten) who advanced arguments for freedom and engaged in efforts to end enslavement, insisting that freedom should apply to everyone in the colonies. The actions of a small number of wealthy White men and women (e.g., Benjamin Rush, Judith Sargent Murray, Charles Thomson) indicate their agency in speaking out against injustices like enslavement, unfair treaties, and gender inequalities.

By paying attention to the culturally informed principles of indigenous voice and a collective humanity, we were able to write at grade level about the voices of Haudenosaunee and African people who, through their actions, defined the common right of culture and the oneness of humanity. Using the principle of accurate scholarship, we wrote about a small sub-group of White colonists—men and women who spoke out against enslavement and gender inequality and advocated for just relations with Native Americans. Being mindful of ways to encourage critical thinking resulted in a question at the end of the Lesson: "Why do you think that when there is real freedom, every group of people is able to keep their culture?" This question asks students to assess the relationship between freedom and culture. Critical thinking was also encouraged for teachers and students by providing divergent ideas about cultural preservation, rather than the unstated but assumed dominant view in standard social studies materials that only Europeans had this right. Mindful use of the above four culturally informed principles when writing for students made it possible to connect and write knowledge from the narratives of the Haudenosaunee, Africans in the Diaspora, and European/White colonists into this lesson.

Lesson 6

Lesson 6 is entitled "Working People, Freedom, and Democracy." Alterity themes in the narrative of Africans in the Diaspora, and a marginalized theme of a sub-group of White colonists and a dominant theme of White

colonists—both in the narrative of European/White colonists—were identified in the historical record during the process of researching and writing
identity-group narratives. These themes direct us to include typically omitted or distorted knowledge about both identity-groups. Black working people pursued freedom by resisting enslavement and restrictions of freedom and
through practices that were congruent with ideas they expressed by petitioning
and in other actions; and a sub-group of White colonists acted as advocates of
freedom and justice as seen in their efforts to end English rule as a first step in
gaining more rights for themselves. A dominant group theme describes that
rights and freedom were only for wealthy White landowning men. This last
Lesson in *Freedom and Democracy* combines alterity, marginalized, and dominant
themes to add "faces" to Black and White working people who sought freedom
and democracy for themselves and others.

In order to maintain Afrocentric theoretical concepts in framing the content
in Lesson 6, we kept in mind the concepts of Centrality/Location, Subjects
with Agency, and Reclamation of Cultural Heritage in order to frame knowledge about Black and White working people who sought freedom and more
rights before and after the Revolutionary War. Vignettes of individuals and
groups position working people of African and European descent as locations
for knowing about this era as seen in the decisions they made and the actions
they took. Presenting these workers as, in some measure, part of a common
pursuit—showing the varied ways in which they acted for justice—consciously
reclaims the identity of working people as part of Revolutionary history. For
White working people (e.g., Sybil Ludington, Deborah Sampson), their socio-
economic position was a way for them to know the value of democracy for all
citizens. For Black working people (e.g., Crispus Attucks, Paul Cuffee), their
race and socioeconomic position, as well as their heritage knowledge, were
ways for them to know about the value of equity and freedom, and that without
these ideas—and the practices related to them—there would be no democracy.

By paying attention to the culturally informed principles of inclusion, representation, accurate scholarship, and a collective humanity, we were able to
write at grade level about the substantive participation of working people as
central to life in their communities and key players in the events leading up
to the Revolutionary War. The principle of representation made it possible
to write about four individuals and two groups (male apprentices and female
spinners and weavers) as normative subjects within, not separated from their
communities and cultural contexts. So, for example, Deborah Sampson dis-
guises herself as a man to fight in the Revolutionary War, but the class context
of her poor White farming family and the hardships she faced contextualize
her actions. The principles of accurate scholarship and a collective humanity
facilitated the writing of content about working individuals and groups who
are shown as equally valued within the human collective. Critical thinking is
encouraged by content provided about Crispus Attucks' ancestry and about his

belief in freedom that lead to his personal and political agency. An-end-of-Lesson question asks students: "Why do you think most working people did not get more rights after the Revolutionary War? This question asks students to synthesize information from the Lesson to assess what might be the reasons for working people—who contributed so fully to the independence effort—not receiving more rights after the war. Mindful use of the above five culturally informed principles when writing for students brought content from the narratives of Africans in the Diaspora and European/White colonists into this Lesson.

CONTRIBUTORS

Linda Campbell, Rochester City School District   As a life-long resident of Rochester, New York, Linda Campbell has chosen to make the Rochester City School District her home for teaching and learning. Ms. Campbell has had teaching experience at each of the grades K-6 and is currently teaching Grade 3. She works collaboratively with the Rochester Teacher Center to acquire knowledge about students, teaching, and learning, and the educational systems that promote effective practices able to enhance the life chances and opportunities of all.

Adrienne C. Goss, Georgia State University   Adrienne C. Goss is a doctoral candidate in the Educational Policy Studies Department at Georgia State University and a research fellow in the Alonzo A. Crim Center's Urban Education Think Tank (UETT). Her research interests include parental involvement, African centered epistemology, and the impact of educational policy on children of color. She has over 11 years of teaching experience at the middle and high school levels.

Joyce E. King, Georgia State University   Joyce E. King, Ph.D., holds the Benjamin E. Mays Endowed Chair for Urban Teaching Learning and Leadership at Georgia State University and is Professor of Educational Policy Studies and affiliated faculty in the Department of African American Studies. Her research and publications address a transformative role for culture in teaching and teacher preparation, Black Studies curriculum theorizing, community-mediated research, and "dysconscious" racism, the term she coined. King has international experience teaching, lecturing, and providing professional development in Brazil, Canada, England, Jamaica, New Zealand, and Senegal. She is the 2014–2015 president of American Educational Research Association (AERA).

Shonda Lemons-Smith, Georgia State University Shonda Lemons-Smith, Ph.D., is an assistant professor of mathematics education in the Department of Early Childhood Education at Georgia State University. Her research and teaching focus on mathematics education in urban school contexts— specifically, teacher development, issues of equity, and culturally responsive pedagogy. Dr. Lemons-Smith has over 20 years of experience in the field of mathematics education at the K-12 and college/university levels. In addition, she is very active in the education community at the national, state, and local levels as well as internationally.

Ericka López, Rochester City School District Ericka López is currently an ESOL teacher in Rochester, New York. She received her undergraduate degree in International Studies from Nazareth College in Rochester. She also holds a master's degree in Islamic Religion, Society, and Power from The School of Historical, Philosophical and Religious Studies at Arizona State University. Her second master's degree in TESOL is from Nazareth College.

Sherell A. McArthur, Georgia State University Sherell A. McArthur has been an elementary school teacher for 5 years and is now a doctorate student at Georgia State University in the Educational Policy Studies department. Her research and teaching interests include urban education, Black girlhood, popular culture, teaching about Hip-hop from the perspective of race and gender, media literacy, and images of Black and Brown girls and women.

Ellen E. Swartz, Education Consultant Ellen E. Swartz, Ph.D., is an education consultant in curriculum development and the construction of culturally informed instructional materials for K-12 teachers and students. As the Frontier Chair in Urban Education at Nazareth College, Dr. Swartz conducted research on the knowledge base of pre-service teachers in urban education as part of identifying how teacher educators can more effectively prepare teachers for urban schools. She has also published in the areas of education history, emancipatory pedagogy, and the concept of "re-membering" as an approach to achieving more comprehensive accounts of the past.

INDEX